T0319970

Institutional Competition

NEW THINKING IN POLITICAL ECONOMY

Series Editor: Peter J. Boettke
George Mason University, USA

New Thinking in Political Economy aims to encourage scholarship in the intersection of the disciplines of politics, philosophy and economics. It has the ambitious purpose of reinvigorating political economy as a progressive force for understanding social and economic change.

The series is an important forum for the publication of new work analysing the social world from a multidisciplinary perspective. With increased specialization (and professionalization) within universities, interdisciplinary work has become increasingly uncommon. Indeed, during the 20th century, the process of disciplinary specialization reduced the intersection between economics, philosophy and politics and impoverished our understanding of society. Modern economics in particular has become increasingly mathematical and largely ignores the role of institutions and the contribution of moral philosophy and politics.

New Thinking in Political Economy will stimulate new work that combines technical knowledge provided by the 'dismal science' and the wisdom gleaned from the serious study of the 'worldly philosophy'. The series will reinvigorate our understanding of the social world by encouraging a multidisciplinary approach to the challenges confronting society in the new century.

Recent titles in the series include:

Governance and Economic Development
A Comparative Institutional Approach
Joachim Ahrens

Constitutions, Markets and Law
Recent Experiences in Transition Economies
Edited by Stefan Voigt and Hans-Jürgen Wagener

Austrian Economics and the Political Economy of Freedom
Richard M. Ebeling

Anarchy, State and Public Choice
Edited by Edward Stringham

Humane Economics
Essays in Honor of Don Lavoie
Edited by Jack High

Public Choice and the Challenges of Democracy
Edited by José Casas Pardo and Pedro Schwartz

Fiscal Sociology and the Theory of Public Finance
An Exploratory Essay
Richard E. Wagner

Institutional Competition
Edited by Andreas Bergh and Rolf Höijer

Institutional Competition

Edited by

Andreas Bergh

Research Fellow, Ratio Institute and Lund University, Sweden

Rolf Höijer

Senior Science Officer, Swedish Research Council, Associate Research Fellow, Ratio Institute, Sweden and London School of Economics – Public Policy Group, UK

NEW THINKING IN POLITICAL ECONOMY

Edward Elgar

Cheltenham, UK • Northampton, MA, USA

© Andreas Bergh and Rolf Höijer, 2008

All rights reserved. No part of this publication may be reproduced, stored in a retrieval system or transmitted in any form or by any means, electronic, mechanical or photocopying, recording, or otherwise without the prior permission of the publisher.

Published by
Edward Elgar Publishing Limited
Glensanda House
Montpellier Parade
Cheltenham
Glos GL50 1UA
UK

Edward Elgar Publishing, Inc.
William Pratt House
9 Dewey Court
Northampton
Massachusetts 01060
USA

A catalogue record for this book
is available from the British Library

ISBN 978 1 84720 669 5

Printed and bound in Great Britain by MPG Books Ltd, Bodmin, Cornwall

Contents

Contributors

Andreas Bergh, Ratio Institute and Lund University, Sweden

Peter Bernholz, Universität Basel, Switzerland

Victoria Curzon-Price, University of Geneva, Switzerland

Lars P. Feld, Philipps-Universität Marburg, Germany

Rolf Höijer, Ratio Institute, Sweden and London School of Economics, UK

Viktor Vanberg, Walter Eucken Institut, Germany

Roland Vaubel, University of Mannheim, Germany

Erich Weede, University of Bonn, Germany

Michael Wohlgemuth, Walter Eucken Institut, Germany

Foreword

In today's globalized world institutional competition, or competition between political units through institutional design, is potentially important. The idea is that communities, regions, nations and even continents can engage in competition over moveable resources, such as people, capital, investments, jobs and companies, using their institutional structures and the incentives they create. Both formal and informal institutions could matter. The scope of this kind of competition and its effects on these political units are the theme of this volume.

The book is written within the research project *Institutional Competition and the Outcomes of Politics* at the Ratio Institute in Stockholm, Sweden (for further information, see www.ratio.se). A number of outstanding scholars from several different countries have contributed to the analysis, which introduces a number of new themes into the analysis of institutional competition, for example, the learning and information effects of competition and how institutional competition affects government efficiency.

The Torsten and Ragnar Söderberg Foundations have provided invaluable financial assistance to the project.

Nils Karlson, President and CEO
The Ratio Institute
Associate Professor
Stockholm, Sweden

Preface

Andreas Bergh and Rolf Höijer

In the policy debate there has been much talk about institutional competition – or the new systems competition, as some prefer to call it. It has been argued, for example, that institutional competition leads to a race to the bottom in terms of eroding government revenues, redistributing wealth from workers to capitalists, and limiting democracy by forcing politicians to please international investment capital instead of working for their voters. Negative assessments of institutional competition have thus predominated.

This volume introduces new perspectives into this debate, basically by turning the argumentation on its head. Why is institutional competition regarded as something bad, when competition is regarded as good in all other economic contexts, and the absence of competition regarded as a bad thing in all other standard analyses? The volume analytically and empirically explores a number of issues surrounding this question. Some important themes that recur in different chapters in this volume consider:

- Whether institutional competition might facilitate liberty and democracy, rather than inhibit it;
- The extent to which competition might involve experimentation and learning that can be beneficial for society;
- How institutional competition may act as a corrective force to reduce inefficiencies and rent-seeking;
- Institutional competition can enable governments to become allocatively efficient in relation to their constituents' preferences;
- Whether institutional competition really does lead to a decline in government revenues.

These perspectives recur in different chapters, but the chapters also differ in many respects. Though there are some overlaps, each contributor is, of course, responsible for what is expressed in their chapter alone.

The volume opens with Höijer's conceptual discussion of institutional competition. He conceptually discusses both 'institutions' and 'competition'. Institutions have been conceived in different ways, for example as (equilibrium) behaviours, as rules, or as rules enforced by sanctions and actors. Höijer notes that each perspective has its own merits and short-comings, but suggests that when considering institutional competition it might be most meaningful to consider a more extensive concept of institutions as consisting of both behavioural rules and the sanctions and actors that enforce them.

Höijer next considers in which sense institutions can be said to compete with each other. Arguing that the economic contribution of institutions is to coordinate actors, and solve information and governance problems, Höijer suggests that institutions also compete with each other in terms of supplying a specific coordination service. According to this view institutions basically compete in a factor market and supply a distinct production factor: 'coordinating rules'. Höijer notes that some difficulties with externalities and pricing such coordination services might exist, but maintains that in principal competition and pricing are possible.

Importantly, Höijer notes that, in general, when we speak of institutional competition, we in fact mean competition between states or governments. States are institutions that are particular in that they 'monopolize' the use of violence for the purpose of enforcing their institutional rules. However, they only nominally monopolize the use of violence; from an international perspective many states exist and no state monopolizes use of violence in the entire world. What states do is to establish partitioned markets, in which each state is a 'local monopolist' in each particular market segment, and it is difficult for consumers of their services to switch from one supplier to another. Competition between states is, however, possible and as the costs consumers incur from switching between governments decrease, we may also expect that competition intensifies and induces governments to set taxes and outputs of public services at levels in line with the demand of their constituents.

In the following chapter, Roland Vaubel traces the history of thought on institutional competition, from David Hume's 1742 statement that 'Nothing is more favourable to the rise of politeness and learning than a number of neighbouring and independent states' until contemporary times, where he discusses Hans Werner Sinn's critical analysis of institutional competition. Using extensive citations Vaubel demonstrates that the most important liberal thinkers in history have held positive opinions about institutional competition, generally much more so than theorists in the last 20–30 years. He introduces the idea that institutional competition might be conducive to the establishment of liberty and democracy, and shows that historical writers such as Montesquieu, Adam Smith, Kant and Lord Acton, argued in favour of institutional competition largely for this reason. (Modern writers, on the other hand, have focused more frequently on how institutional competition might effect the economic allocation of resources.)

Vaubel also introduces the important distinction between 'yardstick competition' and 'resource-based competition'. The point of yardstick competition is that if different competing governments exist, then they may compare themselves with each other, and also learn from each other. This introduces the idea that competition might be conducive to experimentation and learning. In Vaubel's words 'diversity, by extending the scope for comparison promotes learning and innovation'. Vaubel notes that yardstick competition has been taken to promote learning in such different fields as 'arts and sciences', 'political life', 'industry', or creativity in general.

Resource-based competition, on the other hand, concerns how governments compete for mobile capital. According to Max Weber, for example, 'The competitive struggle among the European nation-states created the largest opportunities for modern western capitalism. The separate states had to compete for mobile capital.' Vaubel notes that according to historical writers the exit mechanism may operate either through the movement of capital or the movement of labour (though in contemporary discussion it is often presumed that only capital is mobile). Vaubel also discuss the landmark contributions by Tiebout and Hirschman, and draws a parallel between resource-based competition and Hirschman's 'exit' mechanism.

Vaubel concludes that while modern writers have largely focused on resource-based competition the historical writers were more concerned with yardstick competition.

In the last section of his chapter Vaubel discusses Hans Werner Sinn's influential criticism of institutional competition. He notes that Sinn objects only to resource-based competition, but argues that 'mobility-based competition cannot be appraised without reference to yardstick competition. For whoever proposes to restrict or suppress mobility-based competition by international coordination or centralization (as Sinn does) necessarily restricts or suppresses yardstick competition as well.' He also argues that Sinn adopts heroic assumptions about the benevolence and efficiency of governments, and argues that if we instead assume that some governments are less benevolent or efficient, then competition may act as a corrective force which compels those governments to more closely satisfy the demands of their constituents (a theme that recurs in several other essays as well). As opposed to Sinn's charge that competition between governments leads to the erosion of welfare states, Vaubel argues that empirical evidence points in the other direction; social expenditure and redistributive efforts have not decreased in modern periods of intensified institutional competition – an observation discussed further in the contributions by Victoria Curzon Price and Andreas Bergh.

An important mechanism in competition is the ability to learn from competitors. In Chapter 3, Michael Wohlgemuth introduces the reader to the theme of institutional learning through experimentation. Wohlgemuth describes creative learning as mostly out of reach for neoclassical mainstream theories. On the other hand, Austrian views of competition as a discovery procedure, identify important links between competition and learning. Hayek's argument, that competition would be pointless if we were certain beforehand who would do best, applies to institutional competition as well.

According to Wohlgemuth, institutions always have to prove their adequacy in view of changing problem situations. Rapidly changing circumstances increase the desirability of institutional pluralism and make it less likely that a benevolent central planner could plan the best institutional arrangement. In his contribution, Wohlgemuth also discusses the feedback mechanisms between individual choices of institutions – voting with one's feet – and the collective design of institutional arrangements, what Wohlgemuth calls 'institutional entrepreneurship'. A main point is that competing jurisdictions improve both citizens' and politicians' knowledge base and their incentives to react to shortcomings of present policies. Furthermore, parallel experimentation is superior to sequential or consecutive experimentation. Under institutional pluralism, bad policies will not necessarily imply great damage. On the other hand, when a political union is forced to follow one grand idea or all-embracing political theory, the potential social costs are extremely high. This is especially so if the size of the political union is large. In other words, size matters in a fundamental way for institutional competition. This theme is further developed by Peter Bernholz, in Chapter 4, who notes that competition may occur on different levels: the domestic competition for political power, on the international level in terms of military and foreign policy measures, and the competition between favourable institutional frameworks.

On the level of international military competition and so on, Bernholz notes that in Europe feudalism gave rise to many different power centres and rulers who each sought to maintain and extend their powers. In order to become competitive they were induced to consider the well-being of their subjects and introduce reliable property rights, free markets and limited taxes. Thus international rivalry and competition resulted in domestic liberalizing and democratizing reforms. This conclusion echoes some of the historical arguments for institutional competition that were introduced in Vaubel's chapter.

On the level of domestic political competition, Bernholz considers the competition between different interest groups in pluralist societies. He argues that where certain interest groups have a 'concentrated interest' in receiving certain government subsidies, but the costs of such subsidies are spread thinly over a larger population, then the smaller interest group will usually succeed in getting such subsidies introduced. In a society of competing interest groups this means that different interest groups will each lobby for increased government expenditure, leading to an ever-increasing expansion of the sphere of government and public expenditures. This reminds us of Vaubel's argument that institutional competition may act as a corrective force to rent-seeking activities and so on.

Bernholtz also considers the allocation of decision competencies in systems of multilevel governance. He notes that one meta-decision is most important: who (or what level) is granted the right to determine at what government levels different competencies should be allocated? Ultimately it is a normative question, but in terms of non-normative, economic, analysis it can be useful to investigate what distribution of competencies might be most appropriate instrumentally, in order to attain one's given normative concerns. Bernholtz notes that in terms of static analysis it is usually argued that if one promotes redistributive measures such decision authority normally needs to be centralized rather than decentralized. Furthermore, to the extent that economies of scale or externalities exist, decision authority should be allocated to those agencies that in size most closely correspond to the relevant economies of scale, or the extension of the externalities. Bernholtz himself considers dynamic arguments more important, and here he comes out in favour of extensive decentralization to lower levels of government. Decentralization is superior, he argues, because the decentralized distribution of decision competencies to many diverse units of government allows for a wider experimentation regarding solutions to different social problems, echoing Wohlgemut's argument regarding the importance of experimentation in institutional competition. Such competitive experimentation allows for better solutions to be identified and for different government units to learn from each other.

The important question as to how institutional competition might affect democracy is the central concern of Viktor Vanberg in Chapter 5. As demonstrated in Professor Vaubel's chapter, many historical thinkers have maintained that institutional competition might enhance democracy, but modern writers have often argued that institutional competition impedes democracy in that elected politicians must sometimes refrain from serving their constituents' interests in order to try to attract internationally mobile capital instead. Vanberg considers these conflicting views, and argues that competition between governments might indeed enhance democracy, since it can assist democratic governments to advance the *common* interests of the citizenry.

While many writers define democracy in terms of majority decision rules (and other procedural aspects), Vanberg argues that democracies are properly conceived as cooperatives that are jointly owned by their citizens, and as such should be evaluated on their ability to serve the interests of those citizens. More precisely, democracies should be evaluated by their ability to serve the *common* interests of all citizens, not by the ability of majorities to serve their own particular interests. Vanberg argues that the granting of privileges to certain groups at the expense of others invariably imposes costs on the citizenry at large. This costly activity may be difficult to sustain under competitive pressure. Institutional competition can limit the scope for such privilege granting. By limiting the ability of majorities (or strong interest groups) to transfer resources to themselves, Vanberg maintains that institutional competition serves to enhance democracy in the sense of promoting the *common* interests of the citizenry.

Vanberg thus returns to the idea that (also regarding democracy) institutional competition may serve as a corrective force against rent-seeking and so on. Ultimately Vanberg's argument appears to have the form of a hypothetical imperative: if one agrees with Vanberg's normative position that redistributive transfers are undemocratic and undesirable, then institutional competition is means for limiting such transfers. (Needless to say, some persons would instead maintain that redistribution is a highly desirable activity for governments to engage in.)

Höijer (Chapter 6) focuses on tax harmonization, that is, the absence of tax competition. Such harmonization agreements between (otherwise competing) governments can in fact be considered analogous to a cartel on a private market, according to Höijer. He notes that otherwise it is generally assumed that competitive markets function better than non-competitive markets and that in other contexts anti-competitive measures are called, for example, 'collusion', 'cartelization' or 'monopolism', and are viewed with great suspicion. Yet in fiscal matters it is tax *competition* that is regarded as harmful and anti-competitive measures are being advocated as beneficial. Competition on ordinary markets puts pressure on prices and output decisions to more closely match the preferences of consumers. Apparently governments do not wish to be exposed to the same pressure themselves. Instead they form cartels.

Before analysis demonstrates why cartels would not be harmful in this particular context, one is left wondering why governments are so eager to form cartels themselves. Are there market failures that need to be addressed? In order to answer this question Höijer considers the contemporary policy debate regarding tax competition, and considers three prominent arguments that are invoked to defend tax harmonization: (1) tax competition distorts investments and violates capital export neutrality,

(2) tax competition undermines the financing of ambitious welfare states, and (3) tax competition will shift the tax burden from capital to labour.

Höijer, however, concludes that if governments provide valuable services, then tax rates would – under competitive taxation – only reflect the relative value of such services, not distort investments. He also notes that on other markets one does not propose the introduction of government monopolies/cartels, or similar interventions, unless some 'market failure' (such as externalities, information asymmetries, or the presence of monopolies) has been identified. The arguments against tax competition, however, do not concern such Pareto-relevant market failures, but usually simply concern cases where an actor is out-competed by another actor. No market failures are thus identified which need to be remedied. Instead it is simply suggested that a form of quasi-monopoly – cartels – should be introduced. Why introduce a market failure (a cartel) as a remedy to no market failure, Höijer asks?

In the following two chapters, Victoria Curzon-Price and Andreas Bergh deal with the effects that institutional competition has on rich OECD countries – in Bergh's case especially on a Scandinavian welfare state such as Sweden. They deal empirically with the question of whether institutional competition has indeed led to a decline in government revenues. Interestingly, they both find that although many tax rates have recently become lower, there is no 'race to the bottom' in tax revenues which, if anything, have risen.

Several mechanisms can explain this. Both Bergh and Curzon-Price point to tax-shifting induced by increased competition: from capital to labour, and from mobile parts of the work force to less mobile. Bergh notes that when the Scandinavian welfare states put a larger share of their tax burden on relatively few mobile production factors, this means that they tax middle- and low-income earners more heavily.

Curzon-Price also identifies another mechanism to explain the absence of a race to the bottom: dynamic Laffer-effects mean that lower tax rates do not necessarily imply lower tax revenue. While top marginal income taxes as well as tax rates on corporate income have fallen, and while value added taxes (VAT) have increased only slightly during the last 20 years or so, government revenue has not suffered.

Curzon-Price goes on to suggest that if tax revenues were to decline because of increased competition, governments might want to think about reducing expenditure before immediately seeking to 'make up the shortfall' in revenue. If governments tend to maximize rather than optimize their expenditure, increased competition may be beneficial rather than harmful.

Bergh notes that increased mobility of labour may potentially cause problems of strategic welfare migration for big welfare states, if people enjoy tax-financed benefits without paying the taxes to finance them. It is demonstrated, however, that big welfare states have already responded by tying benefits more closely to labour force participation. In all, it is not necessarily the case that the biggest welfare states will decrease in size as a result of institutional competition – but they will most likely become less redistributive (in line with Vanberg's argument that institutional competition may serve to limit redistribution). The process can be understood as one where the welfare state is altered beneficially for those voters whose position is strengthened by institutional competition. Using several examples from Sweden, Bergh illustrate that this process has already begun.

Our volume ends with two empirical chapters, one quantitative and one descriptive. In Chapter 9, Lars P. Feld notes that if institutional competition has positive effects on economic development, these effects should be possible to measure and estimate. Existing empirical evidence summarized by Feld, however, yields no clear verdict. As already discussed, there are substantial problems with quantification of institutional competition, potentially explaining the lack of robust empirical results.

Feld embarks on an empirical investigation of his own, using a measure of the decentralization of tax revenue in 19 OECD countries from 1973 to 1998 to try to capture the degree of sub-central fiscal autonomy. The aim is to examine whether higher decentralization, measured this way, has any effects on economic growth. Interestingly, Feld fails to find a robust impact of fiscal autonomy on economic growth. One obvious complicating factor is that several beneficial effects of institutional competition may require a long time to appear. For example, the effects of learning through institutional experimentation (as described by Wohlgemuth) can hardly be expected to show up in the growth data for a 25-year period.

Feld does find, however, that when sub-central governments co-determine tax rates or tax bases in systems of joint taxation, this negatively effects growth. This empirical finding fits well with Höijer's idea that supranational political organizations may work in ways similar to a tax cartel, and can be harmful for economic development.

Finally, Erich Weede provides an example of institutional competition between two large countries (India and China) over a long period of time. Weede asks why China and India fell behind the West during the past three hundred years, and also seeks to explain the relative success of these two countries in recent times.

The explanatory factors that Weede points out are institutional: Europe and the West benefited from institutional competition which the Asian giants did not, and as a consequence weak and inadequate property rights, a lack of scarcity prices, and deficiencies in economic freedom developed in Asia's giants as compared to the West. Furthermore, political fragmentation in the West resulted in limited government and comparatively free markets. Similarly, China was able to do better than India and start to catch up with the West only after climbing out of the socialist trap via a de facto improvement of property rights and economic freedom.

The role Weede proposes for property rights and the incentives thereby created, relates both to the classics, such as Adam Smith, and to contemporary writings, such as Hernando de Soto. However, like Wohlgemuth, Weede also relies rather heavily on Hayekian thinking: a central idea is that knowledge is wasted without economic freedom and decentralized decision-making. Thus, institutions characterized by the latter two will make better use of existing knowledge and for this reason also enjoy a superior economic development.

This volume represents the collaborative efforts of all the contributing authors. We gratefully acknowledge the financial support from the Torsten and Ragnar Söderberg Foundation which made this possible, and also the institutional support of the Ratio Institute – especially Nils Karlson and Niclos Berggren.

To summarize, the chapters in this volume introduce a number of new themes to the analysis of institutional competition. Many of the chapters, for example, draw attention to positive learning and information effects from competition that are not discussed otherwise. The contributions also draw attention to how institutional competition might enable governments to become allocatively efficient.

In contemporary discussions a particularly important argument is perhaps the presumption that institutional competition leads to a reduction in government revenues. As a consequence those who favour big government often fear institutional competition, while those who want small government appreciate institutional competition. These tendencies might also be reflected in some of the chapters in this volume. Interestingly, however, the empirical contributions find no strong support for the notion that institutional competition reduces government revenues. And analytically, the contributions in this volume do not clearly point to any reduction in the size of government revenues. What is predicted is instead that institutional competition will enable governments to reduce inefficiencies, and also enable them to more closely match their supply of services with their constituents' preferences, as they are revealed in a competitive price system. These consequences may be palatable to those who favour big governments, as well as those who prefer smaller governments.

1. The concept of institutional competition

Rolf Höijer

1.1 INTRODUCTION

Increased international trade and globalization have recently focused attention on institutional competition. In contemporary discussions such 'institutional competition' is often understood as competition between governments
over tax revenues, and it is argued that institutional competition results in the
depletion of the finances necessary to sustain welfare states. While these are
interesting arguments they skip several important questions. For example,
are governments the only institutions whose competition might be interesting, or can institutions be discussed more generally? And before discussing
what consequences might result from institutional competition; is it not
worth discussing what attributes 'institutional competition' in itself (that is,
as an independent variable) might have? For these reasons it may be worth-
while to discuss institutional competition from a conceptual point of view,
before other chapters in this volume progress to discuss the consequences of
competition between governments.

'Institutional competition' is a composite phrase, consisting of two concepts: 'institution' and 'competition'. This chapter briefly discusses each of
these. The chapter, however, is far from exhaustive; many conceptual questions regarding institutions are certainly left untouched.[1]

In Section 1.2 I discuss the concept of 'institution' and different categories of institutions. I suggest that more or less extensive conceptions of
'institutions' may be proposed (but personally favour a view that emphasizes the importance of sanctions). In Section 1.3 I discuss institutional
'competition' and suggest that this most importantly means a competition
between systems of coordinating rules and is best analysed in standard
ways of understanding competition. In Section 1.4 I discuss 'states' as particular kinds of institutions and suggest that competition between states
may enable them to more closely align their output of services with the
preferences of their citizens.

1.2   ANALYSING INSTITUTIONS

The concept 'institution' may be defined in different ways. In this chapter I will expose a view most familiar from new institutional economics (or 'rational choice institutionalism'), but will also show that even within this perspective there is scope for different conceptions. Recently, for example, institutions have been analysed in terms of game theory. According to this perspective institutions may be regarded either as *actors* that are involved in playing some game, or the *rules* of the game, or institutions may be conceived as the *equilibrium behaviours* of the game.[2]

Kasper and Streit, for example, define institutions as 'man made rules which constrain possibly arbitrary and opportunistic behaviour in human interaction'.[3] This view regards institutions as *rules*, but also draws attention to the *actors* who make the rules.

A more demanding view regards institutions as systems of social control, as defined by Ellickson: 'a system of social control will be defined as consisting of *rules* of normatively appropriate human behaviour. These rules are enforced through *sanctions* . . .'[4] Besides focusing on rules, this view also draws attention to *sanctions*.

This brief exposition shows that it is possible to regard institutions in different ways, focusing on different aspects. Depending on one's point of view, an 'institution' may be said to consist of (either):

1.2.1   Some set of (equilibrium) actions or behaviours
1.2.2   Some set(s) of rules that constrain what actions may be performed
1.2.3   Some set(s) of sanctions (or incentives) that enforce these rules
1.2.4   Some set(s) of individual actors (who determine the rules and administer the sanctions)

Each of the elements 1.2.1–1.2.4 may be considered separately, and different specific concepts of 'institution' may be discussed, depending on which of the elements are emphasized in each concept. Different conceptions might be considered more or less extensive (or demanding) depending on whether they involve more or fewer of these elements.[5] According to a minimalist conception an institution may, for example, be defined only in terms of the *rules* that it involves, while according to a maximalist conception institutions may be defined in terms of *rules*, *sanctions*, and *actors*.

All of the above points (1.2.1–1.2.4) may be further analysed. Different categories of institutions may also be identified depending on what rules, sanctions, actors and so on that they involve. The remainder of Section 1.2 will be devoted to this task.

1.2.1 Institutions as Behaviours and Equilibrium Behaviours

Some academics regard institutions as patterns of behaviour. At least two different versions of this view exist: a sociological view that regards institutions as predictable reciprocal patterns of behaviour, and a game theoretic view that regards institutions as equilibria.

Berger and Luckman described the first, sociological, perspective on institutions and institutionalization. Institutionalization occurs, they argue, when certain behaviours become 'habitualized', and different actors become able to reciprocally anticipate each other's actions. Habits narrow choices for actors, they argue, and habits also enable an actor to 'typify' another actor's actions, and thus render them predictable. Reciprocal habits therefore constitute institutionalization according to these authors.[6] Wrong summarizes this perspective as follows: 'Repeated interactions gives rise to habits, they are perceived by the actors and become expectations in the sense of predictions or anticipations of behavior. Aware of what is expected by the other, each actor feels constrained to live up to the expectation . . .'[7] This sociological view regards institutions as habitual patterns of behaviour which are predictable.

This view of institutions can be criticized, however. First of all, such habits are probably not robust to changes in rules and sanctions. For example, in 1974 only 35 per cent of Swedish motorists were in the habit of using seat-belts in cars, but when new laws introduced sanctions against persons who did not use seat-belts, then habits changed and 85 per cent of motorists started using seat-belts in 1975.[8] This suggests that if sanctions are applied then habits will change – it is usually sanctions rather than habits that determine behaviour.

A second weakness is that the view of institutions as predictable habits may classify too many social situations as institutions. Generally, it is risky to rely only on observing some regular behavioural pattern (for example, habit) in order to establish that an institution is active in modulating behaviour. Not all habits are governed by institutions – for example, most people sleep every night (and are expected to sleep each night), even though they are not induced to do so by any system of social control.[9]

As such, predictability – or habits – would not seem a sufficient criterion for defining institutions. Institutions certainly contribute towards making behaviour predictable, but not all predictable behaviour constitutes institutions. We might need some additional criteria in order to identify when institutions exist.

The second, game theoretic, perspective regards institutions as *equilibrium behaviours* in games.[10] (An equilibrium represents a set of behaviours/actions that have the characteristic that an actor will have no incentives to change his behaviour unless the other actors in the game change theirs.) Calvert explicitly claims that an '*Institution* is just a name we give to certain parts of certain kinds of equilibria.'[11] Aoki similarly argues that 'A reasonable way of approaching institutions . . . is then to conceptualize an institution as an equilibrium outcome of a game.'[12] According to such a view institutions are identical to equilibria (that is, the concepts are co-extensive).

To view institutions as equilibrium behaviours allows for a conception of institutions which is not very extensive, in the sense it does not rely on making reference to other concepts such as rules or sanctions.

Academics who regard institutions as equilibria often support their position by arguing against the conception of institutions as rules, or rules enforced by sanctions. They suggest that if institutions consist of rules and sanctions, then it must be explained how some actors are incentivized to define these rules and enforce them, that is, how each institution is nested in a second order institution that governs the actions of rule definers and enforcers. But in such a case it must also be explained how some other actors define and enforce the rules of the second order institution, that is, how these are nested in third order institutions and so on. This is a general problem for discussions of institutions, and opens for infinite regress – each institution needs to be nested in a higher order institution. To avoid infinite regress some game theorists argue that at some level institutions must involve each player playing an equilibrium strategy.[13]

An important strength of the equilibrium view is, indeed, that it points out the need for institutions to be in equilibrium, but some criticisms may also be raised. A central question is whether the concept 'institutions' is co-extensive with 'equilibria'. Analytically we may imagine (A) institutions that are equilibria, (B) institutions that are not equilibria, and (C) equilibria that are not institutions. The two concepts are co-extensive only in case (A). This raises two questions:

(1.2.1.1)   Does each institution need to be an equilibrium?
(1.2.1.2)   May equilibria exist which are not institutions?

Consider question (1.2.1.1). The 'equilibrium to avoid infinite regress' argument does not imply that every institution needs to be in equilibrium. It only implies that any given first order institution (that is not itself in equilibrium) needs to be nested in another second order institution that is in equilibrium (so that enforcers are properly incentivized to enforce the rules of the first order institution). Clearly then, this argument allows the possibility that some (first order) institutions are not in equilibrium (case (B)).

We next turn to question (1.2.1.2). Let us, for the sake of argument, ignore the above criticism and admit that the 'equilibrium as a method to avoid infinite regress' argument suggests that it is difficult to imagine stable institutions that are not in equilibrium. Even if correct this does *not*, however, imply (¬C) that all equilibria need to constitute institutions (which would be necessary in order to maintain that institutions are identical to equilibria). Indeed, even Calvert admits that 'Not every equilibrium behaviour pattern is an institution.'[14] And Greif et al. (by whom this tradition is inspired), argue that some outcomes appear implausible as institutions even though they represent equilibria.[15]

Some equilibrium behaviours may, for example, be too malevolent to be conventionally regarded as institutions. A Prisoner's Dilemma might illustrate this. For each PD player there (1) exists a strategy which is strictly dominant, (2) the intersection of these strategies represent an equilibrium and (3) this outcome is also strictly Pareto inferior to another outcome. Since PDs involve equilibria they should presumably be regarded as institutions within this tradition (and would also qualify as Berger and Luckman's predictable reciprocal behaviour patterns). But commonsensically I doubt whether we would regard most PD situations as institutions. A main reason is that PD situations are often regarded as so unsatisfactory that it is argued that some institutions need to be introduced specifically in order to solve the PD (for example, the institution 'state' must be introduced to save us from an anarchical Hobbesian state of nature). PDs are thus often represented as a lack of institutions, rather than their presence. This suggests that all equilibria do not constitute institutions.

Jointly the answers to questions (1.2.1.1) and (1.2.1.2) entail both that 'all institutions need not be equilibria' and that 'all equilibria need not be institutions'. This leaves the relation between institutions and equilibria open. That something constitutes an equilibrium does not seem sufficient to establish that it is an institution. Some additional criteria would be needed to tell us which equilibria should be regarded as institutions.

Indeed some of the proponents of the 'institutions as equilibria' position recognize that some games involve multiple equilibria, and consider how specific equilibria are attained.[16] Knight argues that institutions structure choices toward the achievement of particular equilibrium outcomes, and may be regarded as devices for choosing between multiple equilibria.[17] Focal points are important such devices.[18] Aoki also argues that institutions represent self-sustaining systems of shared beliefs about which actions will be chosen and which equilibria attained.[19]

The 'institutions as equilibria' view has a strength in avoiding infinite regress, and the view of institutions as equilibrium selection devices is interesting. However, if institutions are regarded as mechanisms for equilibrium selection, then such institutions are no longer explained in terms of constituting game theoretic equilibria, but rather reduce to some form of rules for selecting among equilibria. Overall, the 'institutions as equilibria' view does not appear entirely self-sustaining, but at some points seems to need to make reference to exogenous criteria – that is, it involves some more extensive view of institutions.

1.2.2 Institutional Rules

Douglass North emphasizes that institutions should be regarded as the 'rules of the game in a society, or, more formally, [institutions] are the humanly devised constraints that shape human interactions'.[20] *Rules*, in the context of institutions, may be defined as 'prescriptions that define what actions (or outcomes) are *required, prohibited* or *permitted*'.[21] Rules constrain the set of feasible actions that a relevant actor may perform (or at least attach higher costs to performing certain actions).

To conceive of institutions as consisting only of rules is to use a conception of institutions that is not very extensive, in the sense that it does not rely on making reference to elements such as 'sanctions' or 'actors' and so on.

In this tradition it is often assumed that institutions represent mechanisms to economize on transaction costs. North argues that 'The major role of institutions in society is to reduce uncertainty by establishing a stable . . . structure to human interaction.'[22] According to him institutions solve information problems by reducing the set of alternatives that bounded rational actors need to consider. Institutions also inhibit opportunism and solve governance problems because their rules serve to reduce and limit the set of actions that an actor might perform, or perceive as possible to perform.

Institutional rules impose costs. Since rules limit an actor's opportunity to carry out the actions he would prefer, such rules may be regarded as imposing costs on the actors that are subject to the rules. In the context of group solidarity theory Hechter argues that such costly obligations may be regarded as a tax that the relevant group imposes. Institutions can accordingly be classified according to the extent of the tax imposed upon their members.[23] According to Hechter a higher tax can be imposed by groups when the relevant actors are more dependent on the group for the provision of whatever goods it produces. If there is no alternative provider of the relevant good, then greater obligations may be imposed.[24] Accordingly, if actors depend on a single institution for defining rules that can coordinate their actions, then this institution may impose higher fees on these actors for supplying this service.

Different institutions may involve different kinds of rules. One important distinction may be made between:

- prescriptive rules, and
- prohibitive rules

Prescriptive rules contain instructions for precisely what actions people should undertake in order to achieve some specified outcome(s). Prohibitive rules, on the other hand, 'rule out certain classes of unacceptable behaviour'.[25] A single institution may incorporate both prescriptive and prohibitive rules. A state for example, can establish both prescriptive rules that 'citizens must pay taxes', and prohibitive rules that 'citizens must not murder each other'.

Prohibitive rules presumably impose less cost on actors than prescriptive rules do, since prohibitive rules allow actors to adjust on more margins. To illustrate this, imagine an actor who faces a set of feasible actions consisting of actions {A, B, C, D, and E}, over which the actor has some preference ordering. If a prohibitive rule rules out the actors most preferred action (say A), then the actor may instead choose to perform his second most preferred action (say B), rather than any of the other, less preferred, actions. If a prescriptive rule instead determines that an actor must perform some specific action, which is not his top priority, then it does not allow him to choose his second-best action, but only allows him to perform the specific action prescribed in the rule. As such a prescriptive rule generally imposes greater costs than a prohibitive rule, in the sense that it more sharply constrains the set of actions that the actor can choose to perform. It will probably also be more costly for the principals of any institution to induce compliance with prescriptive rules.

Kasper and Streit note that prescriptive rules are generally also more information-demanding than prohibitive rules. They argue that:

> Those who prescribe actions – who give directions and direct – will normally need much more specific knowledge than those who only rule out certain types of action. The one who prescribes the behaviour of others must be aware of the means and capabilities of the actor as well as possible conditions for and consequences of the prescribed action.[26]

Even if exceptions to this statement may exist, it appears generally plausible that the application of prescriptive rules involves solving greater information problems than the application of prohibitive rules does.

In two ways, then, prescriptive rules appear more costly to establish and maintain than prohibitive rules. They are more information-demanding, and they impose greater costs on those actors whose behaviour is supposed to be governed by the rule. As such, institutions involving prescriptive rules would seem to encounter greater obstacles to evolutionary success in competitive environments. Different kinds of institutions may be identified depending on the rules they involve.

According to the view presented here rules constitute institutions (or, minimally, indispensable parts of institutions). Alternatively stated, institutions establish rules.[27] To consider institutions only in terms of rules represents a rather minimalist view of institutions in the sense that it does not consider other possible elements of institutions (such as 'sanctions', 'actors' and so on).

1.2.3.   Enforcing Institutional Rules

Another view of institutions emphasizes the sanctions that are supposed to enforce the relevant rules.[28] This view regards the minimalist view of 'institutions as only rules' as insufficient since it does not specify incentives that would induce actors to comply with the relevant rules, and points to a more extensive conception of institutions as rules enforced by sanctions. Kasper and Streit, for example, argue that 'Institutions . . . are always backed up by some sort of sanctions. Institutions without sanctions are useless.'[29]

This perspective suggests that institutions actually shape the actions that will be performed. If one rejects the notion that there may exist latent institutions (that is, institutional rules that do not affect human behaviour), then strong reasons would exist to involve sanctions in the analysis of institutions. (This is a view I personally favour.) Ellickson, for example, argues that 'A guideline for human conduct is a rule only if the existence of the guideline actually influences the behaviour either of those to whom it is addressed or those who detect others breaching the guideline.'[30] According to this perspective institutional rules are sociologically relevant only if they influence the behaviour of those persons whose actions they should govern. If the rule does not affect the behaviour of those persons whom it is supposed to govern, then it is at best an aspirational statement, and at worst only a paper artefact. In the following I call an institutional rule that significantly influences behaviour an *effective rule*, while a rule that does not influence behaviour may be called a *nominal rule*.

Ellickson further argues that 'The best, and always sufficient, evidence that a rule is operative is the routine . . . administration of sanctions – whether rewards or punishments – upon people detected breaking the rule.'[31] According to this view sanctions are central to effective rules. A (nominal) rule does not in itself alter behaviour, unless actors are given some good motives to actually follow that rule. It is through the incentives provided by sanctions that relevant actors are induced to follow the behavioural recommendations that the rule specifies.

When being exposed to an 'institution' an actor is placed in a particular kind of decision situation. Institutions do not (normally) make it strictly impossible to perform the actions it prohibits, or strictly necessary to perform any actions it prescribes. Only physical necessity renders actions impossible or necessary. Normally an institution does not eliminate action alternatives in the feasible set, but either (1) changes the payoff schedule associated with each action, or (2) alters the probability that particular actions will result in specific outcomes, or (3) provides some cognitive limits as to what set of actions are perceived as feasible. By such means an institution alters the balance of desirability between the different actions that an actor may choose to perform.

Those who regard sanctions as important argue that a characteristic of the situation in which an institution places an actor is that the actor is exposed to whatever sanctions are assigned by the relevant institution (if s/he breaks the relevant rules). Sanctions provide incentives for actors to choose (or avoid) specific actions that the institutional rules identify. Sanctions as discussed here may consist in either positive 'rewards' or negative 'punishments'.[32] Most sanctions, in the context of institutions, probably consist in attaching greater costs to the actions that the institution discourages. Sanctions change the opportunity costs of performing the actions that an institutional rule defines as more or less desirable.

According to this line of argument a rule can be rendered inoperative if the relevant actors fail to administer the sanctions that provide the incentives to follow that rule. Changing the sanctions accordingly changes the way that the institution alters behaviour (regardless of what any nominal rule may recommend). If the sanctions that are administered give actors reason to choose to perform action A, even if a nominal rule recommends action B, then it is (probably) the sanctions rather than the 'rule' that determines the way that actors behave. In this case an effective (even if implicit) rule prescribing action A will in fact override the nominal (even if articulated) rule prescribing action B. From a descriptive point of view it could therefore be argued that how the sanctions are administered does in fact define the (effective) rule.

As such it may often be the application of sanctions that transform nominal rules into effective rules, which actually alter the behaviour of actors. The administration of sanctions may de facto define the effective behavioural rules. Accordingly, a more extensive view of institutions can also be formulated, which emphasizes both rules and the sanctions that enforce rules as integral and important parts of institutions.

1.2.4 Actors and Institutions

In this section I turn to institutions and actors. Some scholars regard institutions as actors, for example, they regard firms acting on a market as institutions. North, on the other hand, objects to regarding institutions as actors. He sharply distinguishes between organizations which he regards as active actors, and institutions which he regards as passive rules.[33] Organizations, to North, are the players in some game, but institutions are instead the rules of the game they play. According to his view institutions should not be regarded as actors, because it would only confuse analysis to conflate the rules of the game with the actors who should play according to those rules.[34]

Even if one accepts North's position on this point it could still be possible to favour a more extensive concept of institutions, which incorporates actors in addition to rules and sanctions. Actors may have different relations to institutional rules, and we may distinguish at least three categories of actors:

1.2.4.1   Actors who define the rules of an institution
1.2.4.2   Actors who enforce the rules of an institution
1.2.4.3   Actors whose actions are governed by the rules of an institution
          (for example, 'the players of the game')

North, in fact, only objects to regarding institutions as the actors who should play according to the rules of some game (1.2.4.3). Without disagreeing with North it could still be interesting to analyse different categories of institutions by considering what different actors define and enforce the institution's rules. Here I will briefly indicate how distinctions between different categories of actors who enforce institutional rules might, for example, serve to more clearly analyse the popular distinction between formal and informal institutions.

One common view is simply that 'government' institutions constitute 'formal' institutions – which would imply that no non-governmental institution could be a formal institution. This position seems overstated to me. As I will argue later governments are characterized by relying on (a monopoly on) violence as their method for sanctioning rule-breakers. Personally I do not think all formal institutions need to involve violence as a sanction (or rely on the state to carry out such sanctions for them). Ostracism or poor credit ratings could, for example, constitute other forms of sanctions employed by other formal institutions.

Another common view regards formal institutions as those institutions with rules that are intentionally and explicitly defined. According to the argument presented in Section 1.2.3, however, the way in which effective rules are enforced may be more important than how nominal rules are defined. This suggests that it could be useful to consider the organization for administering sanctions when analysing formal institutions.

What different kinds of actors might, then, enforce the rules of institutions? Taylor introduces a distinction between *centralized* and *decentralized* (external) solutions to collective action problems. In centralized solutions the responsibility for solving the relevant collective action problem rests only on some few well-coordinated actors, while in decentralized solutions the initiative for solving the problem is dispersed among numerous independent actors.[35] We can, similarly, distinguish between institutions that are centralized in the sense that the responsibility for administering sanctions is clearly assigned to only some few individuals, and decentralized institutions in which this responsibility is not assigned to some specific set of actors.

Other distinctions are also possible. In economics literature exchanges between two actors {A, B} are often discussed. In this context it is possible to distinguish between:[36]

- First-party enforcers
- Second-party enforcers
- Third-party enforcers

Say that for some reason actor A has an obligation to deliver a certain good to actor B. What reasons can A have to fulfil this obligation? One reason might be that A himself feels impelled to fulfil this obligation; if, for example, his conscience impels him to do so. This is first-party enforcement. Another reason might be that A delivers the good to B because he fears that B will punish him if does not fulfil his obligation (as in Axelrod's tit-for-tat strategies). This constitutes second-party enforcement. If A and B have a legally binding contract, then B might turn to a state court and ask that this court imposes sanctions on A if he does not fulfil his obligation. In relation to actors A and B the court constitutes an external party, and this is called third-party enforcement.

In general, then, it would seem possible to classify institutions both according to whether the enforcement agents are centralized or decentralized, and according to whether they involve first, second, or third-party enforcers. Jointly these distinctions may enable us to clarify the distinction between formal and informal institutions.

A formal institution, I suggest, may be:

(a) An institution in which specific agents are assigned a special responsibility for enforcement (and adjudication)
(b) Where these assigned agents are third-party enforcers

Conversely, institutions that do not fulfil these criteria would not be regarded as formal institutions. According to this view the distinction between formal and informal institutions depends on how the administering of sanctions is organized.[37]

If, in addition to rules and sanctions, we also involve actors in the conception of institutions, then this clearly makes for an even more extensive view of institutions. We have seen that North, for example, rejects the idea of regarding institutions as actors, but have also seen that analytically there may be scope for considering some actors (rule-definers and enforcers) in the analysis of institutions. That sanctions provide motives to follow effective rules, which may be more important than how (nominal) rules are defined, suggests that it may be important to consider the actors that can render rules inoperative if they do not apply the sanctions.

1.2.5 Institutions: A Summary

Different perspectives on institutions clearly exist (even within the new institutional economics tradition). Depending on one's point of view an 'institution' may be said to consist of (either):

1.2.5.1   Some set of (equilibrium) actions or behaviours
1.2.5.2   Some set(s) of rules that constrain(s) what actions may be performed by relevant actors
1.2.5.3   Some set(s) of sanctions (or incentives) that enforce(s) these rules
1.2.5.4   Some set(s) of individual actors, who determine(s) the rules and administer(s) the sanctions

Differing conceptions of institutions focus on different elements; some focus on (equilibrium) behaviours, other focus on rules and so on. The brief review above has indicated that each perspective has its own strengths and weaknesses. More or less extensive conceptions may also exist, depending on how many different elements they involve. A minimal conception may regard institutions as consisting only in rules, while more extensive conceptions may consider institutions also in terms of sanctions and actors (that facilitate the effective functioning of the rules) as shown in Table 1.1.[38]

Depending on which kind of conception we employ, different kinds of social systems can be regarded as institutions. Some social systems, such as states, can clearly be subsumed under a rather extensive concept of institutions. (States define (legal) *rules*, impose *sanctions* (fines, imprisonment) on rule breakers (criminals), and special *actors*, (judges and police officers and so on) are responsible for defining the rules and administering the

Table 1.1   More and Less Extensive Concepts of Institutions

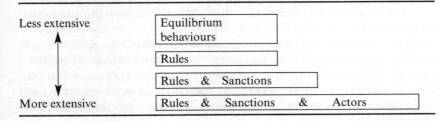

Less extensive	Equilibrium behaviours
More extensive	Rules
	Rules & Sanctions
	Rules & Sanctions & Actors

sanctions.) On the other hand, under this stricter conception it would not appear possible to regard, for example, a market price mechanism as an institution (although Austrian economists have tended to do so).

It is also possible to analyse different categories of institutions, depending on which kinds of rules and sanctions they involve. A formal institution with prohibitive rules might, for example, be quite different from an informal institution with prescriptive rules.

Which conception of institutions is adopted is partly a matter of the intellectual preferences of individual academics, but may also be a function of what is suitable for the particular analysis at hand. To me, it seems that when we discuss institutional *competition*, it is important to consider some actors that actively compete. For competing institutions it would also appear important to offer effective rules, not only nominal rules, because for selection processes (including competition) it would appear important that there exist attributes that selection may work upon, and such attributes need to interact with their environment in some tangible way. As such I favour an extensive view of institutions when analysing competition, but others might disagree.[39]

1.3   COMPETITION BETWEEN INSTITUTIONS

Above I have discussed institutions. To discuss 'institutional competition' one must also discuss 'competition', however. This section briefly addresses questions such as in which sense institutions could be said to compete, and what differentiates 'institutional competition' from other kinds of 'competition'?

Most contemporary discussions of institutional competition focus on the consequences that follow from institutional competition. (It is argued, for example, that institutional competition will result in depleting the revenues that are necessary to maintain costly welfare states.) In this chapter, however, I wish to focus primarily on competition as such (as an independent variable), rather than the consequences of institutional competition.

Unless it has been specified why institutional competition might differ substantively from other forms of competition, one should presumably analyse it according to conventional economic models, and generally institutional competition should be contrasted to situations of institutional monopoly. Questions therefore arise about whether institutional competition is distinct from other competition. What do institutions compete with, and what, more specifically, is said to be competing when institutional competition occurs?

An illustrative example, from current discussions of globalization, is whether or not the West European economic system will be out-competed because labour costs are currently much lower in Poland than in, say France (and even lower in China). Loosely speaking one could perhaps say that France and Poland each represent one institution (or one bundle of institutions), and are engaged in institutional competition with each other. More strictly speaking I would, however, say that this is not a case of competition between institutions (at least as they are discussed here), instead this is a competition between the production factor 'Polish labour' and the production factor 'French labour'.

If we wish to analyse the nature and impact of institutional competition specifically, then it is probably wise to separate this particular production factor analytically from competition between other production factors, that is, to hold constant any competition between other production factors, as *ceteris paribus* conditions. What, then, is the specific (productive) contribution of institutions to the economic system?

If institutions are regarded as (equilibrium) patterns of behaviour, then it is not clear what would differentiate such actions or behaviours from other productive actions; especially it would not be possible to differentiate institutions from labour (considered as production factors).

However, if institutions are regarded as rules (possibly enforced by sanctions and actors), then it is easier to identify a specific economic contribution of institutions. Oliver Williamson argues that institutions on exchange markets arise as responses to the twin challenges of:

- the information problem of bounded rationality coupled with uncertainty, and
- the governance problem of opportunism coupled with small number markets.[40]

According to Williamson it is difficult to specify contracts that adequately coordinate and govern transactions. Bounded rationality implies that actors are not omniscient – they cannot overview and assess all relevant alternatives. This problem is especially grave in situations of uncertainty, when non-predictable changes make it impossible to specify in advance what situations might arise. This makes it impossible to specify a perfect contract to govern continuous transactions between actors, since it is impossible to specify in advance what responses should be undertaken if numerous different contingencies arise. This information problem makes it difficult to coordinate different actors.

Opportunism implies that actors will not always act faithfully to fulfil their perceived obligations. Instead actors might choose to perform actions detrimental to their counterparts if this improves their own position. Williamson argues that the scope for acting opportunistically is greatest on markets that involve small numbers of actors (since on perfectly competitive markets there is no scope for any single actor to affect market outcome by behaving opportunistically). This is a governance problem.

According to North institutions coordinate actors and solve information problems by reducing the set of alternatives that bounded rational actors need to consider.[41] 'The computational limitations of the individual are determined by the capacity to of the mind to process, organise, and utilize information . . . The consequent institutional framework, by structuring human interaction, limits the choices of actors.'[42] And, 'Under conditions of limited information and limited computational ability, constraints reduce the costs of human interaction as compared to a world of no institutions.'[43]

Institutions are also widely considered to solve governance problems. Institutions might be introduced which inhibit detrimental actions and facilitate coordination between actors. For example, institutions are often said to solve free-riding and public goods problems, including common pool resource problems.[44]

To sum up, institutions (defined as rules) arguably fulfil the economic function of coordinating different actors' actions in order to enhance mutual benefits, aiming to solve information and governance problems.[45] The rules solve the coordination problems by reducing and limiting the set of actions that an actor might perform, or perceive as possible to perform.

The production factors that are conventionally discussed in economic analysis are labour, land, and capital. Sometimes one also analyses 'management' and perhaps even 'company culture' as additional production factors. The above discussion suggests that the production factor offered by institutions is (enforced) rules, and that they serve to coordinate the actions of different actors. Institutions appear to offer coordination through rules, and presumably it is in the market for such services that they compete with each other.

If coordination is the contribution of institutions, then institutions offer a production factor that is similar to that offered by management within firms. Management serves to coordinate actors within organizations and determine in which proportions different production factors are combined. There are, however, also differences between management and institutions considered as production factors. One is that management may be implemented through discretionary and partial decision-making, while institutions operate through more universal and semi-permanent rules. Additionally, management is usually aimed at mobilizing a group of people's resources towards specific goals, while institutions may involve prohibitive rules, not aim at mobilizing resources, and be more open-ended in terms of their goals.

If institutions offer the production factor 'coordinating rules' this may suggest some particular problems with institutional competition. One problem is that institutions do not, generally, seem to have easily enforceable property rights in relation to the coordination services that they offer. In comparison it is easier for institutions to maintain that they have property rights over other production factors, such as their capital and land.

It may, for example, be impossible to exclude free-riders from benefiting from a system of institutional rules. Rule-governed behaviour may confer benefits even on those who do not pay for the efforts of defining and enforcing the rules, and sometimes even on actors who do not follow the rules themselves. (For example, even individuals who do not pay taxes enjoy the benefits of reduced crime that follows from police activities, and so on.) Thus, it is not easy to maintain property rights that are enforceable in the sense of being able to exclude non-payers from utilizing the services in question.

In the limiting cases where there is no possibility of excluding anyone from consuming the services produced by institutions, and there is no rivalry in consumption, the institutions that supply coordination services are simply conferring positive externalities on indefinite numbers of persons. In such cases it may not be meaningful to talk of competition between institutions at all, because effectively there is no scarcity of resources. (This is indeed an unusual case, though.)

A more realistic reason why institutional competition may be problematic is that coordinating rules are not easily separable from other bundles of production factors. Coordinating rules do not represent a production factor that can simply be added to, or subtracted from, other production factors. Rather, rules predicate over other production factors, and define what attributes other production factors have, in the sense of regulating what aspects of these production factors may be put to productive use. (For example, labour legislation may determine minimum wages, whether workers can work on Sundays, undertake dangerous tasks and so on.)

Since coordinating rules are not strictly separable from other production factors, but only exist bundled with other goods, it can be difficult to determine the separate price for the production factor 'institutional rules'. The productivity of institutional coordination is not easily measured, it is difficult to determine what value this production factor (as opposed to other production factors, including labour, capital and land), has added to the value of some consumption good. Neither is there a specific market for pricing coordinating rules, since coordinating rules appear as attributes of other goods they are not priced independently. As such, competitive markets may not easily result in unproblematic pricing of the production factor 'coordinating rules'.

In summary, institutional competition may encounter some specific problems. That positive externalities may be conferred by institutional rules, and that it may be difficult to value the contribution of the specific production factor 'coordinating rules' (as opposed to other production factors), suggests that it is uncertain to what extent ordinary market competition easily results in an effective pricing system for such services.

Neither competition nor pricing systems are entirely inhibited, however. Tiebout, for example, shows that if we discuss local public goods – that is goods that it is possible to exclude non-members of a community from consuming, but which must be made available to all members of that given community – then pricing may be possible for such goods. In Tiebout's analysis it is also the case that each community in effect offers a bundle of goods and services and it is this bundle that is priced in the process of competition between communities.[46] Even if this does not arrive at imputing a price to each specific component of the bundle it nevertheless produces a price for the bundle as a whole. As such Tiebout's analysis shows that the problems of market competition and pricing are surmountable, even if the process and results are not perfect.

The ability to compete, and arrive at pricing systems, suggests that even when we are dealing with institutions there is some potential for competition, and in general we may expect such competition to have the effect of making prices reveal consumer preferences and aligning institutions' supply with such consumer preferences. Generally, it appears best to analyse institutional competition in the same manner as other competition, even if it is a somewhat particular case. (How competitive markets are, for example, is often measured in terms of distribution indices, such as the Gini coefficient, Herfindahl's index and so on. There exists no a priori reason why these indices might not be used when measuring institutional competition. For example, it is possible to measure the number of taxpayers a state has in relation to the number of potential taxpayers in some larger territory and so on.)

1.4 STATES, COMPETITION AND STATE-FORMATION

As we have seen it is possible to discuss many different kinds of institutions, which might compete. Frankly, though, what is called 'institutional competition' is almost always competition between governments or states, which this section will discuss.

1.4.1 States as Institutions

States can be subsumed under an extensive concept of institutions (and, *ergo*, also under less extensive concepts). States define (legal) rules, impose sanctions (fines, imprisonment) on rule breakers (criminals), and special actors (judges and police officers and so on) are responsible for defining the rules and administering the sanctions. States are thus institutions, and in cases where states compete we may say that institutional competition occurs.

Furthermore, states are *formal institutions* according to the definition suggested in Section 1.2.4, that is, they employ enforcement officers with a clearly assigned responsibility for enforcing relevant rules (police officers and so on), and (at least in relation to many of the rules they enforce) these enforcement officers constitute third-party enforcers.

States are also institutions that exchange resources with their environment. States collect tax revenues from their taxpayers/citizens, and governments provide services and goods to these taxpayers/citizens. As such they can engage in competition over scarce resources.

To briefly summarize: states are institutions, furthermore they are formal institutions, and organizations which exchange resources with their environment. It could be maintained that states are the kind of institutions that can clearly be said to compete.

1.4.2 The Defining Characteristics of States

If we discuss states as institutions, what is it that set states apart from other institutions? What are the specific defining characteristics of states? Max Weber provided the classical definition of a state: 'the modern state is a compulsory association which organizes domination. It has been successful in seeking to monopolize the legitimate use of physical force as a means of domination within a territory'.[47] By the phrase 'physical force' Weber means 'violence' – 'The state is considered the sole source of the 'right' to use violence.'[48] Weber defines the state as a monopolist of the legitimate use of violence.

Weber's definition is minimalist in the sense that it focuses on what is the least common denominator of all states.[49] He argues that 'There is scarcely any task that some political association has not taken in hand, and there is no task that one could say has always been exclusive and peculiar to . . . the state.'[50] As a means for administration, however, he argues that 'force is a means *specific* to the state'.[51] Weber thus explicitly argues that there are no specific purposes ('tasks') towards which states work (or should work); instead he argues that violence is a state's *means* for attaining whatever purposes it is interested in. If institutions are defined extensively in terms of rules, sanctions and actors, then it follows from Weber's definition that states are institutions that are specific in that *violence* is the instrument that they employ for administering sanctions in order to enforce rules. Since states may work towards different purposes the content of the rules they specify may vary, but violence is states' particular method of enforcing rules. This characteristic sets states apart from other institutions. (An objection to Weber's definition is that it 'places excessive emphasis on the coercive aspects of political life'.[52] However, Weber does not suggest that states always engage in violence, but merely observes that if and when necessary, they can resort to violence to enforce their rules.[53])

1.4.3   Do States Exchange or Appropriate Resources?

States define and enforce many laws that protect their subjects from criminal behaviour, and also delineate and enforce property rights and so on (that is, states solve governance problems).[54] States (as institutions) define coordinating rules and enforce them, and these enforced rules constitute the service that governments, most characteristically, offer their constituents (who may be regarded as analogous to their customers).[55] In return states extract payment through taxation.

An analogy to a market would suggest that a state ruler supplies a service – coordination through enforced rules – that the subjects independently demand. In exchange the subjects surrender a stream of (tax) incomes to the ruler(s) of the relevant state(s) as payment.

Following Hechter, we could plausibly maintain that institutions such as states can impose a higher tax when the relevant actors are more dependent on that institution for the provision of whatever goods it produces. If there is no alternative provider of the relevant good, then greater tax obligations may be imposed.[56] Accordingly, if actors depend on a single state institution for defining rules that coordinate their actions, then this institution may impose higher taxes/fees on these actors for supplying this service. If demand price elasticity is low even higher taxes can be collected.

It is unclear whether states engage in voluntary exchanges, however. Subjects of a state may be unable to abstain from receiving or 'consuming' the services that state rulers supply to them. Subjects cannot choose to flout their government's laws (without risking that their government imposes sanctions). Furthermore, taxpayers are normally not in a position to refuse to pay taxes demanded by their state (without facing sanctions).[57] If subjects cannot abstain from paying taxes, then appropriation of taxes can occur without any exchange, since state rulers need not necessarily deliver any goods or services to their subjects in order to elicit payments. For these reasons states do not necessarily engage in the 'voluntary' exchange that characterizes ordinary markets. (This is not to claim that many subjects/taxpayers would not agree to make such exchanges with their governments, only that if they do not agree then they are in no position to abstain.)

From a domestic perspective, of course, each citizen faces a monopolist state, and cannot abstain from either 'consuming' the services it offers (that is, abstain from being governed by its laws), nor abstain from paying the taxes it demands.

1.4.4 Competition between States and State-formation

Weber's definition indicates that a state is in some respects a monopolist (domestically, vis-à-vis its own subjects). However, no state is a monopolist in the true sense of the word – that it has no (possible) competitors. In the international arena any given state is merely one among many similar actors; it is not a monopolist. The rulers of every state are exposed to actual and potential competition, both from other states and from important groups within their own states.[58]

The reason that a state's subjects may experience their state as a monopolist is probably not because there is any lack of alternative providers of violence and protection (other states do exist), but because it is very costly for citizens to change allegiance between different states.[59] Moving from one state to another is costly since a subject cannot normally bring all his/her resources with him when he moves. There are sunk costs that inhibit exit. A state ruler may also make migration even more costly by imposing exit barriers. States are therefore not necessarily monopolies, but they establish *partitioned* markets, and in each segment of a partitioned market one state dominates the exercise of violence and may act as a monopolist. (It appears, in general, that barriers are lower for mobile capital, than for immobile physical persons.)[60]

In economics literature a standard distinction is made between differently competitive markets, as follows:

1.4.4.1   Perfectly competitive markets
1.4.4.2   Monopolies w
1.4.4.3   Monopolistic competition
1.4.4.4   Oligopolies

Perfectly competitive markets are characterized as markets with a large number of small suppliers of homogeneous goods, none of which can affect market price. The market outcome is presumed to be Pareto optimal, and (low) prices set equal to marginal costs. In monopoly markets there exists only one supplier of the good, who restricts output and increases prices in order to earn monopoly rents (to the detriment of consumers). Prices exceed marginal costs. Under monopolistic competition there exist a large number of small suppliers, but the goods are not homogeneous – producers may employ product differentiation as a competitive strategy (which in effect partitions the market). Since products are differentiated it is costly for consumers to switch between substitutes, which enables the supplier to (imperfectly) restrict output and raise prices (somewhat resembling monopolists). In oligopolistic markets there exist a small number of suppliers whose actions are mutually dependent upon each other. Oligopolists have some scope for reducing output and increasing prices, but each company depends on the reactions of the other alternative suppliers. Consequently outcomes are often indeterminate.

In addition to the above categories it is also common to discuss cases of collusion and cartels, which concern markets in which there exist a number of firms, but where these firms form agreements with each other to limit competition and to act jointly in ways similar to a monopolist.

There exists no obvious reason why competition between institutions might not be analysed in terms of the above categories. The partitioned markets that appear characteristic of competition between governments most closely match monopolistic competition, and probably yield similar outcomes. In both cases the market is partitioned by increasing the costs for consumers to switch to substitutes. This suggests that there are good reasons to assume that the analysis of institutional competition should follow the same lines as analysis of other forms of competition, and that institutional competition should be considered in standard terms of market concentration.

The theoretical opposite of the state is anarchy, which denotes a society in which no state exists.[61] If Weber's perfectly consolidated state is represented by a society in which the capacity to exercise violence is monopolized, then it follows that 'anarchy' is conversely represented by a society where the capacity to exercise violence is perfectly decentralized.[62] A state system can therefore possibly be characterized in terms of its 'degree of market concentration', and *state-formation* can plausibly be defined as changes in the degree of market concentration. Even a political scientist who was very critical towards discussing states at all (Watkins) accordingly argues that the state could be usefully discussed if one recognized that:

> the distinctive feature of the state . . . is its attempt to monopolize coercive power within its own territory . . . From the standpoint of a purely descriptive political science it is sufficient, therefore, to define the state in terms of the limit and to study the conditions that accompany the greater or lesser degrees of monopoly that have been achieved in particular times and places.[63]

If state-formation may be defined as variations in the degree of some market concentration, then it may be useful to note that market concentration may be described in terms of *horizontal integration*. Considering institutional competition in terms of market concentration also implies that the size of states matter; if a geographical region is dominated by some few large states, then institutional competition will be less intense than if many small governments existed in the same area. Territorial integration may be regarded as horizontal integration. Such occurred, for example, when 'Milan, Naples, Navarre, and Sicily disappear[ed] into France and Spain' between 1495–1789.[64] Around 1500 AD there existed as many as 200 political units in Europe that could plausibly be regarded as states. After territorial integration about 35 states exist in Europe today. The majority of the original states disappeared somewhere along the way.[65] Tilly suggests that in 1490 the average territorial size of the 200 state-like units in Europe would have been around 9500 square miles, while in 1890 the 30 state units would have averaged some 63 000 square miles.[66] The declining number of states, and their increasing average sizes, reflects processes of state-formation, increasing 'market concentration' between 1490 and 1890.

1.4.5 Consequences of Competition between States

Monopolist states (or state rulers) do not necessarily engage in the normal kind of exchange with their subjects, instead they may simply appropriate resources from their constituents/taxpayers. (Indeed, by definition, this is how a tax is distinguished from a fee; a fee implies that you get something specific in return for your payment, a tax does not.)

This observation largely fails, however, when it becomes clear that states are not really true monopolists, but are exposed to varying degrees of competition from other states. The reason why states need not necessarily engage in exchanges with their subjects is because subjects (domestically) cannot abstain from paying taxes to their government, and because they cannot abstain from being governed by whatever behavioural rules (laws) their government has defined. From a non-domestic point of view, however, it is clear that when institutional competition exists an individual can move into another state and become subject to its legal and tax codes. By this means this individual can abstain from paying taxes to a given state and can abstain from being governed by its laws, if and when institutional competition occurs.[67]

If institutional competition means that individuals become less dependent on the institutional framework provided by any given state, then this state will also be less able to tax these persons indiscriminately. Individuals can then abstain from paying taxes to a specific government if they are not provided with sufficiently high quality (coordination) services from this government. If taxpayers are mobile, then alternative states may set lower tax rates, and define better behavioural rules, in order to attract subjects/taxpayers. Such a government will be induced to enter into exchanges with such subjects because in order to elicit the payment of taxes state rulers must offer services that their subjects are willing to pay for. Institutional competition should therefore result in partially transforming taxes into fees, and aligning government supply more closely with the preferences of the consumers.

As indicated in Section 1.2 institutional competition may not be perfect. We may be restricted to competition between governments that offer different bundles of goods or services (rather than single goods or services). In such cases migrant subjects may be compelled to buy entire packages of services, some of which they do not really want. To the extent that we discuss government provision of public (not private) goods, then it may also be the case that institutional competition only works well for local public goods (as in Tiebout's analysis). Institutional competition may therefore be imperfect. But there is nothing to suggest that either of the problems would really be better addressed in the absence of competition, instead standard economic analysis suggests that problems would be worse under monopoly.

Competition between governments may, according to the above discussion, be assumed to have at least two consequences:

(1) To transform tax systems where there are no clear exchanges between governments and their subjects/taxpayers into fee systems where there is a clearer correspondence between payments made (by state subjects) and the services offered (by their governments).
(2) To align the output of governments more closely with the preferences of their consumers, and enable tax rates to reflect more closely the relative scarcity of the goods and services that governments offer.

Readers may make their own normative evaluation of these consequences of institutional competition.

1.5   SUMMARY AND FURTHER ANALYSIS

This chapter has discussed conceptual issues regarding institutional competition. Section 1.1 discussed *institutions* and suggested that differently extensive concepts of institutions may be identified. Section 1.2 discussed institutional *competition*, arguing that the benchmark assumption should be to analyse institutional competition in terms of standard economic analysis. I also suggested that institutions specifically provide a particular production factor – coordinating rules. Section 1.3 discussed states as a specific kind of institution that can employ violence in order to enforce whatever behavioural rules they establish. It was also suggested that competition between states can occur, and when it does occur it enhances the ability to conduct exchanges between states and their subjects, because it allows unwilling subjects to abstain from paying taxes.

This chapter clearly leaves many questions open for further analysis. Questions may, for example, be raised by considering the distinction between resource-based competition and yardstick competition.[68] Resource-based competition describes a situation in which several actors attempt to appropriate the same scarce resource and each actor can only appropriate units of the resource by denying the others access to those units. Yardstick competition instead concerns how different competing institutions can learn from each other's comparative successes and failures. I suspect elaborations of this distinction can yield substantial further analysis, perhaps by considering how price mechanisms involve aspects of both kinds of competition.

Another open question concerns the rules of the competition between institutions. In this chapter I have indicated that in many cases institutional competition might enhance outcomes, in the sense of aligning institutional output with the preferences of the institutions' 'customers'. However, this is based on a presumption that competition occurs through the judgement of consumers. In this form of competition a consumer stands as mediator between competing institutions, and it is this consumer's choice of which institution's output he wishes to purchase that determines which institution is most competitively successful. Other rules of competition might instead allow institutions to compete against each other through warfare (or theft), as has often been the case in competition between states. In such cases we cannot expect equally benevolent outcomes from institutional competition. Not only the degree of competition, but also the rules of competition therefore appear interesting. Here too, further analysis would be required.

Yet another important question regards the relation between actors and institutions. On the one hand, academics such as North warn of regarding institutions as actors. On the other hand, if institutions engage in competition it must be important to consider the actors that make institutions take active part in such competition. In any case, important questions arise about how individual actors who maintain institutions (those actors who define and enforce the institutional rules) are provided with motives to carry out these activities, on an individual level. This problem is highlighted by game theorists who note that such matters needs to be resolved or else the analysis of institutions would be subject to infinite regress (see Section 1.2.1).[69] Further analysis is needed of how the incentives for individual actors relate to institutional competition.

Outstanding questions being noted, however, it is fair to say that the main conclusion of this chapter is that unless it has been specified why institutional competition would radically differ from other forms of competition, one should presumably analyse it according to conventional theoretical models. Descriptively I have argued that institutional competition between states is best understood as monopolistic competition. Prescriptively, institutional competition should be compared to institutional monopoly, and almost all economic analysis points to the advantages of competition over monopoly.

NOTES

1. For example, the scope of this chapter does not allow for a discussion of academic traditions such as 'sociological institutionalism', or 'new historical institutionalism' but focuses more narrowly on 'new institutional economics' or 'rational choice institutionalism'. For reviews of such traditions see Peters (1998); Hall and Taylor (1994); DiMaggio and Powell (1991).
2. Aoki (2001, pp. 5, 6, 7).
3. Kasper and Streit (1998, p. 28); Hechter (1987, p. 30).
4. Ellickson (1991, p. 124).
5. I do not use 'extensive' in its semantic meaning here, but to refer to how many elements the definition includes.
6. Berger and Luckman (1966, pp. 71–2).
7. Wrong (1994, p. 48).
8. Höijer (2006, pp. 394–5).
9. Ellickson (1991, p. 129).
10. Calvert (1998, p. 58).
11. Calvert (1998, p. 74).
12. Aoki (2001, pp. 2, 7).
13. Aoki (2001, pp. 2, 14, 15).
14. Calvert (1998, p. 59).

15. Greif et al. (1998, p. 48).
16. Aoki (2001, p. 9).
17. Knight (1998, pp. 96, 98, 110); Knight and Sened (1998, p. 10).
18. Knight (1998, p. 102).
19. Aoki (2001, pp. 10, 11, 13).
20. North (1990, p. 3).
21. Ostrom et al. (1994, p. 38).
22. North (1990, p. 6).
23. Hechter (1987, pp. 10, 41).
24. Hechter (1987, pp. 10, 45, 46).
25. Kasper and Streit (1998, p. 97).
26. Kasper and Streit (1998, p. 97).
27. Knight and Sened (1998, p. 9).
28. I do not know of any academic who attempts to define institutions only in terms of sanctions, without considering the rules that the sanctions are supposed to enforce.
29. Kasper and Streit (1998, p. 28).
30. Ellickson (1991, p. 128).
31. Ellickson (1991, p. 128).
32. Ellickson (1991, p. 124).
33. North (1990, p. 5); see also Kasper and Streit (1998, p. 98).
34. North (1998, pp. 15–16).
35. Taylor (1987, p. 23).
36. Ellickson (1991) p. 126); see also North (1990, pp. 3, 33).
37. Kasper and Streit (1998, p. 106) appear to agree with such a view.
38. The concept of institutions as behaviours seems to stand somewhat by itself, and not involve itself with conceptions based on rules and so on. Indeed the point of endogenizing motives in terms of equilibria is to divorce analysis from the need to discuss sanctions and actors, which is considered to lead to infinite regress.
39. Those who disagree might, for example argue that institutions themselves consist only in rules, and that sanctions only determine whether such institutions are effective or not.
40. Williamson (1975, pp. 7–10).
41. North (1990, pp. 17, 22).
42. North (1990, p. 25).
43. North (1990, p. 36).
44. Ostrom (1990, p. 1).
45. See, for example, Knight and Sened (1998, p. 2). Also note that in some institutionalist analysis it is instead emphasized that institutions have distributional consequences and benefit some actors at the expense of others (rather than resulting in mutual gains). This may well be correct to some extent, but it is unclear how we could analyse institutional competition from this perspective.
46. Equivalently it could be the case that each community (or institution) offers a single good that exhibits a bundle of attributes or characteristics.
47. Weber (1948, pp. 82–3).
48. Weber (1948, p. 78).
49. See, for example, Taylor (1987, p. 1).
50. Weber (1948, p. 77) and (1964, p. 155).
51. Weber (1948, pp. 78–9); see also Weber (1964, p. 154).
52. Watkins (1968, p. 156).
53. Weber (1964, p. 154).
54. Olson (2000) chapter 1).
55. In addition states may offer other services, including teaching, hospital beds and so on, but this does not set them apart from other institutions.
56. Hechter (1987, pp. 10, 45, 46).
57. Brennan and Buchanan (1980, p. 37).
58. North (1981, p. 27); Poggi (1978, p. 87); Tilly (1990, pp. 4, 23); Tilly (1993, p. 37).

59. Hechter (1987, pp. 46–7); Hechter (2000, pp. 31, 67).
60. It appears, generally, that barriers are lower for mobile capital than for immobile physical persons largely due to governments decisions to deregulate and remove barriers that they had earlier introduced to partition the international market.
61. See Weber (1948, p. 78).
62. de Jasay (1989, p. 42).
63. Watkins (1968, pp. 155–6).
64. Tilly (1990, p. 174).
65. Tilly (1993, p. 25).
66. Tilly (1990, p. 46).
67. It may not be possible for individuals to avoid paying taxes to and being governed by the laws of any state. It may be possible for a person so inclined to escape from one state to another, but it may not be possible to escape all states altogether.
68. See Vaubel, Chapter 2.
69. Aoki (2001, pp. 2, 14, 15).

BIBLIOGRAPHY

Aoki, M. (2001), *Toward a Comparative Institutional Analysis*, Cambridge, MA: MIT Press.
Berger, P. and T. Luckman (1966), *The Social Construction of Reality*, Harmondsworth: Penguin.
Brennan, G. and J. Buchanan (1980), *The Power to Tax: Analytical Foundations of a Fiscal Constitution*, Cambridge: Cambridge University Press.
Calvert, R. (1998), 'Rational Actors, Equilibrium and Social Institutions', in J. Knight and I. Sened (eds), *Explaining Social Institutions*, Ann Arbor: University of Michigan Press, pp. 57–94.
Cowen, T. (ed.) (1992), *Public Goods and Market Failures*, New Brunswick: Transaction Publishers.
de Jasay, A. (1989), *Social Contract, Free Ride*, Oxford: Clarendon Press.
DiMaggio, P.J. and W.W. Powell (eds) (1991), *The New Institutionalism in Organizational Analysis*, Chicago: University of Chicago Press.
Ellickson, R. (1991), *Order without Law*, Cambridge, MA: Harvard University Press.
Greif, A., P. Milgrom and B. Weingast (1998), 'Coordination, Commitment, and Enforcement: The Case of the Merchant Guild', in J. Knight and I. Sened (eds), *Explaining Social Institutions*, Ann Arbor: University of Michigan Press, pp. 27–56.
Hall, P. and R. Taylor (1994), 'Political Science and the Three New Institutionalisms', *Political Studies*, **44** (5), 936–57.
Hechter, M. (1987), *Principles of Group Solidarity*, Berkeley: University of California Press.
Hechter, Michael (2000), *Containing Nationalism*, Oxford: Oxford University Press.
Höijer, R. (2006), 'Government Regulation of Behaviour in Public Insurance Systems', in P. Kurrild (ed.), *The Dynamics of Intervention: Regulation and Redistribution in the Mixed Economy*, Oxford: Elsevier, pp. 377–9.
Kasper, W. and M.E. Streit (1998), *Institutional Economics*, Cheltenham, UK and Lyme, USA: Edward Elgar.
Knight, J. (1998), 'Models, Interpretations, and Theories: Constructing Explanations of Institutional Emergence and Change', in J. Knight and I. Sened (eds), *Explaining Social Institutions*, Ann Arbor: University of Michigan Press, pp. 95–120.

Knight, J. and I. Sened (1998), 'Introduction', in J. Knight and I. Sened (eds), *Explaining Social Institutions*, Ann Arbor: University of Michigan Press, pp. 1–14.

Knight, J. and I. Sened (eds) (1998a), *Explaining Social Institutions*, Ann Arbor: University of Michigan Press.

Kurrild, P. (ed.) (2006), *The Dynamics of Intervention: Regulation and Redistribution in the Mixed Economy*, Oxford: Elsevier.

North, D.C. (1981), *Structure and Change in Economic History*, New York: W.W. Norton Company.

North, D.C. (1990), *Institutions, Institutional Change and Economic Performance*, Cambridge: Cambridge University Press.

North, D.C. (1998), 'Five Propositions about Institutional Change', in J. Knight and I. Sened (eds), *Explaining Social Institutions*, Ann Arbor: University of Michigan Press, pp. 15–26.

Olson, M. (2000), *Power and Prosperity*, New York: Basic Books.

Ostrom, E. (1990), *Governing the Commons*, Cambridge: Cambridge University Press.

Ostrom, E., R. Gardner and J.Walker (1994), *Rules, Games and Common-pool Resources*, Ann Arbor: University of Michigan Press.

Peters, G.B. (1998), *The New Institutionalism*, London: Cassells.

Poggi, G. (1978), *The Development of the Modern State: A Sociological Introduction*, Stanford: Stanford University Press.

Sills, D.L. (ed.) (1968), *The International Encyclopedia of the Social Sciences*, vol. 15, New York: The Macmillan Company and the Free Press.

Taylor, M. (1987), *The Possibility of Cooperation*, Cambridge: Cambridge University Press.

Tiebout, C. (1992), 'A Pure Theory of Local Expenditures', in T. Cowen (ed.), *Public Goods and Market Failures*, New Brunswick: Transaction Publishers, pp. 179–92.

Tilly, C. (1975), 'Reflections on the History of the European State-making', in C. Tilly (ed.), *The Formation of National States in Western Europe*, Princeton: Princeton University Press, pp. 3–84.

Tilly, C. (ed.) (1975a), *The Formation of National States in Western Europe*, Princeton: Princeton University Press.

Tilly, C. (1990), *Coercion, Capital, and European States*, Oxford: Blackwell Publishers.

Tilly, C. (1993), *European Revolutions, 1492–1992*, Oxford: Blackwell Publishers.

Watkins, F. (1968), 'State', in D.L. Sills (ed.), *The International Encyclopedia of the Social Sciences*, vol. 15, New York: The Macmillan Company and the Free Press, pp. 150–7.

Weber, M. (1964), *The Theory of Social and Economic Organization*, New York: The Free Press.

Weber, M. (1948), 'Politics as a Vocation', in M. Weber, *Essays in Sociology*, trans. H. Gerth and C. Wright Mills, London: Routledge, pp. 77–128.

Weber, M. (1948a), *Essays in Sociology*, trans. H. Gerth and C. Wright Mills, London: Routledge.

Williamson, O. (1975), *Markets and Hierarchies*, London: The Free Press.

Wrong, D. (1994), *The Problem of Order*, Cambridge, MA: Harvard University Press.

2.   A history of thought on institutional competition

Roland Vaubel

INTRODUCTION

Economists distinguish between competition and anarchy. Competition is a social order in which individuals are free to make their choices without interference from others. They enjoy the right of property and freedom of contract. Interactions among individuals are based on mutual consent. Thus, competition is by definition peaceful. War is not a means of competition.[1]

Anarchy may not be peaceful. As Thomas Hobbes (1651/1962) warned, it may lead to a war of everybody against everybody. The 'anarchistic equilibrium' (Buchanan 1975) must not be confused with a competitive Pareto-optimum. However, even in conditions of anarchy, there may be many peaceful competitive transactions. Anarchy is likely to permit more competition than despotism, and insecurity of possession prevails not only in anarchy but also in any real-world state.

Competition may not only prevail among individuals or private firms in a market, it may also take place among public institutions. Usually, these public institutions belong to different states but the term 'institutional competition' has also been applied to competing legal orders within the same territory.

Just as competition in the market can be improved by a competitive order, that is, public institutions which maintain market competition within each country, (monopolistic) competition among the public institutions of different countries can benefit from an international competitive order which preserves peace and prevents governments from colluding with each other at the expense of third parties, notably their citizens.

Historically, the rivalries among the rulers of different states have hardly ever been entirely peaceful. But besides the constant bickering and international anarchy, there was also a peaceful competition for mobile resources and institutional innovation. Even the tribal system of the Stone Age was more favourable to technical progress than a monopolistic empire would have been (Baechler 2002, Ch. I).

Successful interjurisdictional competition has been a fact long before scholars began to think about it. The best-known instances are the Sumerian civilization of the third millennium BC, China in the late Chou era (722–221 BC) and during the Song period (960–1275 AD), ancient Greece, the Phoenician civilization (seventh to fourth centuries BC) and Renaissance Italy.[2] However, the political thinkers of the time do not seem to have understood the secret of their civilizations' success. Machiavelli, for example, was longing for the political unification of Italy. It is true that the ancient Greeks valued competition (αγων) very highly[3] and that Plato and Aristotle favoured polities that were small both in territory and in population.[4] There is also a well-known quotation from a Roman historian of the first century AD who praises emulation as the path to genius and the highest perfection.[5] But there is no mention of institutional competition. Furthermore, there are authors like the German Protestant Johannes Althusius of Emden (1557–1638) who argue forcefully against large empires. But the reasons they adduce are the heterogeneity of preferences and the increasing cost of law enforcement, notably the problem of corruption – not institutional competition.[6] This changes in the eighteenth century.

THE CLASSICS

As far as we know, the first to realize the benefits of institutional competition was David Hume. We read in his Essay 'Of the Rise and Progress of the Arts and Sciences' (1742/1985, pp. 119, 120):

> Nothing is more favourable to the rise of politeness and learning than a number of neighbouring and independent states connected together by commerce and policy . . . Where a number of neighbouring states have a great intercourse of arts and commerce, their mutual jealousy keeps them from receiving too lightly the law from each other in matters of taste and reasoning and makes them examine every work of art with the greatest care and accuracy.

His prime example was Greek antiquity:

> Greece was a cluster of little principalities which soon became republics; and being united by their near neighbourhood and by the ties of the same language and interest, they entered into the closest intercourse of commerce and learning. There concurred a happy climate, a soil not unfertile and a most harmonious and comprehensive language so that every circumstance among that people seemed to favour the rise of the arts and sciences. Each city produced its several artists and philosophers who refused to yield the preference to those of the neighbouring republics. Their contention and debates sharpened the wits of

men. A variety of objects was presented to the judgement, while each challenged the preference to the rest, and the sciences, not being dwarfed by the restraint of authority, were enabled to make such considerable shoots as are even at this time the objects of our admiration. (pp. 120f.)

Thus, Hume noted two crucial advantages of mutual jealousy among neighbouring and independent states connected together by commerce and learning:

1. Variety sharpens the wits of men.
2. Science is not dwarfed by the restraint of authority.

In the modern literature on institutional competition, the first mechanism has been called 'yardstick competition' (for example, Salmon 1987; Besley and Case 1995): diversity facilitates comparisons, learning and innovation. The second benefit is freedom. However, it is not clear whether Hume meant freedom from *political* authority or freedom from the authority of prejudice. In the same essay, it is true, he also referred to the need for political freedom: 'It is impossible for the arts and sciences to arise, at first, among any people unless that people enjoy the blessing of a free government' (p. 115). But, unlike later authors, he did not explicitly state that mutual jealousy between neighbouring and independent states is favourable to free government.

Hume contrasted ancient Greece with the European Middle Ages and China:

After the Roman Christian or catholic church had spread itself over the civilized world and had engrossed all the learning of the times, being really one large state within itself and united under one head, this variety of sects immediately disappeared and the peripatetic philosophy was alone admitted to all the schools to the utter depravation of every kind of learning. But mankind having at length thrown off this yoke, affairs are now returned nearly to the same situation as before, and Europe is at present a copy at large of what Greece was formerly a pattern in miniature. (p. 121)

But China is one vast empire ... The authority of any teacher, such as Confucius, was propagated easily from one corner of the empire to the other . . . This seems to be one natural reason why the sciences have made so slow progress in that mighty empire. (p. 122)

If we consider the face of the globe, Europe, of all four parts of the world, is the most broken by seas, rivers and mountains and Greece of all countries of Europe. Hence, these regions were naturally divided into several distinct governments. And hence the sciences arose in Greece; and Europe has been hitherto the most constant habitation of them. (pp. 122f.)

As we shall see, Hume's comparison of Europe with China and his geographic explanation of Europe's political fragmentation foreshadow the well-known work of Eric Jones (*The European Miracle*, 1981). Modern scholars who, like Hume and sometimes quoting Hume, attribute the 'Greek miracle' (Renan 1884) to geographic and political fragmentation, institutional competition and freedom are Kathleen Freeman (1950, Ch. 11), Christian Meier (1993, pp. 135f., 64) and Alexander Zaicev (1993, pp. 38–40, 197).[7]

Six years after David Hume, Montesquieu made a similar point in his book 'L'Esprit des Lois' (1748/1989, pp. 283f.):

> In Asia one has always seen great empires; in Europe they were never able to continue to exist. This is because the Asia we know has broader plains . . . and its smaller rivers form slighter barriers.
>
> Therefore, power should always be despotic in Asia. For if the servitude there were not extreme, there would immediately be a division that the nature of the country cannot endure.
>
> In Europe, the natural divisions form many medium-sized states in which the government of laws is not incompatible with the maintenance of the state; on the other hand, they are so favourable to this that without laws this state falls into decadence and becomes inferior to all the others.
>
> This is what has formed a genius for liberty, which makes it very difficult to subjugate each part and to put it under a foreign force other than by laws and by what is useful to its commerce.

Once more, Asian empires are contrasted with political fragmentation in Europe, and once more the difference is explained by geography. But there is also a new message: political fragmentation favours liberty because, without the liberty provided by laws, a medium-sized state would decay and be weaker than the others. But why does (the prospect of?) such inferiority lead to liberal laws? The explanation may be in another chapter of the book where Montesquieu praises the invention and expanding use of the bill of exchange:

> In this way commerce was able to avoid violence and maintain itself everywhere, for the richest trader had only invisible goods which could be sent everywhere and leave no trace anywhere . . . Since that time princes have had to govern themselves more wisely than they themselves would have thought, for it turned out that great acts of authority were so clumsy that experience itself has made known that only goodness of government brings prosperity. (p. 389)

In other words, the mobility of capital among jurisdictions limits government interference. Following Hirschman (1971), this has been called the 'exit' mechanism (as opposed to yardstick competition or 'voice').

Another French-speaking philosopher arguing for smaller rather than larger states is Jean Jacques Rousseau. In his 'Contrat Social' (1762), he gave the following reasons:

1. 'Long distances make administration more difficult.'
2. 'The people has less affection for its rulers whom it never sees.'
3. 'The same laws cannot suit so many diverse provinces with different customs, situated in the most various climates and incapable of enduring a uniform government.'
4. 'Talent is buried . . . among such a multitude of men . . . gathered together in one place at the seat of the central administration.'
5. 'The measures which have to be taken to maintain the general authority . . . absorb all the energy of the public so that there is none left for the happiness of the people.' (Book II, Ch. 9; 1968, pp. 37f.)
6. As the population of a democracy increases, each 'vote . . . has . . . less influence . . . From this follows that, the larger the state, the less the liberty.' (Book III, Ch. I; 1968, p. 48)

He concluded:

> It may be said that the reason for expansion [of the state's territory] ought to be subordinate to the reasons for contraction. (Book II, Ch. 9; 1968, p. 39)

Even though institutional competition is not among Rousseau's reasons, his point 6 is a type of 'voice' mechanism: citizens monitor the government but they do so without the aid of interjurisdictional comparisons. (This is another type of 'voice' from the citizens which, in following, 1 shall call 'voice II'.)

Institutional competition came back to the fore in Adam Ferguson's 'Essay on the History of Civil Society' (1767) which explicitly extended Hume's point to political life:

> Among the advantages which enable nations to run the career of policy as well as of arts . . . we should reckon every circumstance which enables them to divide and to maintain themselves in distinct and independent communities. The society and concourse of other men are not more necessary to form the individual than the rivalship and competition of nations are to invigorate the principles of political life in a state. Their wars, and their treaties, their mutual jealousies, and the establishments which they devise with a view to each other, constitute more than half the occupations of mankind, and furnish materials for their greatest and most improving exertions. For this reason, clusters of islands, a continent divided by many natural barriers, great rivers, ridges of mountains, and arms of the sea, are best fitted for becoming the nursery of independent and respectable nations. (Part III, Ch. 1; 1966, p. 119)

Like Hume and Rousseau, Ferguson emphasized 'voice' rather than 'exit':

> Small communities, however corrupted, are not prepared for despotical govern-
> ment: their members, crowded together and contiguous to the seats of power,
> never forget their relation to the public; they pry, with habits of familiarity and
> freedom, into the pretensions of those who would rule . . . In proportion as ter-
> ritory is extended, its parts lose their relative importance to the whole. Its inhab-
> itants cease to perceive their connection with the state . . . Distance from the
> feats of administration and indifference to the persons who contend for prefer-
> ment teach the majority to consider themselves as the subjects of a sovereignty,
> not as the members of a political body . . . Among the circumstances, therefore,
> which . . . lead to the establishment of despotism, there is none, perhaps, that
> arrives at this termination with so sure an aim as the perpetual enlargement of
> territory. (Part VI, Section 5; 1966, pp. 271f.)

In 1776, Adam Smith in his *Wealth of Nations* returned to the theme of Montesquieu that countries – their 'sovereigns' and their 'societies' – compete for mobile capital which responds to international differences in taxation:

> The . . . proprietor of stock is properly a citizen of the world and is not neces-
> sarily attached to any particular country. He would be apt to abandon the
> country in which he is exposed to a vexatious inquisition in order to be assessed
> a burdensome tax and would remove his stock to some country where he could
> either carry on his business or enjoy his fortune at ease. A tax that tended to
> drive away stock from a particular country would so far tend to dry up every
> source of revenue both to the sovereign and society . . . The nations, accord-
> ingly, who have attempted to tax the revenue arising from stock, instead of any
> severe inquisition . . . have been obliged to content themselves with some
> very loose and, therefore, more or less arbitrary estimation. (1976, Vol. 2,
> pp. 375f.)

Adam Smith did not only say that tax competition restrains taxation. He also came out in favour of fiscal decentralization:

> The abuses which sometimes creep into the local and provincial administration
> of a local or provincial revenue, however enormous so ever they may appear, are
> in reality, however, almost always very trifling in comparison with those which
> commonly take place in the administration and expenditure of the revenue of a
> great empire. They are, besides, much more easily corrected. (1976, Vol. 2, p. 253)

This is quite similar to Althusius' argument about corruption (see note 6).

The first author of the German enlightenment who advocated political decentralization was the protestant Justus Möser of Osnabrück.[8] In his 'Patriotische Phantasien' and an associated essay (1777/1958), he suggested in or around 1777:

His majesty's empire is too large and his subjects . . . are too different in their customs, nourishment, manners and needs to be governed by uniform laws. Thus, it would be better, if each province proposed its own laws and if his majesty confirmed them and instructed the judges to adjudicate in each province according to its law. (1958, Vol. 9, no. 102, p. 344, my translation)

If we look back at the great glory of the many small Greek republics and ask why so many small townships, which nowadays would not even be mentioned, made such a stir at the time, the reason turns out to be that each created its own religious and political constitution and, by this means, increased its strength to an extraordinary extent. (1958, Vol. 6, p. 65, my translation)

In 1778, in a very insightful remark, Turgot extended the 'exit' idea to the mobility of labour:

The asylum which (the American people) opens to the oppressed of all nations must console the earth. The ease with which it will now be possible to take advantage of this situation, and thus to escape from the consequences of a bad government, will oblige the European governments to be just and enlightened. (1810, p. 389)

In 1784, Immanuel Kant gave the first coherent account of why institutional competition favours freedom from government interference. He wrote in his 'Idee zu einer allgemeinen Geschichte in weltbürgerlicher Absicht' (1784/1959):

Now the states are already in the present day involved in such close relations with each other that none of them can pause or slacken in its internal civilization without losing power and influence in relation to the rest; and hence the maintenance, if not the progress, of this end of nature is, in a manner, secured even by the ambitious designs of the states themselves. Further, civil liberty cannot now be easily assailed without inflicting such damage as will be felt in all trades and industries and especially in commerce; and this would entail a diminution of the powers of the state in external relations. This liberty, moreover, gradually advances further. But if the citizen is hindered in seeking his prosperity in any way suitable to himself that is consistent with the liberty of others, the activity of business is checked generally; and thereby the powers of the whole state are again weakened. Hence the restrictions on personal liberty of action are always more and more removed, and universal liberty even in religion comes to be conceded. And thus it is that, notwithstanding the intrusion of many a delusion and caprice, the spirit of enlightenment gradually arises as a great good which the human race must derive even from the selfish purposes of aggrandizement on the part of its rulers, if they understand what is for their own advantage. This enlightenment, however, and along with it a certain sympathetic interest which the enlightened man cannot avoid taking in the good which he perfectly understands, must by and by pass up to the throne and exert an influence even upon the principles of government. (1959, p. 31)

Kant repeats Montesquieu's claim that the existence of several inter-dependent states leads to civil and even universal liberty, and he provides a general explanation: the states are in such close relations with each other that any ruler who assails civil liberty inflicts such damage in all trades and industry and especially in commerce as to diminish the external powers of his state ('im äußeren Verhältnis'). However, Kant does not explicitly say what he means by 'close relations'. Economic relations? Cross-border trade, capital movements, migration? Or Hume's flow of ideas, that is, yard-stick competition?

The fact that Kant praised the rivalry among rulers of different states in his 'Universal History', that is, prior to the French Revolution, may appear to be incompatible with his essay 'Zum Ewigen Frieden' (Perpetual Peace) which he wrote under the impression of the post-revolutionary war in 1795. In the latter piece he suggested that an 'international state (civitas gentium)' established by common accord is the 'only . . . rational way in which states coexisting with other states can emerge from the lawless condition of pure warfare' (1795/1991, p. 105). However, he continued:

> But since this is not the will of the nations, according to their present concep-tion of international right, the positive idea of a world republic cannot be realised. If all is not to be lost, this can best find a negative substitute in the shape of an enduring and gradually expanding federation likely to prevent war . . . A federative association of states *whose sole intention is to eliminate war* is the only lawful arrangement which can be reconciled with freedom. (pp. 105, 129, italics mine)

Thus, the competency of the federation or, a fortiori, of the interna-tional state would be limited to the military field, it would not extend to the economy. Kant aims exclusively at peace-preserving cooperation. He thus prefers competition to anarchy but he also prefers 'the separate exis-tence of many independent adjoining states' to 'an amalgamation of the separate nations under a single power which has overruled the rest' (p. 113) because the former would prevent 'universal despotism' (p. 114). If there are separate independent states, linguistic and religious diff-erences

> may certainly occasion mutual hatred and provide pretexts for wars, but as culture grows and men gradually move towards greater agreement over their principles, they lead to mutual understanding and peace . . . This peace is created and guaranteed by an equilibrium of forces and a most vigorous rivalry. Thus, nature wisely separates the nations. (p. 114)

In other words, Kant prefers interjurisdictional anarchy to centralized despotism.

It is interesting that Kant, in his 'Universal History', attributed the 'great good' of enlightenment (and liberty) to 'the selfish purposes of aggrandizement on the part of the rulers, if they understand what is for their own advantage' (p. 31, as already quoted). This is reminiscent of the point made by Adam Smith that the self-interested actions of competing suppliers benefit consumers in a market:

> It is not from the benevolence of the butcher, the brewer or the baker that we expect our dinner but from their regard to their own interest. We address ourselves not to humanity but to their self-love and never talk to them of our own necessities but of their advantages. (1776/1976, Vol. 1, p. 18)

In modern economic terminology we would say that producers who lower their marginal cost curve in order to raise their profits, unwillingly but automatically also increase consumer surplus. Hence, there is another analogy between institutional competition among the rulers of different states and market competition among private suppliers in that both derive the common good from self-interested behaviour.[9]

In 1787, the case for decentralization was argued by the American anti-federalists (Storing 1981). Their main point was that the proposed federal constitution did not allow for the heterogeneity of the thirteen colonies: 'One government and general legislation alone never can extend equal benefits to all parts of the United States: Different laws, customs and opinions exist in the different states which by a uniform system of laws would be unreasonably invaded' ('Federal Farmer', 8 October 1787). But the need for intergovernmental competition and the danger that politicians might collude also played a role:

> The people in a small state can unite and act in concert and with vigour; but in large territories, the men who govern find it more easy to unite, while people cannot . . . The strength of the government and the confidence of the people must be collected principally in the local assemblies: every part or branch of the federal head must be feeble and unsafely trusted with large powers. A government possessed of more power than its constituent parts will justify will not only probably abuse it but be unequal to bear its own burden. . . ('Federal Farmer', 12 October 1787)

It is interesting to note that both federalists and anti-federalists were aware of Montesquieu's arguments for decentralization. Alexander Hamilton wrote in his Federalist Paper No. 9: 'The opponents of the plan proposed have, with great assiduity, cited and circulated the observations of Montesquieu on the necessity of a contracted territory for republican government.'

Also in 1787, Edward Gibbon in his *History of the Decline and Fall of the Roman Empire* returned to Montesquieu and Kant's explanations of freedom in Europe:

> Europe is now divided into twelve powerful, though unequal, kingdoms, three respectable commonwealths, and a variety of smaller, though independent states . . . The abuses of tyranny are restrained by the mutual influence or fear and shame . . . monarchies have imbibed the principles of freedom, or at least of moderation; and some sense of honour and justice is introduced into the most defective constitutions by the general manners of the times. In peace, the progress of knowledge and industry is accelerated by the emulation of so many active rivals. (Vol. 3, p. 636)

> The division of Europe into a number of independent states, connected, however, with each other by the general resemblance of religion, language and manners, is productive of the most beneficial consequences to liberty and mankind . . . but the empire of the Romans filled the world. (Vol. 1, p. 100)

Like Turgot, Gibbon emphasized that in Europe 'a modern tyrant' would soon find out that 'the object of his displeasure would easily obtain, in a happier climate, a secure refuge, a new fortune adequate to his merit (and) . . . the freedom of complaint' (Vol. 1, p. 100).

In 1793, Wilhelm von Humboldt in his essay on the study of Antiquity returned to Hume's point about the close intercourse of learning among the Greek city states. But he went beyond Hume and stressed competition among the cities, that is 'the mutual jealousy that one city could not afford to neglect the advantages by which the other might gain superiority; and at least this jealousy of energies set each in more active motion' (1793/1961, section 30, pp. 17f., my translation).

In the nineteenth century, Alexis de Tocqueville is well known for opposing centralization and empire-building. We read in his *Democracy in America* (1835/1945): 'The more numerous the people, the stronger the prince . . . Small nations have therefore always been the cradle of political liberty . . . If none but small nations existed, I do not doubt that mankind would be more happy and more free. Nothing is more opposed to the well-being and the freedom of men than vast empires' (Vol. I, pp. 166–8).

He gave several reasons:

1. 'In small states, the watchfulness of society penetrates everywhere . . .' (p. 165)
2. 'The efforts and resources of the citizens are turned to the internal well-being of the community and are not . . . likely to be wasted upon an empty pursuit of glory.' (p. 165)

3. 'The temptations that the government offers to ambition are too weak and the resources of private individuals are too slender for the sovereign power easily to fall into the grasp of a single man.' (p. 166)
4. 'In great centralized nations the legislator is obliged to give a character of uniformity to the laws which does not always suit the diversity of customs and of districts.' (p. 169)

However, he did not mention competition among governments.

The second major author of the nineteenth century is Lord Acton, a member of the English Catholic minority. He wrote in his essay 'The History of Freedom in Antiquity' (1877/1985a):

> If the distribution of power among the several parts of the state is the most efficient restraint of monarchy, the distribution of power among several states is the best check on democracy. By multiplying centres of government and discussion it promotes the diffusion of political knowledge and the maintenance of healthy and independent opinion. It is the protectorate of minorities and the consecration of self-government. (p. 21)

And he added: 'It is bad to be oppressed by a minority but it is worse to be oppressed by a majority' (p. 13). Thus, political fragmentation restrains political power not only in the case of autocratic rulers but also in democracies. Lord Acton gives two reasons which he does not separate, however:

1. The distribution of power among several democratic states protects minorities and independent opinion. This is the exit mechanism which we first found in Montesquieu: minorities, especially intellectual elites, can leave the country at low cost.
2. The distribution of power among several democratic states promotes the diffusion of political knowledge. This is the yardstick competition which we first found in Hume and Ferguson. However, while Hume refers to knowledge in the arts and sciences generally, Lord Acton, like Ferguson, expressly mentions political knowledge. In a democracy, such knowledge will primarily be used by, and benefit, the majority.

Like David Hume, Lord Acton regarded institutional competition as the key to understanding the success of Greek antiquity: 'But although (the distribution of power among several states) must be enumerated among the better achievements of practical genius in antiquity, it arose from necessity, and its properties were imperfectly investigated in theory' (p. 21). Lord Acton seems to be the first to note that freedom is also protected by institutional competition between different legal orders within the same territory. The source is his essay 'The History of Freedom in Christianity' (1877/1985b):

The only influence capable of resisting the feudal hierarchy was the ecclesiastical hierarchy; and they came into collision . . . To that conflict of four hundred years we owe the rise of civil liberty. If the Church had continued to buttress the thrones of the king whom it anointed, or if the struggle had terminated speedily in an undivided victory, all Europe would have sunk down under a Byzantine or Muscovite despotism . . . But although liberty was not the end for which they strove, it was the means by which the temporal and the spiritual power called the nations to their aid. (p. 33)

This foreshadows the work of Berman (1983, 1998), Tierney (1995) and Vaubel (2005b). Acton's emphasis that freedom was an unintended consequence, both in the Middle Ages and in Greek antiquity, is reminiscent of Adam Smith's analysis of market competition and Friedrich Hayek's theory of spontaneous evolution.

Eleven years later, in his study of American federalism, Lord James Bryce, a Scotsman like Hume, Ferguson and Smith, presented a new argument in favour of decentralization and institutional competition: 'Federalism enables a people to try experiments which could not safely be tried in a large centralised country' (1888/1901, Vol. 1, p. 353). Thus, decentralization and competition serve as a discovery procedure (Hayek 1968/1978), and piecemeal innovation is safer than 'holistic' experiments (Popper 1945/1966).[10]

In the early twentieth century, a crystal-clear account of how the potential exit of capital has checked the power of governments in Europe can be found in Max Weber's *General Economic History* (1923/1961): 'The competitive struggle [among the European nation states] created the largest opportunities for modern western capitalism. The separate states had to compete for mobile capital, which dictated to them the conditions under which it would assist them to power' (p. 249). This is the first time that we find the economic term 'competition' ('Konkurrenzkampf') rather than jealousy (Hume) or rivalry (Kant) or emulation (Gibbon) in this literature.

Finally, I mention Arnold Toynbee. In his monumental *Study of History* (1939), he argued in some detail that decline tends to be associated with standardization (Vol. VI, p. 322) and that the final break-up of a civilization tends to be preceded by 'the establishment of the universal state', that is, a unitary political structure (Vol. VI, pp. 283ff., 327).

So far I have given a strictly chronological account of the development of thought on political fragmentation and institutional competition. I shall now distinguish the various strands of thought in a structured synopsis (Table 2.1).

The first distinction is between arguments for institutional competition and other arguments for political fragmentation. Within institutional competition, we have the bifurcation between interjurisdictional and

Table 2.1 The classical case for political fragmentation and institutional competition: a synopsis

Institutional competition				Other arguments in favour of political fragmentation	
Interjurisdictional			Intra-jurisdictional		
Exit mechanism		Yardstick competition (voice I)	Freedom	Government close to the citizens (voice II)	Other arguments
Capital	Labour				
Montesquieu (1748)	Turgot (1778)	Hume (1742): arts and sciences	Montesquieu (1748)	Rousseau (1762)	Plato (4th century BC)
Smith (1776)	Gibbon (1787)	Ferguson (1767): political life	Rousseau (1762)	Ferguson (1767)	Aristotle (4th century BC)
		Gibbon (1787): knowledge and industry	Ferguson (1767)		Althusius (1603)
			Smith (1776)		Rousseau (1762)
			Turgot (1778)		Smith (1776)
			Kant (1784)		Möser (1777)
			Gibbon (1787)		

41

Table 2.1 (continued)

	Institutional competition				Other arguments in favour of political fragmentation	
	Interjurisdictional		Intra-jurisdictional	Freedom	Government close to the citizens (voice II)	Other arguments
	Exit mechanism	Yardstick competition (voice I)				
Capital	Labour					
		von Humboldt (1793)		Anti-federalists (1787)	Tocqueville (1835)	Anti-federalists (1787)
				Tocqueville (1835)		Tocqueville (1835)
		Acton (1877): political knowledge	Acton (1877)	Acton (1877)		
						Bryce (1888)
						Weber (1923)

Toynbee (1939)

Note: Bold indicates that political fragmentation is thought to strengthen freedom for reasons other than institutional competition.

intrajurisdictional institutional competition. Moreover, there is a column indicating whether the author believes that institutional competition of either sort enhances freedom. In the field of interjurisdictional competition, the classic distinction is between the exit mechanism and yardstick competition, a type of voice (voice I). The exit mechanism may operate through capital mobility (Montesquieu, Adam Smith and Max Weber) or through the mobility of labour (Turgot, Gibbon). It is familiar to writers from many countries. Yardstick competition may relate to 'the arts and sciences' (Hume), 'political life' (Ferguson, Acton) 'industry' (Gibbon) or creativity in general (von Humboldt). As can be seen, this line of thought is predominantly British: diversity, by extending the scope for comparison, promotes learning and innovation. The case for intrajurisdictional institutional competition is also most prevalent among Anglo-Saxon authors (Acton and later Berman and Tierney). The increase in freedom due to institutional competition (or voice I) is a common attraction to French, German, English and American authors. Among the other arguments in favour of political fragmentation, the importance of bringing the government closer to the citizens (voice II) is mainly emphasized by French-speaking writers (Rousseau, Tocqueville). So much for the classics.

THE MODERN LITERATURE

The modern literature on institutional competition starts with Charles Tiebout's (1956) famous article in the *Journal of Political Economy*. In Tiebout's model, city managers 'seek to attract new residents to lower average costs' (1956, p. 419) and the 'consumer-voter may be viewed as picking that community which best satisfies his preference pattern for public goods' (p. 418). In the absence of interregional externalities, such voting with the feet improves efficiency. However, in Tiebout's world, the rationale of institutional competition is not to prevent governments from abusing their power. Each city manager 'follows the preferences of the (initial) residents of the community' (p. 419) even in the absence of competition. Voter mobility merely serves to optimize the number of residents in the presence of heterogeneous preferences for local public goods. Thus, Tiebout is closer to Rousseau and Tocqueville than to Montesquieu.

In the following year, Tiebout received support from Chicago economist George Stigler. In a statement before the Joint Economic Committee of Congress Stigler declared: 'Competition of communities offers no obstacles but opportunities to various communities to choose the types and scales of governmental functions they wish' (1957/1998, p. 6). He extended the case to regulatory competition, suggesting that local enterprises which are subjected to local regulations against their will ought to be compensated by the local government (p. 5).

At the latest since Henry Simons, the Chicago school had favoured decentralization. Simons had suggested that, apart from security and trade policy,

> [the] other powers and functions (of the nation states) must be diminished in favor of states, provinces, and, in Europe, small nations . . . The good political order is one in which small nations and governments on the scale of American states are protected in their autonomy against neighbours and protected against federalisms or unions which appropriate their powers. (1948, p. 125)

In the 1960s and 1970s, under the influence of the Musgrave school, the reaction to Tiebout was overwhelmingly negative, however, and the emphasis shifted to internalizing interregional spillovers (for example Musgrave 1959; Oates 1972). I shall address these types of criticism in the last section when reviewing Sinn's *The New Systems Competition*.

The situation changed in 1980 when Brennan and Buchanan published *The Power to Tax*. In their public-choice approach, the political decision-makers are not necessarily benevolent city managers assiduously implementing the wishes of their citizens but self-interested agents aiming at political rents. In these circumstances,

> the potential for fiscal exploitation varies inversely with the number of competing governmental units . . . The potentiality for collusion among separate units varies inversely with the number of units. If there are only a small number of nominally competitive governments, collusion among them with respect to their mutual exercise of their assigned taxing powers may be easy to organize and to enforce . . . Total government intrusion into the economy should be smaller, ceteris paribus, the greater the extent to which taxes and expenditures are decentralized . . . Tax competition among separate units rather than tax collusion is an objective to be sought in its own right. (pp. 180, 185, 186)

Brennan and Buchanan's book has spurred a considerable amount of empirical research indicating that fiscal decentralization and competition tend to lower government spending relative to GDP (for example, Schneider 1989; Vaubel 1994; Moesen and Cauwenberge 2000; for surveys of the empirical literature, see Dowding and John 1994 and Kirchgässner and Feld 2004). There is also evidence that decentralization reduces political corruption (Fisman and Gatti 2002) as the classics (Althusius, Smith, the 'Federal Farmer' and Tocqueville) had claimed. Finally, it has been demonstrated that voters, in evaluating the performance of their government, do not only take account of their own tax burden but also of taxation in neighbouring states (Besley and Case

1995).[11] Once more, the objections to tax competition will be discussed in the last section.

An interesting extension of Brennan and Buchanan's approach is the concept of 'Functionally Overlapping Competing Jurisdictions' (FOCJ) popularized by Frey and Eichenberger (for example, 1999). The citizens themselves would determine the domains of the jurisdictions, and the latter could differ by function. Obviously, competition is stronger if the size of the jurisdiction may vary. For the same reason, Buchanan and Faith (1987) and others have argued for the right of secession, that is, potential institutional competition.

Four years before Brennan and Buchanan's plea for fiscal competition, Hayek came out in favour of monetary competition. While Brennan and Buchanan reacted to the rapid growth of government expenditure in the 1970s, Hayek was motivated by the experience of high and rising inflation. Initially, in his 'Choice in Currency' (1976a), he merely proposed competition among central banks:

> There could be no more effective check against the abuse of money by the government than if people were free to refuse any money they distrusted and to prefer money in which they had confidence. Nor could there be a stronger inducement to governments to ensure the stability of their money than the knowledge that, so long as they kept the supply below the demand for it, that demand would tend to grow. Therefore, let us deprive governments (or their monetary authorities) of all power to protect their money against competition . . . I prefer the freeing of all dealings in money to any sort of monetary union also because the latter would demand an international monetary authority which I believe is neither practicable nor even desirable. (pp. 18, 21)

Half a year later, in his 'Denationalisation of Money' (1976b), he even suggested that the competing currencies could be supplied by private banks. While Hayek focused on the exit mechanism, voice is also likely to play an important role in monetary competition (Vaubel 1987, p. 283). Hayek's analysis and proposals have sparked an extensive literature which, however, cannot be surveyed here.

It may be interesting to note that Hayek did not start his academic life as a decentralizer. Initially, under the influence of his Austrian mentor Ludwig von Mises, he wanted to return to the gold standard, and, under the impression of a devastating war, he – like Kant – proposed to establish an international federation and authority. We read in *The Road to Serfdom* (1944):

> There must be a power which can restrain the different nations from action harmful to their neighbours, a set of rules what a state may do, and an authority capable of enforcing these rules. The powers which such an authority would need are mainly of a negative kind; it must, above all, be able to say 'No' to all

sorts of restrictive measures . . . But this does not mean that a new super-state must be given powers which we have not learned to use intelligently even on a national scale, that an international authority ought to be given power to direct individual nations how to use their resources. (pp. 232, 231)

Hayek went beyond Kant: he wanted to eliminate not only war but all negative international externalities. However, he favoured decentralization within the existing states: 'It is even to be hoped that within a federation . . . the process of centralisation of the past may in some measure be reversed and some devolution of powers from the state to local authorities become possible' (p. 234). In *The Constitution of Liberty* (1961), he did not explicitly advocate the decentralization of government. But he noted that 'while it has always been characteristic of those favouring an increase in governmental powers to support maximum concentration of powers, those mainly concerned with individual liberty have generally advocated decentralisation' (1961, p. 263).

In the second half of the 1970s, interjurisdictional institutional competition was increasingly threatened by attempts to coordinate macroeconomic policies. This provoked opposition from the adherents of institutional competition – notably Feldstein (1988), Kehoe (1987), Rogoff (1985), Stefan Sinn (1992), Tabellini (1990) and myself (Vaubel 1980, 1983, 1986, 1988). From the viewpoint of institutional competition, the following considerations are important:

- 'The problem about [the economic case for coordination] is that it fails to make a distinction between technological and pecuniary externalities' (Vaubel 1983, p. 10), that is, between non-market interdependence and interdependence through the price mechanism.
- 'Competition [among national macroeconomic policies] is a mechanism of discovery[12] . . . Competition produces more of the public good of knowledge than the uniformity which tends to result from coordination' (ibid. p. 15).
- 'Policy competition is a way to desynchronise business cycles or even to randomise the underlying policy shocks internationally and thus to reduce business-cycle uncertainty and risk through diversification' (ibid. pp. 15f.).
- 'Rational politicians and bureaucrats have an incentive and the power in a democracy to act against the interest of the majority of their voters, let alone the welfare of society at large . . . International collusion strengthens this power' (ibid. p. 18).
- 'A regime in which governments conduct monetary policy independently may produce lower time-consistent inflation than a regime in which central banks cooperate' (Rogoff 1985, p. 211).

- 'Our politicians and those of other leading countries should not be allowed to escape their responsibilities by blaming poor domestic economic performance on the policies pursued abroad' (Feldstein 1988, p. 11).
- 'In order to mitigate the principal-agent problem, it is desirable to reduce the cost of monitoring and to increase the scope for corrective sanctions. This can be attained by assigning clear responsibilities to each policymaker . . . This requires that the number of targets should not exceed the number of policy instruments. However, in these circumstances, the game-theoretic case for international policy coordination is no longer valid' (Vaubel 1988, p. 297).

Since the 1980s, a large body of research on institutional competition has accumulated – on the concept, the causes and the effects of such competition. This is the current debate rather than its history, and I lack space to survey it. But I mention some of the most important English sources in the note below.[13] The common point is that institutional competition shifts the citizens' demand curve, or willingness to pay for their government's services, to the left while at the same time increasing its (absolute) price elasticity.

From a historical perspective, it is more interesting to return to the role of institutional competition in the rise of European civilization because the postwar integration of Europe has led many economic historians to look more deeply into this subject.

The first book to mention is Leopold Kohr *The Breakdown of Nations* (1957/1978). This is a passionate plea for small jurisdictions rather than a scholarly study but it looks at many examples of interjurisdictional competition in European history: ancient Greece, the Holy Roman Empire (which, as Lord Bryce once remarked, was neither holy, nor Roman, nor an empire), the British Isles in the sixteenth century, Switzerland and Italy before its unification. Kohr argues that the rulers of small states compete for cultural accomplishments whereas the rulers of large states aim to suppress competition by empire-building and war:

From the moment the small interstate strife had ceased amongst the Italian and German principalities and republics, they began to cultivate imperial ambitions . . . And their prime concern was not the creation of art but . . . war. (p. 128)

Creative individuals cannot flourish in the consuming atmosphere of large powers. (p. 129)

Bigness in its ultimate form cannot be maintained except by a totalitarian organization. (p. 130)

A small-state world would not only solve the problem of social brutality and war; it would solve the equally terrible problems of oppression and tyranny. (p. 79)

Democracy, in turn, is inseparably connected with the smallness of the collective organism of which the individual is part – the state. (p. 98)

[Without] the little-state world from which our individualistic Western civilization has sprung . . . it cannot continue . . . Our statesmen seem to have nothing at all on their minds except our unification that will . . . doom our civilization. (p. 131)

The first modern writer to develop Max Weber's explanation of the rise of capitalism is the French sociologist Jean Baechler. His original article (1968) and his first book (1971) are in French. I shall quote from the English translation of the book (*The Origins of Capitalism*, 1975). Baechler referred to Max Weber repeatedly, also to Weber's *General Economic History*, but not to Weber's above-mentioned statement that 'the competitive struggle [among the European nation states] created the largest opportunities for modern Western capitalism'. Yet this is precisely the explanation on which Baechler focuses and elaborates:

The expansion of capitalism owes its origins and its raison d'être to political anarchy . . . Internal anarchy inherited from the feudal order was the motor of capitalist expansion . . . A limitation of power to act externally and the constant threat of foreign assault [the two characteristics of a multipolar system] imply that power is also limited internally . . . Fundamental springs of capitalist expansion are, on the one hand, the coexistence of several political units within the same cultural whole and, on the other, political pluralism which frees the economy. (pp. 77, 78, 80)

He contrasts political fragmentation in Europe with the empires of Byzantium, China and Japan but is careful to add:

Each time China was politically divided, capitalism flourished. The fact is very clear for . . . the end of the T'ang and especially the Song period . . . The same evolution may be found in the more distant past: the so-called period of the Warring Kingdoms (453–221 B.C.), probably the richest and most brilliant of all Chinese history, the period of the Three Kingdoms (A.D. 220–280) and finally the period of the Six Dynasties (A.D. 316–580). (p. 82)

He makes the same exception for Tokugawa Japan which 'never ceased to be internally an international social order' (p. 83). These findings are confirmed by the case studies assembled in Bernholz and Vaubel (2004) to which he contributes.

Also in 1971 but independently of Baechler, Max Weber and all the rest, a group of socio-psychologists directed by Raoul Naroll published the first quantitative historical analysis of whether political fragmentation affects individual creativity. Their sample covers four civilizations (China, India, the Islamic Middle East and Europe) from 500 BC to 1899 AD. The dependent variable is the number of famous scientists as listed in Kroeber (1944). The explanatory variables are political fragmentation, wealth, area, political centralization within the states and the frequency of war for the largest state. The pooled rank correlation analysis demonstrates that the number of famous scientists is significantly affected by only one variable: political fragmentation. The effect is positive.

Simonton (1975), in a Harvard dissertation, confined the investigation to a time series analysis of Western civilization from 700 BC to 1839 AD but he disaggregated the data, looking at periods of 20 years rather than centuries. Once more, political fragmentation provides the most robust explanation (with a lag of 20 years) but the number of famous scientists and artists is also significantly – negatively – affected by political instability during the preceding period. In 1976, Simonton showed that creativity is even better explained by contemporaneous ideological diversity as measured by Sorokin (1937) but ideological diversity is shown to depend significantly on political fragmentation in the preceding period. Thus, the results of Simonton (1976) give more weight to yardstick competition than to mobility-based competition.

Economic historians discovered the subject in the early 1980s. The crucial publication is *The European Miracle* by Eric Jones (1981). Jones had been unaware of most of his predecessors (Jones 2004) and did not want to study the history of thought. But like Hume and Montesquieu, he explained Europe's political fragmentation by geography: 'Natural barriers helped to hold the ring between various ethnic and linguistic groups making up the European peoples' (1981, p. 226). He then exploited the geographic explanation more fully:

> Europe's very considerable geological, climatic and topographical variety endowed it with a dispersed portfolio of resources. This conduced to long-distance, multilateral trade . . . Important political, and therefore eventually market, consequences stemmed from an extensive trade . . . Sheer distance from the Central Asian steppes offered some protection from the worst ravages of their horse nomads . . . Finally, Europe's Atlantic seaboard location proved, when activated, to give relatively cheap access to the rich, graspable resources of the Americas and the oceans and to large external markets. (p. 227)

He also provided a detailed comparison with the politico-economic systems of the Ottoman Empire, the Mughal empire in India and the Ming and Manchu dynasties in China:

Despite great creative surges in times when Europe had still been primitive, despotic Asian institutions suppressed creativity or diverted it into producing voluptuous luxuries. (p. 231)

But how did Europeans escape crippling exploitation by their rulers? . . . The rulers of the relatively small European states learned that by supplying the services of order and adjudication they could attract and retain the most and best-paying constituents . . . European kings were never as absolute as they wished. The power dispersed among the great proprietors was a check on them, as was the rising power of the market. (p. 233)

Europe offered a series of refuges to the oppressed and its history might be written as a saga of the escape of refugees from its wars, invasions and religious persecutions. (p. 119)

Thus, Jones emphasized mobility-based institutional competition. But he also mentioned yardstick competition and the insurance effect of diversification:

European states were alike enough to learn to solve problems precisely because they could see that some neighbouring state had solved them, i.e., by stimulus diffusion. (p. 123)

What Europe had hit on in addition in the states system and in the nation state was a framework in which decentralisation could offset malfunction in one part and yet where unity was provided by competitive exchanges of know-how and factors of production. (p. 236)

Also in 1981, Douglass North published his famous book *Structure and Change in Economic History*. His primary explanation of Europe's success is the rise of property rights, especially rights over innovations (patents). However, he also referred to institutional competition (as a possible explanation of the rise of property rights in Europe):

The state is constrained by the opportunity cost of its constituents since there always exist potential rivals to provide the same set of services. The rivals are other states, as well as individuals within the existing political-economic unit who are potential rulers. The degree of monopoly power of the ruler, therefore, is a function of the closeness of substitutes for the various groups of constituents. (pp. 23f.)

He expanded on this idea in 1995 and 1998, favouring a Schumpeterian or Hayekian explanation of the European 'miracle' and supporting Montesquieu's hypothesis that political fragmentation is good for freedom:

It was the dynamic consequences of the competition amongst fragmented political bodies that resulted in an especially creative environment . . . The key to the story is the variety of the options pursued and the increased likelihood [as compared to a single unified policy] that some would turn out to produce economic growth . . . It was precisely the lack of large scale political and economic order that created the essential environment hospitable to economic growth and ultimately human freedoms. (1998, p. 22)

In 1983, Harold Berman, a Harvard professor of legal history, returned to Lord Acton's theme, the institutional competition between the secular and the ecclesiastical order during the Middle Ages: 'There was cooperation and competition – sometimes acute competition – between the state-level church and the state-level secular authorities, as well as among state-level secular authorities themselves' (p. 553). His view that institutional competition between the medieval church and the secular rulers contributed to the ultimate supremacy of law comes out most clearly in his 1998 article:

In the Western legal tradition diverse jurisdictions and diverse legal systems coexist and compete within the same community. This characteristic originated in the late eleventh century with the church's establishment of an 'external forum', a hierarchy of ecclesiastical courts, with exclusive jurisdiction in some matters and concurrent jurisdiction in others. Laymen, though governed generally by secular law, were also subject to ecclesiastical law, and to the jurisdiction of ecclesiastical courts, in matters of marriage and family relations, inheritance, spiritual crimes, contract relations where faith was pledged, and a large number of other important matters . . . The pluralism of Western law was a source of legal sophistication and of legal growth. It was also a source of freedom. (pp. 38f.)

Another author who developed Lord Acton's theme is Brian Tierney (1995):

The most obvious way in which medieval popes contributed (unintentionally, of course) to the growth of modern liberty was by their insistence on the freedom of the church from control by secular rulers. In the Middle Ages there was never just one hierarchy of government exercising absolute authority but always two – church and state to use the language of a later age – often contending with one another, each limiting the other's power. (p. 66)

Since, in the conflicts between church and state, each side always sought to limit the power of the other, the situation encouraged theories of resistance to tyranny and constitutional limitations on government. (p. 69)

The principal contributions of the medieval church to the development of Western freedom were these: a limitation of state power in matters of religion; a well-developed theory of consent as the basis of legitimate government; new techniques of representation; significant adaptations of the old idea of a mixed constitution; a nascent theory of natural rights. (p. 100)

In the 1980s and 1990s, the view that Europe's success has been due to political fragmentation and institutional competition took hold among economic historians. Europe's race to the top became a commonplace theme as the following citations show:

> Dozens of . . . refuges for entrepreneurs were scattered across the face of Europe, thanks to its peculiarly fragmented political geography. Under these circumstances, command simply could not prevail against the market as a way to marshal men and resources. (Mc Neill 1982, p. 114)

> In the West, the absence of an empire removed the crucial bureaucratic block on the development of market forces; merchants persecuted in one place could always go with their capital elsewhere. (Hall 1985, p. 102)

> The paradox is that competition between states, economic and political rivalry, and international tension are the best guarantees of continuing progress . . . The very tension which presents the greatest threat to our survival assures that, if we survive at all, some states, in order to compete better, will be obliged to encourage intellectual freedom and progress. (Chirot 1986, p. 296)

> Competition among the political leaders of the newly emerging nation states . . . was an important factor in overcoming the inherited distaste of the rural military aristocracy for the new merchant class. Had the merchants been dealing with a political monopoly, they might not have been able to purchase the required freedom of action at a price compatible with the development of trade. (Rosenberg and Birdzell 1986, pp. 136ff.)

> The political and social consequences of this decentralized, largely unsupervised growth of commerce . . . and markets were of the greatest significance. In the first place, there was no way in which such economic developments could be fully suppressed . . . There existed no uniform authority in Europe which could effectively halt this or that commercial development; no central government whose change in priorities could cause the rise and fall of a particular industry; no systematic and universal plundering of businessmen and entrepreneurs by tax gatherers . . . In Europe there were always some princes and local lords willing to tolerate merchants and their ways even when others plundered and expelled them. (Kennedy 1987, pp. 19f.)

> The availability of alternative nation states for production meant that labour expelled from one nation could find other nations in which to locate, and the possibilities opened for capital mobility could operate as a deterrent to widespread political confiscations. (Engerman 1988, p. 14)

> Western technological creativity rested on two foundations: a materialistic pragmatism based on the belief that the manipulation of nature in the service of economic welfare was acceptable, indeed, commendable behavior, and the continuous competition between political units for political and economic hegemony. (Mokyr 1990, p. 302)

The various European societies complemented one another, and their internal competition gave [Europe] a dynamism that China lacked. (Mokyr 2003, p. 18)

Ironically, then, Europe's great good fortune lay in the fall of Rome and the weakness and division that ensued . . . The Roman dream of unity, authority, and order (the pax Romana) remained, indeed has persisted to the present. After all, one has usually seen fragmentation as a great misfortune, as a recipe for conflict . . . And yet . . . fragmentation was the strongest brake on wilful, oppressive behaviour. Political rivalry and the right of exit made all the difference. (Landes 1998, pp. 37f.)

Other studies which ought to be mentioned are Bernholz (1985), Baechler et al. (1988), Weede (1988, 2000), Mokyr (1999, 2005), Volckart (1999b, 2000), Murray (2003), Vaubel (2005a, b) and Landes (2006). Volckart analysed mobility-based institutional competition in the Holy Roman Empire and showed that political fragmentation does not necessarily entail institutional competition because local institutions (the city guilds) may restrict mobility.[14] Vaubel (2005a) is the first to measure institutional competition (rather than political fragmentation) and to test for its effects. The analysis shows that the average duration of employment of court composers in the Baroque era was significantly shorter in fragmented Italy and Germany than in centralized France and England. Mokyr (2005) analysed the mobility of 1064 European scientists and other creative individuals born between 1450 and 1750. He shows that mobility was generally high – especially in 1450–1600 – and that, for the entire period, British, French and Iberian scientists moved substantially less than German or Dutch scientists did. Vaubel (2005b) studied the security strategies of the medieval papacy and argued that the medieval church did not only contribute to intrajurisdictional institutional competition by providing an alternative institutional order (as Acton, Berman and Tierney have emphasized) but also to interjurisdictional institutional competition by ensuring that no ruler could become too powerful – either in Italy or in Europe as a whole. Murray (2003, pp. 375–7), finally, provided the first direct test of Hume's hypothesis that political freedom is favourable to creativity. Estimating a random-effects model for 312 'significant figures' from 800 BC to 1950 AD, he found that despotic government exerts a significantly negative effect on the frequency of creative individuals. Moreover, his results confirm the decentralization hypothesis: the number of significant figures also depends negatively on the concentration of population in the country's largest city.

Table 2.2 provides a synopsis of the modern literature which is comparable to the synopsis of Table 2.1. As can be seen, the emphasis is mainly on the exit mechanism which was not the case among the classics. This may indicate that international mobility has increased more than learning from foreign policy experiences.

Table 2.2   The modern case for institutional competition: a synopsis

Institutional competition			Other arguments in favour of political fragmentation
Interjurisdictional		Intra-jurisdictional	
Exit mechanism	Yardstick competition		
Public goods			
Tiebout (1956)	Salmon (1987)		Simons (1948)
			Stigler (1957)
Taxation			
Brennan and Buchanan (1980)	Besley and Case (1995)		
Money			
Hayek (1976a)	Vaubel (1987)		
Macroeconomic policy			
Rogoff (1985)	Vaubel (1983) Feldstein (1988)		Tabellini (1990)
European history			
Baechler (1968)	Simonton (1975, 1976)		Kohr (1957)
Jones (1981)	Jones (1981)		Jones (1981)
North (1981)	North (1995, 1998)		
McNeill (1982)			
Hall (1985)		Berman (1983, 1998)	
Chirot (1986)		Tierney (1995)	
Rosenberg and Birdzell (1986)			
Kennedy (1987)			
Engerman (1988)			
Mokyr (1990, 2003, 2005)			
Landes (1998, 2006)			
Vaubel (2005a, b)			

H.-W. SINN's CRITIQUE OF INSTITUTIONAL COMPETITION: A REBUTTAL

No historical survey of the case for institutional competition would be complete without an account of the objections put forward by the critics. The most comprehensive collection of these criticisms is Hans-Werner

Sinn's book *The New Systems Competition* (2003). It is based on a series of lectures given in Helsinki in 1999, and it has been published by a respectable publisher. Instead of surveying the anti-competitive literature, I shall focus on this 'pièce de résistance' in an exemplary fashion.

Sinn is the arch-critic of institutional competition. But he confines his critique to mobility-based institutional competition or, in his words, 'the new systems competition'. The 'old systems competition', in his terminology, is yardstick competition. He recognizes that it has brought the Soviet empire down, and he does not want to object to it.

As a matter of definition, the distinction between mobility-based and yardstick competition is very useful. However, mobility-based competition cannot be appraised without reference to yardstick competition. For whoever proposes to restrict or suppress mobility-based competition by international coordination or centralization (as Sinn does) necessarily restricts or suppresses yardstick competition as well. This is detrimental even to factors like labour whose mobility is low.[15] Alternatively, in a decentralized world, mobility-based competition may weaken yardstick competition and vice versa as Hirschman (1971) has argued.

Moreover, Sinn excludes all principal-agent problems and all problems of majority decision-making by assumption:

> The book does not assume benevolent politicians but it . . . assumes a well-functioning democracy. Selfish politicians who want to be reelected in a democratic voting process maximize domestic rents and choose policy moves that are Pareto-optimal from a national perspective, for if they did not, they would be beaten by others who offer such policy moves. The focus is directed entirely on a study of the effective functioning and possible failures of systems competition when the competing countries themselves [sic!] act rationally in the national interest. (p. 9)

In this way, Sinn assumes away the possibility that mobility-based institutional competition may mitigate government failure and be a necessary condition for a second-best optimum. It is like assuming that monopolists in private markets do not exploit their monopoly position. If private monopolists behaved efficiently, we would not need competition in private markets either.

Apparently, Sinn himself is somewhat uneasy about the restrictiveness of his assumptions but he tries to defend them by analogy:

> The public choice theorist knows that the failures of the internal political competition can only be isolated when clever, maximizing politicians, households and firms are assumed, and the systems economist knows that failures of systems competition can only be isolated when clever, welfare-maximizing governments are assumed. (p. 11)

But the comparison is misleading. For the public-choice theorist, private sector inefficiencies are not a topic because they do not affect the negative evaluation of government failure. For the evaluation of systems competition, however, it is crucial whether there is government failure because systems competition is a possible remedy against government failure. It makes a difference whether relevant or irrelevant circumstances are assumed away.

In spite of the restrictiveness of his assumptions, Sinn believes that his analysis enables him 'to make constructive recommendations for international European policy moves' (p. 207).

After stating and defending his assumptions in the first chapter, Sinn devotes the second chapter to tax competition of the Brennan/Buchanan sort. If capital is more mobile than labour, tax competition lowers the taxation of capital, and since government expenditure is always optimal by assumption, the taxation of labour rises. Sinn acknowledges that the outcome may be efficient but, in his view, 'the distributional implications of this equilibrium are less convincing' (p. 37). He then assumes that the public sector produces with increasing returns to scale (even though, as he concedes, the empirical evidence does not support this assumption). This aggravates his distribution problem: 'Capital receives a net subsidy at the expense of immobile taxpayers. Tax competition not only imposes a race to the bottom, as is often argued, but in a certain sense it also even implies a race *below* the bottom' (p. 43). Sinn's proposed solution is not tax harmonization but an international agreement 'not to subsidize capital and to finance the infrastructure investment exclusively with capital charges' (p. 46). He does not mention that his solution is inefficient: if, under conditions of increasing returns to scale, governments price infrastructure not at marginal but at average cost, too little infrastructure will be demanded and provided.

The third chapter comes under the heading 'The Erosion of the Welfare State'. Since Sinn assumes optimality of the redistributional status quo, he warns: 'Globalization . . . makes the income distribution in the rich countries more unequal and thus increases the need for welfare assistance' (p. 65). 'Redistribution is insurance and as such must be included in the set of state activities which are legitimated by the goal of increasing allocative efficiency' (p. 67). The argument ignores the fact that insurance is costly and that we do not know whether and for whom it is worth its cost. Thus, participation has to be voluntary. Governmental redistribution as we know it is not voluntary. Therefore, the argument is not applicable. For the same reason, it cannot be based on adverse selection (p. 68).

In the next section, entitled 'The End of the Welfare State in Tax Competition', Sinn goes even further: 'An equilibrium in systems competition will not be reached before the welfare states have disappeared' (p. 77). 'The welfare state is being eroded by the pressures of systems competition' (p. 78). This statement is inconsistent with the historical evidence. From 1980 to 2001, social expenditure relative to GDP has increased from an average of 17.9 per cent to 22.9 per cent in the OECD countries (Vaubel 2005c, Table 1). Also in the OECD, until the mid-1990s, the reduction of the Gini coefficient (that is, of income inequality) brought about by government redistribution had increased from 33 to 38 percentage points (ibid., calculated from Table 3). The main reason is that the growth of real labour cost has exceeded the decelerating growth of labour productivity as more and more capital has left the industrial countries of Western Europe. In the emerging economies of Asia and Latin America, which have raised their labour productivity growth by importing more capital, poverty rates have dropped dramatically (Sala-i-Martin 2002, Tables 4A and B). Overall, the world Gini coefficient has declined from 0.662 in 1980 to 0.633 in 1998 (ibid., Table 8).

In Chapter 4, Sinn deals with 'social standards'. He does not plead for harmonization, however: 'Since the decentralized choice of government actions leads to a first-best optimum, there is no social dumping and no need for centralized government actions' (p. 101). In Chapter 5, he takes the same position with regard to environmental policies directed at purely domestic pollution. This is unobjectionable but incompatible with his general principle that 'the failures that originally caused the government to take action will show up again at the higher level of government competition' (p. 6).

In the case of cross-border pollution, Sinn calls for equal Pigou taxes everywhere: 'When it is a question of air and water flowing between countries uniform tax rates are required . . . The tax rates should be harmonized internationally so as to avoid ecological dumping. A factor which is freely tradable internationally needs the same price everywhere' (p. 133). This is not true. The fact that air and water are flowing between countries does not mean that the quality of air or water is the same everywhere. As the willingness to pay for a clean and natural environment has been shown to depend on per capita income, age, population density, geography and so on, pollution tax schedules or per capita quantities of pollution permits ought to differ internationally. International arbitrage by investors will then tend to equalize the marginal price of polluting the environment. The role of governments and international organizations is to establish and enforce international property rights. This is also true in the environmental field.

Chapter 6 deals with product regulations: 'National product standards . . . have a responsibility to protect the consumers from buying lemon goods . . . Deregulation competition may result in a lemons equilibrium' (p. 135). 'An equilibrium in the competition between regulatory authorities is thus characterized by too lax standards' (p. 146). This raises the question of why governments may not confine themselves to publicizing the superior quality information which they are supposed to have. Public quality seals would possess the important advantage that, unlike product regulation, they would allow for differences in individual quality preferences.

If national product regulation is merely to provide information to consumers, it can do so also under regulatory competition (mutual recognition, the origin principle). If the cost of getting informed about the quality (regulations) of foreign products is excessive, domestic consumers can stick to domestic products.

But let us assume with Sinn – for the sake of the argument – that some domestic product regulations are justified in a closed economy because they are the most efficient way of conveying information about product qualities to a majority of voters. If, in these circumstances, regulatory competition is introduced by admitting cheaper goods of lower quality produced abroad, the minority which prefers the cheaper, lower quality goods will be better off without making the majority worse off. Thus, if we allow for the existence of majority decisions, international regulatory competition may be a Pareto-improvement even if domestic product regulation is warranted. This is another exception to Sinn's principle that 'the failures that originally caused the government to take action will show up again at the higher level of government competition'.

Since the information-theoretic case against regulatory competition is dubious, Sinn construes an externality problem as well: 'Because the utility of the foreign consumers is not considered in the calculations of the national government, there is a policy bias implying overly lax consumer protection' (p. 147). This leads him to advocate 'supra-national, European solutions' (p. 147), that is, 'Europe-wide minimum quality standards' and a European 'supervisory authority' (p. 148). However, exported goods need not be subject to the same product regulations as goods bought domestically. Each government has a sufficient incentive to differentiate and, at the same time, to warn and protect its citizens against excessively dangerous import goods. International organizations have to prevent national governments from abusing national quality standards for protectionist aims. However, they tend to ignore the differences in quality preferences when they impose international product regulations themselves.

In the seventh chapter, Sinn argues against institutional competition in the field of financial and banking regulation. He justifies the national regulations by asymmetrically imperfect information of bank creditors and the limited liability of banks. Once more, this raises the question whether and to what extent governments, instead of interfering with the freedom of contract, could not confine themselves to ensuring that the missing information is disclosed – if necessary, by awarding seals of approval to prudent banks. Limited liability is a pervasive feature of the modern market economy. Does Sinn want to regulate all contractual liabilities?

According to Sinn, financial and banking regulation has to be 'harmonized' internationally because the liabilities of banks (including their shares) are partly held by foreigners. Without harmonization, each national regulatory authority would be too lax since it would fail to take the foreign (external) benefits of its regulation into account and since the foreign creditors would be unable to appraise its regulations. Once more, these arguments may justify international negotiations to internalize the international external effects and an international organization which evaluates and compares national regulatory policies. Sinn's call for harmonizing the national regulations is a non-sequitur.

Finally, in the last chapter, Sinn warns against competition among competition policies:

> The competition among competition rules is a race to repeal the national anti-trust law as quickly as possible. (p. 203)

> Once the borders are opened, it is in the interest of any single country to help its national firms to form a cartel and to credibly commit to a common supply decision. The cartel will take on a Stackelberg leadership position if the other countries continue to stick to or do liberal policies. (p. 194)

> The aim is to give the country's own economy a lead in achieving an early Stackelberg position, which it then exploits, as soon as it is allowed to. (p. 203)

> Politicians and company leaders . . . obviously . . . have first mover advantages in mind when they argue that . . . anti-trust laws should be generously interpreted or even abandoned. (p. 188)

However, as Sinn himself admits (p. 206), it is doubtful that such credible commitments to particular supply conditions can be made in the various countries. Without this assumption, his wild-west scenario of 'first mover advantages' breaks down. There may be valid externality-theoretic or politico-economic arguments in favour of internationally agreed competition rules and an international guardian of these rules. However, competition policy is no exception to the case for institutional competition.

Institutional competition does not produce perfect solutions. Some minor externalities are always likely to be present. However, in the long run, institutional competition seems to be the most potent remedy against government failure. In view of the paramount importance of this goal, the disadvantages pale into insignificance.

NOTES

The author thanks Rudolf Adam, Peter Bernholz, Charles Blankart, Eric Jones, Hartmut Kliemt, Alan Peacock, Jean-Jacques Rosa, Pierre Salmon, Manfred Streit, Viktor Vanberg and Michael Wohlgemuth for helpful comments on earlier versions of this chapter.

1. Some authors use the term 'military competition', This can only mean competition in the development of military technology, not the use of these technologies in a war. They argue that the possibility of war can be an important stimulus for innovation and internal liberalization. The first proponent of this view was probably Heraclitus (540–480 BC): 'War is father of all . . . ' (Fragment 53, 1987).
2. For these and other historical instances see the case studies in Baechler et al. (1988), Bernholz et al. (1998) and Bernholz and Vaubel (2004).
3. Already in Homer's Ilias (6, 208), we find the admonition 'always to be the best and to excel the others' (my translation). Hesiod (eighth century BC), in his poem 'Works and Days' (Verse 11–26), asserts that 'strife is useful to mortals . . . because 'it rouses the lazy men to work' (my translation). Heraclitus adds that 'all things come about by strife' (Fragment 8, 1987).

    Jakob Burkhardt, in his *Greek Cultural History* (1898), argues that 'compared with the Scythians and the Asians, the Greek is in continuous competition or "Agon" with his compatriots' (pp. 319f.). 'The orient is not "agonal" because the caste system alone does not permit competition' (p. 320, my translation). Burkhardt also notes the competition among the Greek Gods (p. 320) and each Greek's dislike of the other Greek city states (p. 294). The Olympic games also come to mind.
4. Plato argued for a polis small enough so that citizens would all know each other and would be as friendly as possible towards one another ('Laws', V, 738, 742, VI, 771). Aristotle suggested that the optimum must lie between a population so small that the polis could not be self-sufficient and so large that the citizens could no longer know one another's characters (*Politics*, p. 1326b): 'A state then only begins to exist when it has attained a population sufficient for a good life in the political community . . . But, as I was saying, there must be a limit.'
5. Gaius Velleius Paterculus (born 19 BC) writes in his compendium of Roman history (30 AD): 'Genius is fostered by emulation, and it is now envy, now admiration which enkindles imitation, and, in the nature of things, that which is cultivated with the highest zeal advances to the highest perfection' (translation quoted from Kroeber 1944, p. 34). Paterculus was firmly rooted in the old republican tradition.
6. Althusius writes in his book 'Politica methodice digesta' (1603): 'Mighty imperia manifest many corruptions by which they are gradually worn down . . . Nor can concord, good order and proper discipline be preserved as easily among many persons . . . The Roman Commonwealth is an example. When it was of medium size, it was free from many corruptions. When it grew to a great size, however, with greater might and a larger population, as in the time of Marius, Sulla, Pompey and Julius Caesar, it abounded with corruptions so much that it was thrown into great calamities' (1964, pp. 63f.).
7. Zaicev (1993, pp. 42–7) also gives a number of examples of how famous Greek figures moved from one polis to another. Snodgrass (1986, pp. 61ff.) looks at political rivalry and emulation among the poleis in the field of military technique and the codification of law.
8. Möser's 'localism' has been discussed by Knudsen (1986, pp. 150ff.).
9. A more radical and less economic version of deriving public virtue from private vice is Bernard de Mandeville's *The Fable of the Bees* (1714/1970).
10. 'Blueprints for piecemeal engineering . . . are blueprints for single institutions . . . If they go wrong, the damage is not very great, and a readjustment is not very difficult. They are less risky, and for this reason less controversial' (Popper 1945/1966, Vol. 1, p. 159).
11. There is also considerable evidence that regulators in one jurisdiction tend to imitate the (de-)regulatory policies in other jurisdictions (see, for example, the econometric results of Feld et al. in Bernholz and Vaubel 2007).

12. This test also refers to Hayek's 'Competition as a Discovery Procedure' (1968/1978). While Hayek simply emphasizes the multiplicity of experiments under competition, Popper has presented an additional argument to the same effect in *The Poverty of Historicism* (1957, pp. 88f.): 'Since so much is done at a time, it is impossible to say which particular measure is responsible for any of the results.'
13. Baechler (2004), Bernholz (2000), Bernholz, Vaubel, eds (2007), Blum and Dudley (1991), Breton et al. (1991), Eichenberger (1994), Feld (2000), Gerken (1995), Kerber (2000), Oates and Schwab (1988, 1991), Pecquet (1985), Salmon (1987, 2006), Streit (1998), Vanberg (2000), Vanberg and Kerber (1994), Vaubel (1995, 1999), Vihanto (1992), Volckart (1999a), Wohlgemuth (1995a, b).
14. As Burkhardt (1898, p. 320) and Bernholz and Vaubel (2004, p. 14) suggest, the same may have been the case in India due to the caste system.
15. Moreover, immobile labour benefits from institutional competition if it is complementary to capital.

REFERENCES

Acton, Lord (1877/1985a), 'The History of Freedom in Antiquity', in J. Rufus Fears (ed.), *Selected Writings of Lord Acton*, Vol. 1: *Essays in the History of Liberty*, Indianapolis: Liberty Fund, pp. 5–28.

Acton, Lord (1877/1985b), 'The History of Freedom in Christianity', in J. Rufus Fears (ed.), *Selected Writings of Lord Acton*, Vol. 1: *Essays in the History of Liberty*, Indianapolis: Liberty Fund, pp. 29–54.

Althusius, Johannes (1603/1964), *The Politics of Johannes Althusius*, Boston.

Aristotle (1942), *Politics*, London: Oxford University Press.

Baechler, Jean (1968), 'Essai sur les origines du système capitaliste', *Archives Européennes de Sociologie*, **9**, 205–63.

Baechler, Jean (1971), *Les origines du capitalisme*, Paris: Edition Gallimard.

Baechler, Jean (1975), *The Origins of Capitalism*, Oxford: Basil Blackwell.

Baechler, Jean (2002), *Esquisse d'une histoire universelle*, Paris: Fayard.

Baechler, Jean (2004), 'The Political Pattern of Historical Creativity: A Theoretical Case', in Bernholz and Vaubel (eds) (2004), pp. 18–28.

Baechler, Jean, John A. Hall and Michael Mann (eds) (1988), *Europe and the Rise of Capitalism*, Oxford: Basil Blackwell.

Berman, Harold J. (1983), *Law and Revolution: The Formation of the Western Legal Tradition*, Cambridge, MA: Harvard University Press.

Berman, Harold J. (1998), 'The Western Legal Tradition: The Interaction of Revolutionary Innovation and Evolutionary Growth', in Bernholz, Streit and Vaubel (eds) (1998), pp. 35–47.

Bernholz, Peter (1985), *The International Game of Power*, Berlin: Mouton.

Bernholz, Peter (2000), 'Democracy and Capitalism: Are they Compatible in the Long Run?' *Journal of Evolutionary Economics*, **10**, 3–16.

Bernholz, Peter and Roland Vaubel (eds) (2004), *Political Competition, Innovation and Growth in the History of Asian Civilizations*, Cheltenham, UK and Northampton, MA, USA: Edward Elgar.

Bernholz, Peter and Roland Vaubel (eds) (2007), *Political Competition and Economic Regulation*, Abingdon: Routledge.

Bernholz, Peter, Manfred E. Streit and Roland Vaubel (eds) (1998), *Political Competition, Innovation and Growth: A Historical Analysis*, Berlin: Springer.

Besley, Timothy and Anne Case (1995), 'Incumbent Behavior: Vote Seeking, Tax Setting, and Yardstick Competition', *American Economic Review*, **85**, 25–45.

Blum, Ulrich and Leonard Dudley (1991), 'A Spatial Model of the State', *Journal of Institutional and Theoretical Economics*, **147**, 312–36.

Brennan, Geoffrey and James M. Buchanan (1980), *The Power to Tax*, Cambridge: Cambridge University Press.

Breton, Albert et al. (1991), *The Competitive State*, Dordrecht: Kluwer.

Bryce, James (1888/1901), *The American Commonwealth*, London: Macmillan.

Buchanan, James M. (1975), *The Limits of Liberty: Between Anarchy and Leviathan*, Chicago: Chicago University Press.

Buchanan, James M. and Roger Faith (1987), 'Secession and the Limits of Taxation', *American Economic Review*, **77**, 1023–31.

Burkhardt, Jakob (1898), *Griechische Kulturgeschichte*, Berlin, Stuttgart.

Chirot, Daniel (1986), *Social Change in the Modern Era*, San Diego, CA: Harcourt, Brace, Jovanovich.

Dowding, Keith and Peter John (1994), 'Tiebout: A Survey of the Empirical Literature', *Urban Studies*, **31**, 767–97.

Eichenberger, Reiner (1994), 'The Benefits of Federalism and the Risk of Overcentralization', *Kyklos*, **47**, 403–20.

Engerman, Stanley (1988), 'Reflections on How (and When and Why) the West Grew Rich', paper presented at the Interlaken Seminar on Analysis and Ideology.

The Federalist Papers (1787/1987), ed. I. Kramnick, Harmondsworth: Penguin.

Feld, Lars (2000), 'Tax Competition and Income Redistribution: An Empirical Analysis for Switzerland', *Public Choice*, **105**, 125–64.

Feldstein, Martin (1988), 'Thinking about International Economic Coordination', *Journal of Economic Perspectives*, **2**, 3–13.

Ferguson, Adam (1767/1966), *An Essay on the History of Civil Society*, Edinburgh: Edinburgh University Press.

Fisman, Raymond and Roberta Gatti (2002), 'Decentralization and Corruption: Evidence across Countries', *Journal of Public Economics*, **83**, 325–43.

Freeman, Kathleen (1950), *Greek City States*, New York: Norton.

Frey, Bruno S. and Reiner Eichenberger (1999), *The New Democratic Federalism for Europe: Functional, Overlapping and Competing Jurisdictions*, Cheltenham, UK and Northampton, MA, USA: Edward Elgar.

Gerken, Lüder (ed.) (1995), *Competition among Institutions*, London: Macmillan.

Gibbon, Edward (1787), *The History of the Decline and Fall of the Roman Empire*, London: A. Strahan and T. Cadell.

Hall, John A. (1985), *Powers and Liberties: The Causes and Consequences of the Rise of the West*, Oxford: Basil Blackwell.

Hayek, Friedrich A. von (1944), *The Road to Serfdom*, Chicago: Chicago University Press.

Hayek, Friedrich A. von (1961), *The Constitution of Liberty*, London and Henley: Routledge & Kegan Paul.

Hayek, Friedrich A. von (1968/1978), 'Competition as a Discovery Procedure', in Chiaki Nishiyama and Kurt R. Leube (eds), *The Essence of Hayek*, Stanford, CA: Hoover Institution Press, pp. 254–65.

Hayek, Friedrich A. von (1976a), 'Choice in Currency: A Way to Stop Inflation', Occasional Paper 48, Institute of Economic Affairs, London.

Hayek, Friedrich A. von (1976b), 'Denationalisation of Money', Hobart Paper 70, Institute of Economic Affairs, London.

Heraclitus (1987), *Fragments*, trans. T.M. Robinson, Toronto: University of Toronto Press.

Hesiod (2007), *Theogony, Works and Days*, Cambridge, Mass.: Harvard University Press.

Hirschman, Albert O. (1971), *Exit, Voice and Loyalty*, Cambridge, MA: Harvard University Press.

Hobbes, Thomas (1651/1962), *Leviathan*, London: Collins, The Fontana Library.

Humboldt, Wilhelm von (1793/1961), 'Über das Studium des Altertums und des griechischen insbesondere', in Wilhelm von Humboldt, *Werke*, Vol. II: *Schriften zur Altertumskunde und Ästhetik*, Die Vasken, Stuttgart: Cotta'sche Buchhandlung.

Hume, David (1742/1985), 'Of the Rise and Progress of the Arts and Sciences', in Eugene F. Miller (ed.), *David Hume: Essays, Moral, Political and Literary*, Indianapolis: Liberty Fund, pp. 111–37.

Jones, Eric (1981), *The European Miracle*, Cambridge: Cambridge University Press.

Jones, Eric (2004), 'Foreword', in Bernholz and Vaubel (eds) (2004), pp. x–xii.

Kant, Immanuel (1784/1959), 'Idea of a Universal History from a Cosmopolitan Point of View', in Patrick Gardiner (ed.), *Theories of History*, New York: Free Press, pp. 22–34.

Kant, Immanuel (1795/1991), 'Perpetual Peace', in Hans Reiss (ed.), *Kant: Political Writings*, Cambridge: Cambridge University Press, pp. 93–130.

Kehoe, Patrick J. (1987), 'Policy Cooperation among Benevolent Governments may be Undesirable', Working Paper 373, Federal Reserve Bank of Minneapolis.

Kennedy, Paul (1987), *The Rise and Fall of the Great Powers*, New York: Random House.

Kerber, Wolfgang (2000), 'Interjurisdictional Competition within the European Union', *Fordham International Law Journal*, **23**, S217–S249.

Kirchgässner, Gebhard and Lars Feld (2004), 'Föderalismus und Staatsquote', *Jahrbuch des Föderalismus*, **5**, 67–87.

Knudsen, Jonathan B. (1986), *Justus Möser and the German Enlightenment*, Cambridge: Cambridge University Press.

Kohr, Leopold (1957/1978), *The Breakdown of Nations*, New York: E.P. Dutton.

Kroeber, A.L. (1944), *Configurations of Culture Growth*, Berkeley, CA: University of California Press.

Landes, David S. (1998), *The Wealth and Poverty of Nations*, New York, London: Norton.

Landes, David S. (2006), 'Why Europe and the West? Why not China?', *Journal of Economic Perspectives*, **20**, 3–22.

Mandeville, Bernard de (1714/1970), *The Fable of the Bees*, Harmondsworth: Penguin.

McNeill, William H. (1982), *The Pursuit of Power*, Chicago: Chicago University Press.

Meier, Christian (1993), *Die Entstehung des Politischen bei den Gnechen*, Frankfurt/Main: Suhrkamp.

Moesen, Wim and Philippe van Cauwenberge (2000), 'The Status of the Budget Constraint, Federalism and the Relative Size of Government', *Public Choice*, **104**, 207–24.

Mokyr, Joel (1990), *The Lever of Riches*, New York: Oxford University Press.

Mokyr, Joel (1999), 'Invention and Rebellion: Why do Innovations Occur at all? An Evolutionary Approach', in Elise Brezis and Peter Temin (eds), *Minorities and Economic Growth*, Amsterdam: Elsevier, pp. 179–203.

Mokyr, Joel (2003), 'Why was the Industrial Revolution a European Phenomenon?' *Supreme Court Economic Review*, **9**.

Mokyr, Joel (2005), 'Mobility, Creativity and Technological Development', paper presented at the session 'Creativity and the Economy', German Association of Philosophy, Berlin, September.

Montesquieu, Charles Louis de Secondat (1748/1989), *The Spirit of the Laws*, Cambridge: Cambridge University Press.

Möser, Justus (1777/1958), *Sämtliche Werke*, Oldenburg, Hamburg: Gerhard Stalling Verlag.

Murray, Charles (2003), *Human Accomplishment*, New York: Harper Collins.

Musgrave, Richard M. (1959), *The Theory of Public Finance*, New York: McGraw Hill.

Naroll, Raoul, E.C. Benjamin, F.K. Fohl, M.J. Fried, R.E. Hildreth and J.M. Schaefer (1971), 'Creativity: A Cross-historical Pilot Survey', *Journal of Cross-cultural Psychology*, **2**, 181–8.

North, Douglass C. (1981), *Structure and Change in Economic History*, New York: Norton.

North, Douglass C. (1995), 'The Paradox of the West', in R. Davis (ed.), *Origins of Modern Freedom in the West*, Stanford: The University Press, pp. 1–34.

North, Douglass C. (1998), 'The Rise of the Western World', in Bernholz et al. (1998), pp. 13–28.

Oates, Wallace E. (1972), *Fiscal Federalism*, New York: Harcourt Brace Jovanovich.

Oates, Wallace E. and Robert M. Schwab (1988), 'Economic Competition among Jurisdictions: Efficiency-enhancing or Distortion-inducing?', *Journal of Public Economics*, **35**, 333–54.

Oates, Wallace E. and Robert M. Schwab (1991), 'The Allocative and Distributive Implications of Local Fiscal Competition', in D. Kenyon and J. Kincaid (eds), *Competition among State and Local Governments*, Washington, DC: Urban Institute, pp. 127–45.

Pecquet, Gary M. (1985), 'The Effect of Voter Mobility on Agenda Controllers', *Public Choice*, **45**, 269–78.

Plato (1937), 'Laws', in *The Dialogues of Plato*, trans. B. Jowett, Vol. II, New York.

Popper, Karl (1945/1966), *The Open Society and its Enemies*, London: Routlege & Kegan Paul.

Popper, Karl (1957), *The Poverty of Historicism*, London: Routledge & Kegan Paul.

Renan, E. (1884), *Sovenirs d'enfance et de jeunesse*, Paris.

Rogoff, Kenneth (1985), 'Can Interjurisdictional Monetary Policy Cooperation be Counterproductive?' *Journal of International Economics*, **18**, 199–217.

Rosenberg, Nathan and L.E. Birdzell (1986), *How the West Grew Rich*, New York: Basic Books.

Rousseau, Jean Jacques (1762/1968), *The Social Contract and Discourses*, trans. G.D.H. Cole, London, Dent.

Sala-i-Martin, Xavier (2002), *The World Distribution of Income*, Working Paper 8933, Cambridge, Mass.: National Bureau of Economic Research.

Salmon, Pierre (1987), 'Decentralisation as an Incentive Scheme', *Oxford Review of Economic Policy*, **3**, 24–43.

Salmon, Pierre (2006), 'Horizontal Competition among Governments', in Ehtisham Ahmad and Giorgio Brosio (eds), *Handbook of Fiscal Federalism*, Cheltenham, UK and Northampton, MA, USA: Edward Elgar.

Schneider, Mark (1989), 'Intercity Competition and the Size of the Local Public Workforce', *Public Choice*, **63**, 253–65.

Simons, Henry C. (1948), *Economic Policy for a Free Society*, Chicago: Chicago University Press.

Simonton, Dean Keith (1975), 'Sociocultural Context of Individual Creativity: A Transhistorical Time-Series Analysis', *Journal of Personality and Sociopsychology*, **32**, 1119–33.

Simonton, Dean Keith (1976), 'Ideological Diversity and Creativity: A Reevaluation of a Hypothesis', *Social Behavior and Personality*, **4**, 203–17.

Sinn, Hans-Werner (2003), *The New Systems Competition*, Oxford: Basil Blackwell.

Sinn, Stefan (1992), 'The Taming of Leviathan: Competition among Governments', *Constitutional Political Economy*, **3**, 177–96.

Smith, Adam (1776/1976), *The Wealth of Nations*, Chicago: Chicago University Press.

Snodgrass, Anthony (1986), 'Interaction by Design: The Greek City State', in Colin Renfrew and John F. Cherry (eds), *Peer Polity Interaction and Sociopolitical Change*, Cambridge: Cambridge University Press, pp. 47–58.

Sorokin, P.A. (1937), *Social and Cultural Dynamics*, Vol. 2, New York: American Book.

Stigler, George J. (1957/1998), 'The Tenable Range of Functions of Local Government', in Wallace E. Oates (ed.), *The Economics of Fiscal Federalism and Local Finance*, Cheltenham, UK and Lyme, USA: Edward Elgar, pp. 3–9.

Storing, Herbert J. (ed.) (1981), *The Complete Anti-Federalist*, Chicago: Chicago University Press.

Streit, Manfred E. (1998), 'Competition among Systems, Harmonisation and Integration', *Journal des Economistes et des Etudes Humaines*, **8**, 239–54.

Tabellini, Guido (1990), 'Domestic Politics and the International Coordination of Fiscal Policies', *Journal of International Economics*, **28**, 245–65.

Tiebout, Charles M. (1956), 'A Pure Theory of Local Expenditures', *Journal of Political Economy*, **64**, 416–24.

Tierney, Brian (1995), 'Freedom and the Medieval Church', in R.W. Davis (ed.), *The Origins of Modern Freedom in the West*, Stanford: Stanford University Press, pp. 64–100.

Tocqueville, Alexis de (1835/1945), *Democracy in America*, New York.

Toynbee, Arnold (1939), *A Study of History*, Vol. VI, Oxford: Oxford University Press.

Turgot, Anne Robert Jacques (1778/1810), 'Letter to Richard Price', in Turgot, *Oevres*, Paris: Delance.

Vanberg, Viktor (2000), 'Globalization, Democracy and Citizens' Sovereignty: Can Competition among Governments Enhance Democracy?', *Constitutional Political Economy*, **11**, 87–112.

Vanberg, Viktor and Wolfgang Kerber (1994), 'Institutional Competition among Jurisdictions: An Evolutionary Approach', *Constitutional Political Economy*, **5**, 193–219.

Vaubel, Roland (1980), 'Internationale Absprachen oder Wettbewerb in der Konjunkturpolitik?' Walter Eucken Institut (ed.), *Vorträge und Aufsätze*, **77**, Tübingen: Mohr/Siebeck.

Vaubel, Roland (1983), 'Coordination or Competition among National Macroeconomic Policies?' in Fritz Machlup et al. (eds), *Reflections on a Troubled World Economy*, London: Macmillan, pp. 3–28.

66 *Institutional competition*

Vaubel, Roland (1986), 'A Public Choice Approach to International Organization', *Public Choice*, **51**, 39–58.
Vaubel, Roland (1987), 'Competing Currencies: The Case for Free Entry', in James A. Dorn and Anna J. Schwartz (eds), *The Search for Stable Money*, Chicago: Chicago University Press, pp. 281–96.
Vaubel, Roland (1988), 'Comment on "Macroeconomic Policy Coordination: Where should we stand?" by Gilles Oudiz', in Herbert Giersch (ed.), *Macro and Micro Policies for More Growth and Employment*, Tübingen: Mohr/ Siebeck, pp. 296–300.
Vaubel, Roland (1994), 'The Political Economy of Centralization and the European Community', *Public Choice*, **81**, 151–90.
Vaubel, Roland (1995), 'The Centralisation of Western Europe', Hobart Paper 127, Institute of Economic Affairs, London.
Vaubel, Roland (1999), 'Enforcing Competition among Governments', *Constitutional Political Economy*, **10**, 327–38.
Vaubel, Roland (2005a), 'The Role of Competition in the Rise of Baroque and Renaissance Music', *Journal of Cultural Economics*, **29**, 277–97 (the German version appeared in 2002: *ORDO*, **53**).
Vaubel, Roland (2005b), 'Das Papsttum und der Politische Wettbewerb in Europa', *ORDO*, **56**, 187–92.
Vaubel, Roland (2005c), 'Die Sozialpolitischen Konsequenzen der Globalisierung', in Andreas Freytag (ed.), *Weltwirtschaftlicher Strukturwandel, Nationale Wirtschaftspolitik und Politische Rationalität*, Köln: Universitätsverlag, pp. 143–58.
Vihanto, Martti (1992), 'Competition between Local Governments as a Discovery Procedure', *Journal of Institutional and Theoretical Economics*, **148**, 411–36.
Volckart, Oliver (1999a), 'Institutional Competition: A New Theoretical Concept for Economic History', *Essays in Economic and Business History*, **17**, 75–87.
Volckart, Oliver (1999b), 'Political Fragmentation and the Emergence of Market Economies: The Case of Germany, c. 1000–1800 A.D.', Discussion Paper 01/1999, Max Planck Institute, Jena.
Volckart, Oliver (2000), 'The Open Constitution and its Enemies: Competition, Rent Seeking and the Rise of the Modern State', *Journal of Economic Behaviour and Organization*, **42**, 1–17.
Weber, Max (1923/1961), *General Economic History*, New York: Collier.
Weede, Erich (1988), 'Der Sonderweg des Westens', *Zeitschrift für Soziologie*, **17**, 172–86.
Weede, Erich (2000), *Asien und der Westen*, Baden-Baden: Nomos.
Wohlgemuth, Michael (1995a), 'Economic and Political Competition in Neoclassical and Evolutionary Perspective', *Constitutional Political Economy*, **6**, 71–96.
Wohlgemuth, Michael (1995b), 'Institutional Competition: Notes on an Unfinished Agenda', *Journal des Economistes et des Etudes Humaines*, **6**, 277–99.
Zaicev, Alexander (1993), *Das Griechische Wunder*, Konstanz: Universitätsverlag.

3. Learning through institutional competition

Michael Wohlgemuth

Nothing is more favourable to the rise of politeness and learning than a number of neighbouring and independent states connected together by commerce and policy. David Hume (1742/1985: 119)

3.1 INTRODUCTION

Why is it that the arts and sciences rose to such early and lasting heights in what is called 'Western civilization'? Why have schools, universities, academies emerged and progressed in various parts of Europe – and with them democracy, commerce, and the rule of law? David Hume was amongst the first to ask that question and provide an answer that relates to 'mutual jealousy' between 'neighbouring states' that are 'connected together by commerce and policy' (Hume 1742/1985: 119). Greek antiquity provides an early example:

> Greece was a cluster of little principalities which soon became republics . . . Each city produced its several artists and philosophers . . . Their contention and debates sharpened the wits of men. A variety of objects was presented to the judgement, while each challenged the preference to the rest, and the sciences, not being dwarfed by the restraint of authority, were enabled to make such considerable shoots as are even at this time the objects of our admiration. (Ibid.: 120f.)

According to this account two elements seem to have been most favourable to 'sharpened wits of men' or, for that matter, learning: variety and liberty.[1] One could even attribute the 'sharpened wits' to only one causal factor that combines variety and liberty: competition. Competition as the peaceful rivalry and free mobility between a variety of free producers of arts, ideas, crafts, services, commodities, but also of laws, institutions and policies can be said to be a most distinctive heritage of European or (later) 'Western' civilization and has been argued to be a major explanation of 'How the West Grew Rich' (Rosenberg and Birdzell 1986). Being neither

67

historian nor anthropologist, I have to abstract from many aspects of history and 'culture' in a wider sense (including habits, traditions, tastes, informal norms, values, arts and sciences). Rather, I will concentrate on favourable conditions for 'political learning' in the sense of learning about the qualities of alternative potential legal-political solutions to present-day social problems. And I will argue that competition between institutions (more specifically: between jurisdictions) provides, by ways of peaceful rivalry, an unequalled opportunity for learning about potentially more adequate potential solutions to political-social problems.

The chapter proceeds as follows: in Section 3.2 I will discuss the ability of economic theories of competition to take the phenomenon of learning into account. Neoclassical mainstream theories are able to address many aspects of competition (above all, static efficiency), but creative learning is mostly out of their reach. Therefore I will turn to Austrian, especially Hayekian, views of 'competition as a discovery procedure' in order to show important links between competition and learning. In Section 3.3 I will lay out a first set of important peculiarities of *institutional* competition between jurisdictions. In a spirit of 'consequent fallibilism' I will characterize institutions as hypotheses that always have to prove their adequacy in view of changing problem situations. Only based on this crucial assumption does learning by way of trial and error become an important aspect of political life. Unlike in the realm of economic competition, institutions, however, appear on two distinct levels: not only as rules of the game that channel individual and collective choices *within* rules, but also as objects of individual choices *of* rules by ways of 'exit'. In Section 3.4 I will sketch the feedback mechanisms between individual choices of institutions or 'institutional arbitrage' on the 'demand'-side, and collective choices of rules or 'institutional entrepreneurship' on the 'supply'-side. The capabilities of institutional competition to trigger learning processes in politics are discussed in Section 3.5. Here, a major argument will be that 'parallel experimentation' offers greater hope and scope for evolutionary learning than 'consecutive experimentation'. In Section 3.6 I want to highlight the virtues of institutional competition as a discovery procedure by comparing it to realistic alternatives (isolation, harmonization and centralization). Section 3.7 provides a short outlook with reference to the future of European integration.

3.2 COMPETITION AS A DISCOVERY PROCEDURE AND LEARNING OPPORTUNITY

The mainstream neoclassical approach to competition and other social phenomena can be condensed in one sentence as 'the combined assumptions of maximizing behavior, market equilibrium and stable preferences, used relentlessly and unflinchingly' (Becker 1976, p. 5). Such relentless combinations imply another assumption: 'given knowledge'. And by assuming 'given knowledge' or 'common knowledge' the phenomenon of learning is excluded from the area of investigation right from the start. To be sure, with the advent of the economics of information (for example, Stigler 1961; Stiglitz 2000) 'perfect information' no longer serves as a necessary companion to neoclassical economics. Imperfect and/or asymmetric information can be combined with stable preferences and maximizing behaviour and still yield market equilibriums. Learning in the sense of coping with true uncertainty and facing the potential of error and novelty, however, is something other than optimizing ignorance based on given knowledge.[2] Still, even imperfect information based on 'rational ignorance' leads neoclassical price theory to imply 'imperfect competition' and various forms of 'market failure'. The ideal of welfare economics – 'perfect competition' – demands that homogeneous goods are given and knowledge about their properties is complete. Competition thus seems to be efficient and welfare-enhancing only in the economist's Nirvana where there is nothing left to learn.

'Austrian' or evolutionary approaches are characterized by a more or less relentless rejection of Becker's view. Maximizing representative agents are rejected in favour of bounded rational individuals who differ in their knowledge, skills, expectations, practices and learning heuristics. Expectations and practices can even be wholly mistaken. Static equilibrium is rejected in favour of a process analysis of spontaneous orders characterized by endogenous change based on the permanent creation of novelty, the competitive selection and the (often path-dependent) emulation of potential problem-solutions which are not 'given data' but changing options to be discovered in the process of competition. And with the emergence of novelty, endogenous change and interactive learning, stable preferences become a much more critical assumption that can hardly serve as an adequate starting point in many cases that are of interest – such as the case of learning.

It is above all with Hayek (1937/48) that a new view of the relation between 'Economics and Knowledge' emerged that centred on the phenomenon of a 'division of knowledge' as 'the really central problem of economics as a social science' (p. 50). Economic agents are now assumed to base their individual plans on subjective expectations that reflect personal skills and local, partial knowledge which in its totality can never be known to any single mind. Economic coordination therefore takes place between individuals whose expectations about the behaviour of others are necessarily speculative, different and fallible, since they are based on only partial and conjectural knowledge about the social environment. Individuals always have to adapt to new circumstances that are permanently changed by processes of trial and error. In other words: social interaction involves permanent learning about new, subjective and ephemeral social 'facts'.

'The Use of Knowledge in Society' (Hayek 1945/48) thus is not to be seen as a learning process in the sense of an increasing stock of 'scientific' knowledge about historical facts or universal nomological relations of cause and effect. The knowledge relevant here 'never exists in concentrated form but solely as the dispersed bits of incomplete and frequently contra-dictory knowledge which all the separate individuals possess' (p. 77). With the division of knowledge a form of social learning becomes important that consists of innumerable actors' successful adaptation to changing circum-stances by ways of using knowledge that *others* have and that they them-selves do not have to understand. Hayek's prime example for such a somewhat free-riding use of knowledge is the price system as a 'system of telecommunications' or 'signals' (p. 87) that allows market actors to adjust their subjective plans to a myriad of changes in the economic environment that affect the scarcity of goods and services, and thus to the dispersed knowledge of others that they never command themselves.[3]

'The Meaning of Competition' (Hayek 1946/48), in this context of a divi-sion of knowledge and its social use through price signals, in important respects becomes the exact opposite of the neoclassical view of 'perfect com-petition' based on 'given' circumstances. If one could in fact treat preferences, knowledge and homogeneous goods as given 'data', competition would indeed become meaningless.[4] The true meaning of competition is that of

a process of the formation of opinion . . . It creates the views that people have about what is best and cheapest, and it is because of it that people know at least as much about possibilities and opportunities as they in fact do. It is thus a process which involves a continuous change in the data and whose significance must therefore be completely missed by any theory that treats these data as con-stant. (p. 106)

'Competition as a Discovery Procedure' (Hayek 1968/78) thus implies that '*wherever* the use of competition can be rationally justified, it is on the ground that we do *not* know in advance the facts that determine the actions of competitors . . . it would clearly be pointless to arrange for competition, if we were certain beforehand who would do best' (p. 179). Thus, the need to learn is the main justification for competition. And enhanced learning is the main outcome of competition 'as a procedure for the discovery of such facts as, without resort to it, would not be known to anyone, or at least would not be utilised' (ibid.).

For my purpose of analysing the possibility of learning through institu-tional competition a general assessment of competition is needed, very much like the one that Hayek portrays as 'competition as a discovery procedure'. Such a general view would not have to be limited to the case of market competition and the price system, which are only parts of the overall process of institutional competition (see below). As major elements of an evolutionary view of competition as a process of discovery and social learning one needs only a few assumptions about individual behaviour and social life – which fortunately are much more realistic than those commonly used in mainstream economics. In addition, these assumptions hold for social behaviour in general – for economic as well as political rivalry and coordination.[5]

(1) *Individual behaviour* Human action, on markets as well as in politics or elsewhere outside the realm of irrational exuberance, metaphysical trance, or lovelorn remorse, is based on purposeful theory-guided expectations. The purpose is to achieve one's own chosen ends (satisfy preferences) which may also include a purposeful regard for the welfare of others. Knowledge about the best way to achieve these ends is based on conjectures and beliefs (theories). These conjectures can be mistaken, they take the form of fallible hypotheses.[6]

(2) *Social context* If human action takes place in a competitive environment, the ability to achieve one's own chosen ends depends on the reactions of others. These 'others' are (a) those who voluntarily prefer one's offered problem-solutions to alternative suggestions made by (b) competing providers of potential problem-solutions.

Competition, thus, is a permanent process of trying to persuade others to voluntarily prefer one's own proposed problem-solutions to those of others. It is not a state of rest or 'equilibrium', nor can it be based on objective 'maximizing behaviour', because which and whose hypotheses will prove to be momentarily 'right' and socially rewarded, changes and cannot be known ex ante. It emerges from the process of voluntary interaction with likewise uncertain partners and 'un-given' environments and thus cannot inform the same interpersonal process in a hypothetical state of given antecedents. If all facts that price theory assumes to be given and known were in fact given and known, competition would indeed be a most superfluous and wasteful method of securing adjustment to these 'given' facts. Only if there is no permanent and pre-known 'truth', only if there is something to discover and something new to learn, does competition make social sense. And since one can have no ex-ante preference for something that one can only aspire to discover and learn, even the comfortable assumption of 'given preferences' becomes unsuited for an assessment of the relationship between competition and learning. In short, the mainstream approach based on 'the combined assumptions of maximizing behavior, market equilibrium and stable preferences' (Becker 1976, p. 5) may have many advantages. But as a starting point for exploring 'learning through competition' it does not allow us to account for learning processes as they unfold in real life.

3.3   INSTITUTIONS AS OBJECTS OF INDIVIDUAL CHOICE AND AS RULES OF THE GAME

Similar statements about the inadequacy of neoclassical economics to account for evolutionary properties of market competition have often been made. In addition to the Hayekian insight of the use of (more or less given) dispersed subjective knowledge, (Schumpeterian) creative entrepreneurship needs to be added to those elements that the neoclassical mainstream is ill-equipped to deal with. Both elements – the discovery of dispersed knowledge and the creation of new knowledge – are, of course, central elements of any theory of learning. Learning involves both the discovery and communication of facts and theories that are 'better' and the creation of ideas that may turn out to be 'better'. The criterion for 'better' or 'worse' is easily identified in the realm of individual voluntary transactions in the marketplace: the customer is 'king' – whatever s/he 'buys', according to the 'consumer's sovereignty', is 'better', according to theories about what best satisfies individual needs. Market competition based on free choices and entrepreneurial creations produces both the spontaneous *adaptation to* variety (of preferences, opinions, capabilities and so on) and the spontaneous *creation of* variety (new potential problem-solutions for new potential needs). Both are prerequisites for learning.

There are important differences between typical market competition and interjurisdictional competition, to which I will turn in the next section. Still, institutional competition can be, quite like market competition, reconstructed as a 'discovery procedure' and unique occasion for social learning processes. I define 'institutions' for the purpose of the present task as rules of behaviour that are enforced by various sanctioning mechanisms within a given group of people. In the process of competition between (realms and suppliers of) institutions, such rules relate to two different levels: (i) as objects of individual or collective (political) choice and (ii) as rules of the game defining legitimate procedures and objects of individual or collective (political) choices. I will return to this crucial distinction in due course. First, I want to stress the fallible, conjectural character not only of human action, but also of institutions as human creations: on both levels – as interjurisdictional rules of the game that define how jurisdictions and rules can be individually chosen and as domestic rules that might be individually chosen.

Institutions play a crucial role in stabilizing expectations of uncertain actors, thus reducing transaction costs and making mutual gains from trade with others more likely (for example North 1990). But any collective decision about *which* rules in *which* kinds of combinations with existing formal and informal rules are most adequate for *which* groups of citizens under *which* changing conditions is confronted with formidable knowledge-problems. Such things can never be completely and conclusively known – neither to an enlightened benevolent dictator (or economist) nor to 'the sovereign' in a democracy: the majority of citizens. Based on that simple but fundamental Popperian insight, Albert (1986, pp. 40ff.) calls for a 'consistent fallibilism' which should not only apply to scientific hypotheses, but also to political attempts to solve collective action problems. In terms of a procedural social technology, consequent fallibilism or 'rational problem-solving behaviour' (ibid.) calls for competition in the sense of the creation and comparative evaluation of realizable proposals for the solution of social problems offered by various groups and political 'entrepreneurs' (ibid.). This is the basic rationale for learning through institutional competition (see Section 3.5 below).

But which kinds of proposals can be effectively, legally, realized and which criteria for their evaluation and final implementation should be applied, depends on the rules of the game of collective decision-making. Very much in the way that workable competition in the realm of economics (or of science) depends on the general acceptance of procedural rules of conduct, the workability and effectiveness of institutional competition as a learning device depends on the rules of the game. Of course, these institutions on a procedural level, as rules of the game of interjurisdictional competition or of an interjurisdictional *Wettbewerbsordnung*, are just as conjectural and fallible as are the intrajurisdictional institutional hypotheses themselves. However, combining a constitutional economics 'consent' test and some Austrian economics insights into the preconditions of competition as a discovery procedure, one can arrive at some plausible suggestions about which kinds of rules of the game of institutional competition would be most suited to allow for experimentation and learning in a way that should be in the common constitutional interest of sovereign citizens.

As Hayek and others[7] have argued, both interpersonal justice and the workability of competition as a discovery procedure are best served under rules of the game that pass a 'test of universalizability'. This is a procedural 'test of the appropriateness of a rule' (Hayek 1976, p. 27) with the main criterion for appropriateness being whether we 'can "want" or "will"' that such a rule be generally applied' (p. 28). Applying this Kantian test to the principles of a legal order, Hayek (1966/67, p. 166) distinguishes three essential and interrelated aspects of rules of just conduct:

(1) The rules should refer to concrete individual and political behaviour, not to states of affairs that no one could intentionally have brought about.
(2) The rules would in most cases be prohibitions aimed at the prevention of unjust action.[8]
(3) By prohibiting non-generalizable, discriminatory acts, the rules create protected domains that allow legally equal citizens to pursue self-chosen ends by choosing between an open set of actions that are not prohibited.

With respect to the discussion of international governance (for example, Rodrik 1997; Rawls 1999) these criteria can yield some guidance. It implies that it would be broadly pointless to discuss globalization or institutional competition in terms of market results such as the distribution of incomes across countries or regions or 'terms of trade', as long as they are the unintended results of spontaneous interactions between millions of individuals, which no one could ever have produced (or prevented) by deliberate action. Instead, one would have to look for concrete behaviour on the part of economic or political actors that can be argued to be unjust because it does not pass the test of universalizability, since no one (including those who carry out these acts) would want this kind of behaviour to be *generally* applied. Protectionism provides the perfect example. Tariffs and quotas, as well as cases of deliberately erected non-tariff barriers to trade will be ruled out by the generality test as prejudicial to the myopic interests of specific groups.

The most important rules of just behaviour in an international community of free nations would have to bind *political* agents. They would above all consist of prohibitions of certain *political* actions that obstruct citizens' freedom to engage in mutually beneficial trade with foreigners. To be sure, the removal of barriers to the free movement of goods, services, capital and persons across borders need not be the only task of an international economic order. But it is the foremost task, since without negative guarantees of free trade the market order is not going to develop into an extended abstract order that allows individuals across borders to pursue their self-chosen aims in a regime of mutually beneficial exchange.[9] Other political rules that could facilitate international trade – such as the legal enforcement of border-crossing contracts, or the introduction of international standards and norms – are clearly secondary to the establishment of free trade. In addition, it is far from obvious that these elements of international private law would necessarily have to be laid down and fixed once and for all by an international political authority.[10]

3.4 THE PROCESSES OF INSTITUTIONAL COMPETITION

Evolutionary market competition can be analysed as a compound of two interrelated processes, linked by feedback mechanisms, the power of which depends on the actors' incentives and willingness to invest in information (Streit and Wegner 1992): a selection process driven by choices on the demand side and a process of rivalry between (potential) suppliers of alternative problem-solutions. In its general structure, this concept also describes competition in a democracy with voters selecting between parties and candidates and political rivals competing for attention and votes, triggered by gain-and-loss feedbacks, the quality of which depends on the information costs that the actors are willing to bear. In their substance, however, economic and political processes of selection and rivalry differ considerably.[11] I will now discuss some differences between economic market competition and political competition. At the same time, I will distinguish competition for mandates in a purely representative democracy and interjurisdictional rivalry for mobile resources, which combines elements of economic selection processes ('exit') with those of political rivalry ('voice').[12]

3.4.1 Institutional Choice

In both politics and the market, the intensity of competitive selection and the prospects for discovery and learning during the process critically depend on the freedom of the actors on the demand side to choose, using their individual knowledge and pursuing their individual goals. And the citizens' propensity to invest in information, to potentially 'learn', critically affects the intensity and quality of the selection processes. The more substitutes with differing price–quality combinations can be chosen according to individual preferences and needs, the more actors on the demand side are exposed to high-powered incentives and opportunities to discover these differences.

With regard to these aspects, political competition clearly fails to provide convincing equivalents to normal market competition. A consumer of market goods receives only the goods s/he prefers and for which s/he is willing to pay. A political subject receives a complete bundle of political goods and services, regardless of personal preferences or any reciprocal action. Voters for the winning coalition, voters for losing parties and non-voters all end up with the same election result and have to accept the same policies. Not surprisingly therefore, incentives to search, store and interpret information about political offers (programmes, candidates), political products (laws, regulations) or political systems (rules of the game) are low. This lack of high-powered incentives for knowledge-creation reduces the ability of the political selection process to discover the comparative qualities of political alternatives. In addition, general elections do not *continuously* signal citizens' opinions on *particular* policies. They are only capable of voicing bold aggregate judgements about bundles of promises as incorporated in parties and candidates – and changing their relative political power positions every four or five years.

It is here that interjurisdictional competition differs from purely representative democracy. Institutional competition is based on *individual* choices of jurisdictions as, thus, alternative (bundles of) rules by way of exit of mobile resources across borders.[13] Exit entails the individual choice of rules instead of a collective choice of rulers. It is based on individuals' comparative appraisals of the net benefits when combining their mobile resources with various existing political infrastructures in different jurisdictions. Using exit, individuals can free themselves to some extent from forced consumption of political goods. As an ongoing selection mechanism, exit is therefore much more likely to provide political analogues to evolutionary market competition and the discovery and use of local knowledge.

By confronting actual (and not just potential) political alternatives, institutional competition communicates political preferences much more concretely than general elections. It provokes political opinion formation focused on concrete institutional alternatives, thus leading to the creation and social use of political skills and knowledge in society. Compared to market competition, the selection processes of representative democracy are poorly equipped to discover individual opinions and satisfy individual preferences according to their diversity, intensity and variability.[14] The choice options of individuals within the process of institutional competition are centred somewhere between typical market competition and general elections. Institutions have no individual price tags attached to them. They are not auctioned on a daily basis on a specific 'market'. Hence the use of knowledge about institutions is not directly built on a division of knowledge that can be abstractly communicated by ways of changes in relative prices. By deciding to invest one's capital or labour in a different jurisdiction, one is usually forced to choose a complete bundle of institutions for which one has to pay a more or less fixed overall 'price': taxes. The possibilities of 'cherry picking' – choosing specific institutions of a foreign country while retaining others of one's home country, are limited. And the possibilities of 'free-riding' – using foreign local public goods while not paying for them, should be limited.

As a consequence, exit or 'institutional arbitrage' (Wohlgemuth 1995, pp. 282ff.) sends out abstract and often diffuse signals about the institutional preferences of owners of mobile resources. These signals do not directly and undisputedly tell suppliers of institutional frameworks how to react. The signals have to be interpreted and successful (new) strategies have to be envisaged. This is the formidable task of political entrepreneurs.

3.4.2 Institutional Entrepreneurship

The main motivation of politicians is to acquire or retain power, prestige and income. For that task, institutional competition is only relevant as far as it affects a politician's (party's) prospects for (re-)election. In the end only the home market for votes is relevant for domestic politicians and thus for the supply of institutions in a democracy. But interjurisdictional competition does affect this market in various ways: (a) the withdrawal of mobile resources reduces the productivity of immobile factors. Ensuing income losses of owners of (relatively) immobile resources can lead them to withdraw their support for the government. Especially the 'exit' of capital investments and high-skilled labour has a negative impact on national income and employment – both crucial factors of empirically tested 'popularity functions' of governments (for example, Nannestad and Paldam 1994). In addition, the withdrawal of valuable resources as a tax base has a negative impact on the government's budget and hence its ability to please voters with government transfers and expenditure programmes.

Very much like entrepreneurs on markets for private goods, political entrepreneurs face the difficult task of identifying the often complex causes of the reactions of their 'customers' and finding adequate responses. And as with competition in general, simple imitation of the behaviour of more successful rivals is no guarantee for success. The political entrepreneur's task is even more demanding, since simple institutional emulation often creates frictions and inconsistencies within developed political-legal systems and traditions that display a high degree of functional interrelatedness. Successful political entrepreneurship would therefore very often not consist in imitation of one 'golden' solution, but in institutional innovation, the creation of new problem-solutions that can be more easily adapted to the specific legal-political structures and socio-political needs of the jurisdiction to which they should apply (see also, Mukand and Rodrik 2005).

Market competition based on free choices and entrepreneurial creations enhances both the *adaptation to* variety (of preferences, opinions, capabilities and so on) and the *creation of* variety (new potential problem-solutions for new potential needs). The same is true for institutional competition. And this is a major reason why models of institutional competition that are based on strict neoclassical equilibrium assumptions are inadequate to account for innovation and learning as major advantages of interjurisdictional competition. In Charles Tiebout's (1956) famous model, only the adaptation to given alternatives is discussed. Here 'exit' leads, under strong assumptions (for example, perfect information), to an efficient allocation of given local public goods, because citizens with heterogeneous preferences move to jurisdictions that best fit their given preferences. Competition between jurisdictions thus results in homogeneous communities, with residents who all value public services similarly. In this sorting equilibrium, no individual can be made better off by moving, and the market is efficient. The 'supply' of policies remains constant, only the mobile constituency re-allocates itself efficiently. Other neoclassical models that look at the reactions of political suppliers to the threat of exit also assume given and known alternatives and given and known knowledge about their attributes. Depending above all on the initial assumptions, a 'race to the bottom' or 'race to the top', ending in an equilibrium of 'ex post' harmonization of policies across jurisdictions is deduced and compared to given 'ex-ante' states of affairs or ideal states. Again, these models are not without merit. But they are unsuited for the purpose of discussing learning through (institutional or any other kind of) competition.[15]

3.5 LEARNING THROUGH INSTITUTIONAL COMPETITION

Above, I have introduced the notion of institutions as fallible hypotheses concerning ways to secure beneficial coordination and control in human interaction. Critical-rational learning depends on continuously challenging (falsifying) 'given' theories by creating alternative hypotheses. In some respects, the need for the creation of variety is even greater with what one could call 'institutional fallibilism' than in the realm of critical-rational science. Nomological scientific theories mostly claim universal validity and falsifiability independent of time and place. Political theories – ideas about which policies are most adequate to solve collective action problems – are much more contingent. They can hardly be 'true' once and for all. Thus, political learning is not about finding one eternal and universal 'truth', but about discovering temporarily more suitable solutions to changing problems of groups with different preferences and capabilities. And it is here that variety becomes especially important: 'Only when a great many different ways of doing things can be tried will there exist such a variety of individual experiences, knowledge and skills, that a continuous selection of the most successful will lead to steady improvement' (Hayek 1978, p. 149). Political entities quite naturally fail to support variety on the level of goods and services provided. This is not by itself to be decried as policy failure since the tasks of the protective state (rule of law) and most tasks of the productive state (provision of public goods) require some intrajurisdictional uniformity when it comes their application and enforcement. Most political goods and services are valuable precisely by virtue of their being the same for all citizens within a jurisdiction and their being changed only discontinuously.

At the same time, the variety of trials, together with an effective selection of errors are necessary conditions for the discovery of problem-solutions that are regarded superior by their users. Democracy does introduce variety, but mainly on the level of proposals rather than that of final products (laws, regulations). This restriction of the realm of actual competition limits the evolutionary potential of political competition within a jurisdiction, because in each jurisdiction or 'natural' monopoly of government, there is only one set of political problem-solutions being tested at a time. Political evolution within these bounds is basically limited to learning from *consecutive* trials and errors (Vanberg 1993, pp. 15f.). By introducing 'potential competition' from non-incumbents, democracy creates a variety of ideas and contestability of the status quo, but potential rivals make no actual contribution to an ongoing process of effective trial and error, and hence to a process of knowledge-creation based on actual comparative performance.[16] In this context interjurisdictional competition displays its major virtue as a 'discovery procedure'. By enabling citizens to actively choose between concrete sets of political alternatives, institutional competition triggers a politically effective form of *parallel* – rather than of consecutive – learning from real-life experiences.

Our lack of knowledge about the respective working properties of policies and institutions and the increasing depreciation of our knowledge in the face of changing environments is thus the prime argument in favour of interjurisdictional competition (and not, as our neoclassical friends tend to argue, a prime argument against it). If all the problem-solving qualities of institutions and policies were known once and for all, institutional competition could justly be regarded as a wasteful (transaction-cost laden) method of discovering what we (as economists or politicians) claim to know already. This critique applies to neoclassical opponents and to defenders of institutional competition. Both presume to know the equilibrium outcome based on models with given preferences, given alternatives and given knowledge. In the first class of mechanistic models inefficient solutions crowd out the given efficient one(s) ('race to the bottom'); in the second the one known optimal solution is finally selected. Both models come close to our perfect competition stationary equilibrium model; often the only difference is that in the first case one starts with a perfect set of institutions and omniscient benevolent dictators, in the second, one usually assumes a rotten and corrupt Leviathan.[17] But in both cases the competitive process has no meaning as a discovery procedure nor as a permanent incentive structure to trigger learning and innovation.

Again, institutional competition is above all a most useful procedure if we acknowledge politicians' and citizens' constitutional lack of knowledge concerning present and future social problems and adequate political responses. In addition, decentralization and interjurisdictional competition are the only ways to account for the fact that citizens also have different and changing preferences concerning the institutions and policies that they will have to finance and endure. Institutional competition is no equalizer or 'ex post harmonizer', it is a permanent process of creating, comparing and adopting different responses to different needs, capabilities, and preferences.

Such political learning processes naturally take time, and they need time in order to be based on analytical insight and emerging political consent. Instantaneous adaptation and perfect mobility are elements of a misleading 'perfect competition' Nirvana. Gradual adaptation and 'loyalty'-based inhibitions of immediate 'exit' are not to be deplored as indicators of 'imperfect competition'; they rather serve as necessary implications and even preconditions of a workable discovery and learning process in society. As Hayek (1946/48, p. 103) observed:

> slow adaptation does by no means necessarily mean weak competition. When the variety of near-substitutes is great and rapidly changing, where it takes a long time to find out about the relative merits of the available alternatives . . . the adjustment must be slow even if competition is strong and active . . . competition is the more important the more complex or 'imperfect' are the objective conditions in which it has to operate.

In a very similar vein Hirschman (1970, p. 85) argued that a certain amount of 'loyalty' helps to find the right responses to decline in firms, organizations and states, since it gives entrepreneurs (on markets as well as in politics) time to analyse the situation and convince citizens of the need for political reforms.

Especially with regard to responses to decline in states, the exit signals have to be interpreted, and 'voice' or public opinion, exploring reasons for decline and acceptable responses to it, has to be collectively formed and communicated. Since 'voice' remains the decisive currency in democratic policies, both extremely sensitive and instantaneous 'exit' and extremely acquiescent 'loyalty' (the relinquishment of exit options) would obstruct critical collective learning processes. Extreme 'exit' would lead to the sudden collapse of the community and leave no dissenting voice behind; extreme 'loyalty' would lead to paralysis of the community with no credible threat of 'exit' to lead to political responses. Workable learning processes, in political as well as in economic organizations, are most likely to exist in situations where moderately loyal citizens can credibly threaten to 'exit' if their 'voice' is not heard.[18]

3.6 INSTITUTIONAL COMPETITION AND ITS ALTERNATIVES

In order to appraise the virtues of interjurisdictional competition, the adequate basis of comparison is not an unrealizable state of affairs. Instead of such a 'Nirvana approach', the adequate basis of comparison ought to be the consequences that would arise in the absence of competition (Hayek 1946/48, p. 100). Realistic alternatives to institutional competition are of two kinds:

(1) Unilateral measures of local governments to prevent the 'exit' of their citizens.
(2) Multilateral collusion to prevent competition by ways of harmonization or centralization.

Both the unilateral erection of artificial barriers to exit (or entry) and the multilateral cartelization of would-be competitors have similarly negative effects on potential discovery and learning in politics. Inside the isolated jurisdiction as well as among harmonized or centralized jurisdictions, all we can hope for and learn from are consecutive trials and errors. Institutional competition adds the very important dimension of parallel experimentation: the opportunity to compare and choose among real-world political trials.[19] As a consequence, only institutional competition allows for the continuous discovery and communication of citizens' changing preferences and needs and the continuous reflection of local differences between informed preferences and tested capabilities.

At the same time, decentralization and interjurisdictional competition are the least risky way to correct unavoidable errors. Inadequate harmonized or centralized policies are already less easily identified due to the lack of comparable and selectable alternatives. Presumably this is often what interjurisdictional cartels had in mind in the first place. But even generally recognized fatal errors of harmonized or centralized policies are very hard to revise due to the complex log-rolling arrangements that created many internationally agreed, but obviously non-universalizable and collectively damaging policies (for example the EU's Common Agricultural Policy).

By comparison, a system of competing jurisdictions greatly improves both citizens' and politicians' knowledge base and their incentives to react to the revealed shortcomings of present policies. The effects in terms of risk control are obvious: with local experimentation on smaller scales the refutation of a social-political 'hypothesis' is no great disaster, but if a large encompassing political union is forced to follow one grand idea or all-embracing political theory, its refutation or falsification implies large social costs or even catastrophe. The holistic social experiment of communism is a radical illustration of this point.

One does not have to refer to the end of history or the fall of most communist and many other totalitarian systems to demonstrate the merits of interjurisdictional competition. One can even admit that in many cases there are respectable arguments in favour of harmonization. As an example, harmonized product norms can help reduce transaction costs and this, viewed in isolation, can foster efficiency and competition on product markets. Or more generally one may prefer to forgo some potentials for competitive discovery on a higher level (say, by accepting common basic rules of the game of an internal market), if one can thus create more intensive competition on lower levels. Such arguments have been widely discussed in the classical anti-trust literature, for example regarding standardization cartels (for example, Farrell and Saloner 1985; Blankart and Knieps 1993). The main problem is how to determine the trade-off between concrete and tangible advantages of some harmonization from a static point of view (that is, the efficiency of given, present policies due to, for instance, economies of scale) on the one hand and a reduced potential for competitive discovery on the other. The tangible advantages are more easily modelled (which may be why mainstream economists like them), and they are more easily communicated (which may be why politicians like them).

What is less easily modelled and sold to the public is the inherent danger of standardized 'one-size-fits-all' policies creating institutional path-dependencies that make a spontaneous adaptation to new environments, new preferences and new knowledge much more difficult than it would be in the presence of freedom to develop and choose alternative policies. To be sure, institutional competition could also lead to a reduction of institutional variety. But there are two crucial differences between such unplanned (ex post) harmonization and deliberately arranged (ex ante) harmonization: first, ex post harmonization through competitive selection is the result of voluntary decisions of citizens whereas ex ante harmonization is often the result of barter and collusion between politicians holding coercive power. Second, ex post harmonization through voluntary and revocable choices leaves the option for decentralized units to (re-)introduce (new) political alternatives if they so wish, whereas ex ante harmonization by political compact does not. The costs and benefits of upholding such 'potential competition' as well as those of its deliberate destruction, however, cannot be specified in much detail. This would presuppose that we already knew what we can only hope to learn through institutional competition.

3.7 OUTLOOK: HOW FAR IS BRUSSELS FROM ATHENS?

Let me return to the opening quotation in which David Hume refers to the rivalry between Greek principalities and republics and argues that 'nothing is more favourable to the rise of politeness and learning than a number of neighbouring and independent states connected together by commerce and policy'. Hume (1742/1985, p. 121) went on to claim that 'Europe is at present a copy at large of what Greece was formerly a pattern in miniature'. More than 250 years after Hume wrote this down, Europe certainly looks very different. She saw the emergence of large nation-states often engaged in non-peaceful rivalry with disastrous results. With the advent of the European Community and the European Union, peace on the continent has been restored and more and more nation-states were (once again) to be 'connected together by commerce and policy'. This is no minor achievement, to say the least.

At the same time however, the political integration of Europe seems more and more to legislate away the richness of the European institutional landscape and the potential for learning and innovation that was once the secret of Europe's dynamic growth of civilization. With an 'acquis communautaire' of over 90 000 pages of unified laws and regulations, and incessant demands by EU organizations and member state governments for 'European solutions' – that is, for centralized or harmonized institutional responses to social-economic problems – there is an imminent danger of the European Union degenerating into a political cartel for defending a European 'social model' that nowhere exists as a common heritage and that – in its variant as an overburdened welfare state – has long lost competitive sustainability. Such a 'model' or 'European solution' could easily become a monolithic set of sclerotic institutions that politicians would like to protect. But institutional competition does not stop at the borders of the

EU. If it is true that institutional variety and 'mutual jealousy' were major causes of the 'European miracle' (Jones 1981), present trends towards uniformity within the European Union are in danger of dampening learning processes and social progress on our continent.

NOTES

1. Many other classical authors have noted the peculiar relationships between variety (political decentralization) and liberty in 'old Europe' from Greek antiquity until the advent of nationalism during the nineteenth century. A recurrent account sees Europe's geography as a primary condition that allowed only small and medium-sized jurisdictions to endure. Limited size coincided with limited government mainly because of the necessity to engage in interjurisdictional trade and market-friendly policies in order to attract fairs and merchants, but also artists and scholars who would find a variety of attractive neighbouring locations for employing their talents. Thus liberty may historically have been a by-product of competing variety which, in turn, was necessitated by geography. Roland Vaubel (see Chapter 2) in his survey of the history of thought on institutional competition, refers to Hume, Montesquieu, Kant, Smith, Gibbon, Tocqueville, Acton, to substantiate this claim. Amongst present-day scholars Jones (1981), North (1981), Berman (1983), Rosenberg and Birdzell (1986), Landes (1998), Volckart (2000) or Nemo (2005) point at very similar interrelations.

2. See, for example, Knudsen (1993) or Wohlgemuth (2005, pp. 31ff.) for a critique of the optimizing calculus of 'rational ignorance' based on marginal costs and benefits of an investment in new knowledge – the value of which can by its very nature not be known ex ante.

3. See also Lachmann (1956, pp. 21f.) on the role of changes in relative prices which assist individual learning about new circumstances: 'by observing price changes consumers learn which goods to substitute for which, and producers learn which line of production to abandon and which to turn to . . . We may regard the price system as a vast network of communication through which knowledge is at once transmitted from each market to the remotest corners in the economy.'

4. Hayek later made the even more drastic point that: 'if anyone really knew all about what economic theory calls the *data*, competition would indeed be a very wasteful method of securing adjustment to these data' (Hayek 1968/78, p. 179).

5. In other words, one does not have to use 'bifurcated man' assumptions that would imply that someone who enters the political field would display standards of behaviour that differ from those she uses in economic transactions (see Buchanan (1972) on the methodological inconsistency of using 'bifurcated man' assumptions).

6. See Boulding (1956), Vanberg and Buchanan (1989) or Wohlgemuth (2002) for a more thorough account of the methodological consequences of adding to preferences (goals, tastes: 'what one wants') theories and beliefs about the world and about how to achieve these goals ('what one believes').

7. See Vanberg (2006) for a systematic account of the concepts of common constitutional interests and 'citizen sovereignty'. See also Buchanan and Congleton (1998) and Berggren (1999) on the relationship between common constitutional interests and the formal principle of 'generality' or 'univerzalisability'.

8. The same is true for Kant's famous articles on perpetual peace. All, Kant observes, 'are prohibitive laws' requiring the abolishment of the stated abuses (Kant 1795/1991, p. 97).

9. In Wohlgemuth and Sideras (2004) we argue that the European Union offers both a prime example and a major refutation of an ideal of a competitive 'interstate federalism' based on univsersalizable rules of just (government) conduct, as was early envisaged by Hayek (1939/48). Already in the 1958 treaties creating the European Economic

Community, one finds the crucial universalizable rules governing the conduct of member state governments: the prohibition of barriers to trade between member states and the 'abolition of obstacles to freedom of movement for persons, services and capital'. Prohibitions also include member states' granting of privileges in the form of aids, subsidies, discriminatory taxation and regulation. In addition, private restraints to trade are 'prohibited as incompatible with the common market'. Hence, the freedom to act and to compete *within* the common market is protected by universalizable rules of just conduct against interference of national governments and of private actors. At the same time, individual member states, as long as their actions are not prohibited as incompatible with the common market, are free to develop institutional systems that reflect their own social and economic condition, cultural tradition and public opinion. This interjurisdictional competition can in fact provide, as Hayek (1939/48, p. 268) expected, a 'salutary check' on the states' interventionist endeavours while still allowing or even stimulating 'desirable experimentation'. On the other side, European integration also clearly contradicts Hayek's expectation that interstate federalism would discourage discriminatory regulation and purpose-oriented legislation. Discriminatory laws and policy prescriptions can be found right at the beginning of European integration (for example, the Common Agricultural Policy or European Coal and Steel Community). And they have grown ever since: demanding a 'high level of protection' in health, safety, environmental and consumer protection policies or the establishment of redistributive funds introduced by the Single European Act; ambitious industrial policy targets added by the Maastricht Treaty; or a verbose declaration of aims and purposes in the fields of 'social policy, education, vocational training and youth' added with the Amsterdam Treaty.

10. In fact, border-crossing transactions within the 'international private law society' (Sally 2000, p. 111) do rely quite comfortably on 'a web of private property rights and the enforcement of contracts according to private law *within a multitude of separate national jurisdictions*' (ibid.). International trade flourished well in the absence of unitary private law and of a central enforcer of international contracts. In addition to the choice of national formal private law and jurisdiction, informal, privately-established and enforced norms and conventions governing international transactions have for centuries spontaneously evolved and supported the extending order of global capitalism. Obviously, this unplanned evolution of an order of rules establishing 'stability of possession, of its transference by consent and of the performance of promises' (Hume 1739/1978, p. 126), originating in the mercantile community and spreading across borders of provinces and states by imitation rather than deliberate design is a major vindication of Hayek's trust in social self-organization.

11. See Wohlgemuth (2003) for more details.

12. See Hirschman (1970) for the classic treatment of 'exit' and 'voice' as responses of citizens to a decline in performance of suppliers on markets and in politics.

13. The realization of choice options by way of 'exit' is not necessary for institutional competition to trigger at least some learning effects. Comparative performance evaluation across jurisdictions can also help to inform and strengthen citizens' 'voice' and thus limit monitoring and agency problems of comparatively ill-informed voters. Such 'yardstick competition' can, even in the absence of realized 'exit', serve as a device to discipline rent-seeking politicians (Besley and Case 1995) and to promote policy innovation (Rincke 2005). However, yardstick competition and exit-based competition should not be regarded as alternatives, but rather as complements that mutually reinforce each others' thrust. The effectiveness of yardstick competition certainly also depends on the collective availability of exit-options and the individual decisions whether or not to use these exit-options is based on comparative performance evaluations of citizens who face clear incentives to invest in comparative institutional analysis according to their own individual 'yardsticks'.

14. To be sure, these comparative shortcomings are not 'policy failures', but mostly the necessary consequences of collective action in general and of democratic decision-making under the rule of law in particular. Equality before the law and quality of the law both demand that laws, regulations and political favours are not 'exchanged' in a

market-like fashion. Such activities as one usually welcomes on markets attain negative connotations (favouritism, bribery) on political 'markets'.

15. See below and Wohlgemuth (1995) for further details.
16. This argument is neglected by neoclassical models of both 'contestable markets' (for example, Baumol 1982) in industrial economics and 'efficient political markets' in the Chicago Public Choice literature (for example, Wittman 1995, p. 23). Both claim that 'potential competition' or the threat of entry can lead to results that are exactly equivalent to those to be expected under polypolistic competition – which is true (only) based on the models' assumptions which exclude learning processes by treating all knowledge about alternatives as given.
17. For models that show a 'race to the bottom' from the peaks of benevolent omniscient governments see, for example, Hans-Werner Sinn (2003) and the critique provided by Vaubel (Chapter 2). For a 'Leviathan'-assumption based argumentation, see, for example, Stefan Sinn (1992).
18. Such conditions seem to be particularly well developed in Switzerland, with low legal barriers to exit to neighbouring Cantons in a highly decentralised federal system, combined with a system of direct democracy on the Canton-level which creates a substantial potential for citizens' loyalty and responsibility (see Adamovich/Wohlgemuth 1999).
19. Solely in terms of variety, centralization and harmonization are even more damaging to political learning than isolationism since the latter does not by itself reduce variety and hence the potential of 'yardstick competition' based on empirical observations of comparative success or failure. In terms of liberty (our second major component of competition, see above) however, harmonization seems to be in most cases a less drastic infringement. It does not curtail the freedom to move and choose as such, it 'only' reduces the alternatives from which one can choose.

REFERENCES

Adamovich, Ivan Baron and Michael Wohlgemuth (1999), ' "Exit" und "voice" im Systemwettbewerb: Das Zusammenwirken von Föderalismus und direkter Demokratie in der Schweiz', in Manfred E. Streit and Michael Wohlgemuth (eds), *Systemwettbewerb als Herausforderung an Theorie und Politik*, Baden-Baden: Nomos, pp. 123–49.

Albert, Hans (1986), 'Freiheit und Ordnung. Zwei Abhandlungen zum Problem einer offenen Gesellschaft', Walter Eucken Institut (ed.), *Vorträge und Aufsätze*, 109, Tübingen: Mohr Siebeck.

Baumol, William J. (1982), 'Contestable Markets: An Uprising in the Theory of Industry Structure', *American Economic Review*, 72, 1–15.

Becker, Gary S. (1976), *The Economic Approach to Human Behavior*, Chicago: University of Chicago Press.

Berggren, Niclas (1999), 'A Preference-utilitarian Foundation for the Generality Principle', *Constitutional Political Economy*, 10(4), 339–53.

Berman, Harold J. (1983), *Law and Revolution: The Formation of the Western Legal Tradition*, Cambridge, MA: Harvard University Press.

Besley, Timothy and Anne Case (1995), 'Incumbent Behavior: Vote Seeking, Tax Setting, and Yardstick Competition', *American Economic Review*, 85, 25–45.

Blankart, Charles B. and Günter Knieps (1993), 'State and Standards', *Public Choice*, 77, 39–52.

Boulding, Kenneth E. (1956), *The Image. Knowledge in Life and Society*, Ann Arbor: University of Michigan Press.

Buchanan, James M. (1972), 'Toward Analysis of Closed Behavioral Systems', in James M. Buchanan and Robert D. Tollison (eds), *Theory of Public Choice*, Ann Arbor, University of Michigan Press, pp. 11–23.

Buchanan, James M. and Roger D. Congleton (1998), *Politics by Principle, not Interest. Toward Nondiscriminatory Democracy*, Cambridge: Cambridge University Press.

Farrell, Joseph and Garth Saloner (1985), 'Standardization, Compatibility, and Innovation', *Rand Journal of Economics*, 16, 70–83.

Hayek, Friedrich A. (1937/48), 'Economics and Knowledge', in *Individualism and Economic Order*, Chicago: University of Chicago Press, pp. 77–91.

Hayek, Friedrich A. (1939/48), 'The Economic Conditions of Interstate Federalism', in *Individualism and Economic Order*, Chicago: University of Chicago Press, pp. 255–72.

Hayek, Friedrich A. (1945/48), 'The Use of Knowledge in Society', in *Individualism and Economic Order*, Chicago: University of Chicago Press, pp. 33–58.

Hayek, Friedrich A. (1946/48), 'The Meaning of Competition', in *Individualism and Economic Order*, Chicago: University of Chicago Press, pp. 92–106.

Hayek, Friedrich A. (1966/67), 'The Principles of a Liberal Social Order', in *Studies in Philosophy, Politics and Economics*, London: Routledge, pp. 160–77.

Hayek, Friedrich A. (1968/78), 'Competition as a Discovery Procedure', in *New Studies in Philosophy, Politics, Economics and the History of Ideas*, London: Routledge, pp. 179–90.

Hayek, Friedrich A. (1976), *Law, Legislation and Liberty*, Vol. 2: The *Mirage of Social Justice*, Chicago and London: University of Chicago Press.

Hayek, Friedrich A. (1978), 'Liberalism', in *New Studies in Philosophy, Politics, Economics and the History of Ideas*, London: Routledge, pp. 119–51.

Hirschman, Albert O. (1970), *Exit, Voice and Loyalty*, Cambridge, MA: Harvard University Press.

Hume, David (1739/1978), *A Treatise on Human Nature*, Oxford: Oxford University Press.

Hume, David (1742), 'Of the Rise and Progress of the Arts and Sciences', reprinted in Eugene F. Miller (ed.) (1985), *David Hume: Essays, Moral, Political, and Literary*, Indianapolis: Liberty Fund, pp. 111–37.

Jones, Eric (1981), *The European Miracle*, Cambridge: Cambridge University Press.

Kant, Immanuel (1795), 'Perpetual Peace. A Philosophical Sketch', in Hans Reiss (ed.) (1991), *Kant. Political Writings*, 2nd edn, Cambridge: Cambridge University Press, pp. 93–130.

Knudsen, Christian (1993), 'Equilibrium, Perfect Rationality and the Problem of Self-reference in Economics', in Uskali Mäki, Bi Gustafson and Christian Knudsen (eds), *Rationality, Institutions and Economic Methodology*, London: Routledge, pp. 133–70.

Lachmann, Ludwig (1956), *Capital and its Structure*, London: G. Bell & Sons.

Landes, David S. (1998), *The Wealth and Poverty of Nations: Why Some are so Rich and Some so Poor*, New York: Norton.

Mukand, Sharun W. and Dani Rodrik (2005), 'In Search of the Holy Grail: Policy Convergence, Experimentation, and Economic Performance', *American Economic Review*, **95**(1), 374–83.

Nannestad, Peter and Martin Paldam (1994), 'The VP-function: A Survey of the Literature on Vote and Popularity Functions after 25 years', *Public Choice* 79, 213–45.

Nemo, Philippe (2005), *What is the West?*, Pittsburgh: Duquesne University Press.

North, Douglass C. (1981), *Structure and Change in Economic History*, New York: Norton.

North, Douglass C. (1990), *Institutions, Institutional Change and Economic Performance*, Cambridge: Cambridge University Press.

Rawls, John (1999), *The Law of Peoples*, Cambridge, MA: Harvard University Press.

Rincke, Johannes (2005), 'Yardstick Competition and Policy Innovation', Discussion Paper 05-11, Centre for European Economic Research, Mannheim.

Rodrik, Dani (1997), 'Has Globalization Gone Too Far?', Institute for International Economics, Washington, DC.

Rosenberg, Nathan and L.E. Birdzell (1986), *How the West Grew Rich*, New York: Basic Books.

Sally, Razeen (2000), 'Hayek and International Economic Order', *ORDO*, 51, 97–118.

Sinn, Hans-Werner (2003), *The New Systems Competition*, Oxford: Basil Blackwell.

Sinn, Stefan (1992), 'The Taming of Leviathan: Competition among Governments', *Constitutional Political Economy*, 3, 177–96.

Stigler, George J. (1961), 'The Economics of Information', *Journal of Political Economy*, 69, 213–25.

Stiglitz, Joseph E. (2000), 'The Contributions of the Economics of Information to Twentieth Century Economics', *Quarterly Journal of Economics*, 115(4), 1441–78.

Streit, Manfred E. and Gerhard Wegner (1992), 'Information, Transactions, and Catallaxy: Reflections on Some Key Concepts of Evolutionary Market Theory', in Ulrich Witt (ed.), *Explaining Process and Change – Approaches to Evolutionary Economics*, Ann Arbor: University of Michigan Press, pp. 125–49.

Tiebout, Charles M. (1956), 'A Pure Theory of Local Expenditures', *Journal of Political Economy*, 64, 416–24.

Vanberg, Viktor J. (1993), 'Constitutionally Constrained and Safeguarded Competition in Markets and Politics with Reference to a European Constitution', *Journal des Economistes et des Etudes Humaines*, 4, 3–27.

Vanberg, Viktor J. (2006), 'Democracy, Citizen Sovereignty and Constitutional Economics', Freiburg Discussion Papers on Constitutional Economics no. 06/2, Walter Eucken Institut, Freiburg.

Vanberg, Viktor J. and James M. Buchanan (1989), 'Interests and Theories in Constitutional Choice', *Journal of Theoretical Politics*, 1, 49–63.

Volckart, Oliver (2000), 'The Open Constitution and its Enemies: Competition, Rent Seeking and the Rise of the Modern State', *Journal of Economic Behaviour and Organization*, 42, 1–17.

Wittman, Donald A. (1995), *The Myth of Democratic Failure. Why Political Institutions are Efficient*, Chicago: University of Chicago Press.

Wohlgemuth, Michael (1995), 'Institutional Competition. Notes on an Unfinished Agenda', *Journal des Economistes et des Etudes Humaines*, 6(2/3), 277–99.

Wohlgemuth, Michael (2002), 'Democracy and Opinion Falsification: Towards a New Austrian Political Economy', *Constitutional Political Economy*, 13, 223–46.

Wohlgemuth, Michael (2003), 'Democracy as an Evolutionary Method', in Pavel Pelikan and Gerhard Wegner (eds), *The Evolutionary Analysis of Economic Policy*, Cheltenham, UK and Northampton, MA, USA: Edward Elgar, pp. 96–127.

Wohlgemuth, Michael (2005), 'Schumpeterian Political Economy and Downsian Public Choice: Alternative Economic Theories of Democracy', in Alain Marciano and Jean-Michel Josselin (eds), *Law and the State. A Political Economy Approach*, Cheltenham, UK and Northampton, MA, USA: Edward Elgar, pp. 21–57.
Wohlgemuth, Michael and Jörn Sideras (2004), 'Globalisability of Universalisability? How to Apply the Generality Principle and Constitutionalism Internationally', Freiburg Discussion Papers on Constitutional Economics no. 04/7, Walter Eucken Institut, Freiburg.

4. Institutional competition: international environment, levels and consequences

Peter Bernholz

4.1 INTRODUCTION

Institutional competition between nations, but also within nations, especially in federalized states, has received growing attention in academic debate in recent years. This development has probably been mainly caused by the observation of a growing mobility of capital but also of a growing mobility of labour, related to the opening of borders after the downfall of the communist bloc and the so-called globalization originating from the spreading of the 'capitalist system' to ever greater areas of the globe. The deepening of the European Economic Community to the European Union, the inclusion of many new members and the demand for stronger decentralization in several countries may also have contributed to this phenomenon.

The scientific interest in institutional competition is well founded, for many of the inherent relationships and their consequences are still not well understood. First, institutional competition is a part of systems competition and interrelated with, but different from, other kinds of competition, such as military and foreign policy or market competition. Moreover, institutional competition exists on different levels, for instance on the international, the state or cantonal and the community levels. And its consequences may be quite different depending on which competencies are executed at which level. Moreover, even if the consequences were fully understood, the normative question would arise of how best to assign such competencies to the different levels to reach certain aims. And finally, even after answering this question, there would still remain the problem of how to implement the preferred assignment given the status quo and the forces working within the political system.

Below we will first discuss the different kinds of competition contained under the heading of systems competition, and the relationship of institutional and other kinds of competition. Next we will turn to the meaning and consequences of international institutional competition between nations. After that the assignment of parts of the competencies to different levels of government and the consequences thereof have to be discussed. This is partly a normative exercise, and has, therefore to be complemented by a discussion of the political forces at work and the possible consequences of their interplay. The chapter ends with some concluding comments.

It should be obvious that with the present state of research it is impossible to answer all the questions that will be raised. Instead we will try to give a general categorization of the problems involved and sketch some preliminary results.

4.2 KINDS OF SYSTEMS COMPETITION AND INTERRELATIONSHIPS BETWEEN THEM

Different Kinds of Systems Competition

The discussion concerning systems competition has enjoyed increasing popularity ever since the path-breaking works by Baechler (1975), North (1981), Jones (1981), Hall (1985) and Rosenberg and Birdzell (1986). Two conferences took place on the subject in Jena in 1996 (Bernholz et al. 1998) and in Heidelberg in 2002 (Bernholz and Vaubel 2004), in which an analysis was made of many historical periods of Western and non-Western societies, characterized by competition between many or few states. The association of German-speaking economists, the Verein für Socialpolitik, selected institutional competition as the main subject for its annual meeting in Magdeburg in 2001. However, in studying the subject, it has often been forgotten that many different kinds of competition are covered by the concept of 'systems competition' and that basic ideas concerning it can be found in the writings of Kant (1784/1959), Gibbon (1787) and Max Weber (1923). Kant for instance explains:

> Now the States are already in the present day involved in such close relations with each other that none of them can pause or slacken in its internal civilisation without losing power and influence in relation to the rest . . . *Civil liberty cannot now be easily assailed without inflicting such damage as will be felt in all trades and industries, and especially in commerce; and this would entail a diminution of the powers of the State in external relations. . . And thus it is that,* notwithstanding the intrusion of many a delusion and caprice, *the spirit of enlightenment gradually arises as a great good* which the human race must derive even *from the selfish purposes of aggrandisement on the part of its rulers,* if they understand what is for their own advantage. (1784/1959, p. 31)

And Max Weber points out that:

> The competitive struggle (among the European nation states) created the largest opportunities for modern western capitalism. *The separate states had to compete for mobile capital, which dictated to them the conditions under which it would assist them to power*. (Weber 1923, p. 249)

Even in these early extracts both authors refer to different kinds of competition. Kant mentions the importance of freedom for the development of trade and commerce and thus finally for the power of states in international relations. Max Weber by contrast stresses the competition of states for capital as a means to increase their power. But both recognize that there exists a relationship between foreign policy competition and institutional competition.

Given these early interpretations it seems advisable first to present a schedule defining the different kinds of competition and then to analyse some of their interrelationships (Box 4.1). Mostly, if we speak about competition, we understand by this the competition of firms in markets, in advertising and marketing, undercutting of prices, the supply of better goods and generally by product and process innovation. We have also to include in this *market competition*, the competition by consumers for goods and the competition of firms and workers in labour markets.

BOX 4.1   DIFFERENT KINDS OF SYSTEMS COMPETITION

1   Competition among business firms and consumers in markets
(Market competition)
1.1   Price competition
1.2   Marketing competition
1.3   Quality competition
1.4   Competition by imitators
1.5   Competition by product and process innovation
1.6   Private institutional competition.
2   Competition between interest groups to influence political decisions
Part of Political competition and market structure (like cartelization)
Rent-seeking

---

3   Political competition of parties or oligarchs
Military officers, wealthy citizens, bureaucracy for government power (Political competition)
Short time horizon

4   Competition between rulers or states

4.1   Military and foreign policy competition
Arms races, wars, influence by diplomacy through threats, aid, promises or formation of alliances (Systems competition)
Long time horizon

4.2   Competition by providing favourable institutional frameworks
For example, of the legal system (safe property rights, reliable and enforceable contract law), of taxes, regulations, educational system and monetary stability. (Institutional competition)
Intermediate time horizon

5   Ideological competition

However, since market competition takes place within an institutional and legal framework, our attention is at once drawn to a quite different kind of competition. As soon as a number of more or less independent political units with a certain domain of action are present, they can change institutions, including the legal framework, and thus enter into *institutional competition*. In this respect it seems to be important whether only governmental agencies or subsets of private society as well are allowed to develop institutional innovations.

When considering the political units themselves we observe that within them another kind of competition takes place. This is a competition for the power to take binding decisions and thus to participate in designing and changing institutions. In democracies the competition between parties, bureaucracies and interest groups as well as elections and referenda are part of this process. In autocracies other groups, such as the armed forces, the bureaucracies and certain oligarchs are fighting for power. We may call this kind of competition *domestic political competition*.

The *military and foreign policy competition* between rulers or nations to expand their power, their territory or their influence or to just defend themselves constitutes a further kind of competition. Finally, we have to mention the *competition between ideas and ideologies*, including those of religions.

The different kinds of competition are also differentiated by the level at which they take place. Military and foreign policy competition takes place between nations, apart from civil wars, guerrilla warfare and terrorist activities. Ideological competition tries to win the minds of people and is therefore not limited to geographical units. The participants in market competition, namely firms, groups of people and individuals can live anywhere on the globe if not hampered by institutional limitations. Domestic political competition occurs between political parties, interest groups and voters and can take place on the national but also at the state and communal level. Finally, institutional competition occurs between nations, but also between states and cantons and the communities within them. There may even occur institutional competition between firms, individuals, universities and so on, if the institutional framework set up by the states so allows. To mention only a few examples: neither museums, nor paper money, nor the banking system, the stock exchange nor the joint stock company were invented and introduced by a government bureaucracy. Bureaucracies are, indeed, not very innovative, apart from inventing ever new regulations and taxes.

Reasons for the Evolution and Retention of Institutional Competition

In analysing the relationships between different kinds of systems competition we are mainly interested in the question of why institutional competition favouring free societies with efficient and innovative market economies should arise and be maintained. In this context, the first question to be answered is that of under what conditions such societies could come into existence. Why should the ruling elite in an autocracy agree to strong and secure property rights, to minimal state intervention, to a limitation of taxes, and thus a limitation of its own powers to command and to withdraw goods at their own discretion? It seems that the New Economic Historians and others have tried with a certain success to answer these questions (North and Thomas 1973; Baechler 1975; North 1981; Jones 1981; for comparative historical analyses see also Bernholz et al. 1998 and Bernholz and Vaubel 2004). They have stressed that European disunity has been our good luck. Feudalism, with its many power centres, developed during the Middle Ages and a split opened up between religious and temporal powers. Strong rivalries arose between the many rulers to extend and preserve their powers through foreign policy and military endeavours. This forced them to consider the well-being and loyalty of their subjects and to become concerned with economic development in order to secure a greater tax base and thus to finance stronger armies. However, economic development in turn depended on establishing adequate property rights, a reliable legal system, free markets and limited taxes. As a consequence, those states who were successful in this fierce foreign policy and military competition in the long run were those who, by chance or by design, had made the greatest progress in introducing such institutions. Thus competition between states forced on unwilling rulers a limitation of domestic powers. Institutional competition was the consequence of military and foreign policy competition. The development of competing legal systems, of the rule of law and of property rights was helped not only by interstate competition but also by the increasing separation of church and state, the forestalling of a theocracy (Berman 1984). Because of these developments, limited government and a pluralistic society arose in Europe as a pre-democratic achievement. First capitalism and later democracy were their progeny.

I have argued elsewhere (Bernholz 1995) that international competition between states remains a driving force today, motivating rulers such as those of Japan in the Meiji Era, or Gorbachev and Deng, to limit their domestic powers and to initiate institutional reforms with the purpose of strengthening their economies as a base of international power. Whether the resulting reforms were adequate and thus successful is, of course, another question.

Institutional competition between nations is not – and has not – only been caused by military and foreign policy competition. It is also furthered – especially in an age of mass media and tourism – by the fact that populations in less-developed countries can become aware of the much better living conditions in nations enjoying more favourable institutional frameworks. This leads to dissatisfaction and in relatively open societies to an emigration of the most enterprising individuals and of capital. As a result the pressures on governments grow to initiate reforms of the institutional framework, to remove inadequate regulations and unproductive subsidies, and to lower the tax burden.

But these factors favouring institutional competition are not sufficient to initiate economic development. Ideologies whose creeds supposedly forbid the introduction of some or even many important institutional reforms may be so strong that even the pressure stemming from military and foreign policy competition cannot overcome the obstacles set by such beliefs. One example would be the interpretation of Islam which prevents the adequate education of women and their participation in the workforce and the taking of interest, which was also characteristic of medieval Christianity. It also seems possible that the caste system implied by the Hindu religion prevented that military and foreign policy competition among many states led, in India, to an economic development comparable to the West before the coming of the Muslim conquerors.

The Consequences of Domestic Political Competition in Democracies

In democracies in which the domain of legislators is not strictly limited by constitutional or other institutional safeguards, shifting majorities in

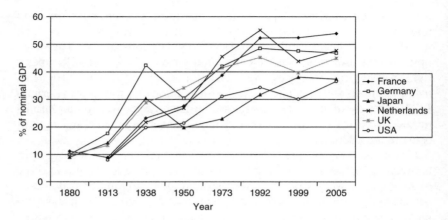

*Figure 4.1   Development of total government as a share of nominal GDP,
              six developed countries*

parliament – that is, small minorities of the population only inadequately
controlled by rationally uninformed voters – can impose their aims on the
rest of the population. Since several parties compete for votes and need
financial support, mainly from interest groups, to cover the expenses for
their organizations and for election campaigns, one has to expect, over
time, an ever-increasing sphere of government activities. Thus we would
expect to see growing public expenditures (Figure 4.1), more and more regulation by government, and the introduction of tax loopholes and subsidies favouring special minority interest and pressure groups to flow from
the incessant activity of legislative bodies. This can happen because the
majority of voters are rationally uninformed about issues. This is true for
issues in which decisions impinge only marginally on the situation of consumers or taxpayers, since they then have little reason to incur the costs of
informing themselves, given the negligible effect of individual votes on election outcomes. Also, whereas the benefits may be concentrated on a limited
number of people – who will be aware of them – the costs are spread over
the majority of voters and taxpayers who may not realize what they are
paying for, especially in a country with growing GDP per capita. Thus the
protection of certain industries against foreign competition, the fixing of
agricultural prices above market clearing levels, subsidies to coal or steel
industries and the toleration or even promotion of cartels can be observed,
even though a majority of voters are affected by higher taxes and/or prices.
On the other hand, whenever changes such as rent increases are perceived
by a majority of voters – since expenditures for rents amount to a substantial part of their budgets – the government will take action in favour of the

majority, for example by introducing rent controls (Downs 1957; Bernholz 1966).

If these arguments are correct, why is it that government activities are not increased at once under the pressure of political competition to a Nash equilibrium level in which each party maximizes votes, if such an equilibrium exists? Why does government activity rise to ever higher levels over decades? Several reasons have been given to explain this empirical fact. Olson (1965, 1982) points out that since it is difficult to form interest groups because they provide public goods to their members, it takes time to organize them (see also Bernholz 1969). The more diverse the interests and the greater the number of potential members, the more difficult the task and the longer the time needed to organize an interest group. As a consequence, cartels can only be formed and influence be exerted on the political system by potential interest groups after they have found enough time to be organized.

Bernholz (1966) has pointed out a second reason for the gradual extension of government, namely continual changes of the industrial structure brought about by economic development. These changes threaten old industries, their capital owners and managers as well as the jobs and the wage levels of the people employed in them. This leads to voter dissatisfaction and thus, under the pressure of political competition, to government intervention to maintain or to win the support of those voters and of their families who suffer from the changes in the industrial structure. A third reason sometimes mentioned in the literature is fairly closely related to the second:

> The need to keep in check the forces which might produce unemployment is not the only root of the expansion of government control over industry and trade, because the sheer growth of complexity of economic structures requires more co-ordination, and the number of tasks which cannot be left to private initiative – such as prevention of soil erosion, traffic control, smoke abatement and so on – grows incessantly. (Andreski 1965, p. 355)

Finally, time is obviously needed to devise new governmental measures, to introduce and to pass new legislation, taxes and subsidies.

If our analysis is correct, state activity will grow over time in democracies. A democratic system with competing parties reacts to the demands of different minorities and majorities of voters and of special interest groups which arise over time. As a consequence, the older and the less disturbed a democracy by wars, revolutions and other crises enforcing a restructuring of the political economic system, the higher the level of regulations, of subsidies, transfers and taxes one would expect at comparable levels of per capita incomes (Olson 1982, 1983). But since excessive state activity also makes for less efficiency, less savings and less innovation one would also expect negative

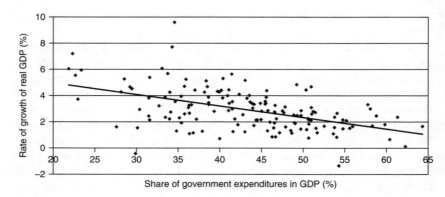

Figure 4.2   Growth of real GDP depending on share of public expenditures in GDP, OECD democracies, 1964–2004 (five-year averages)

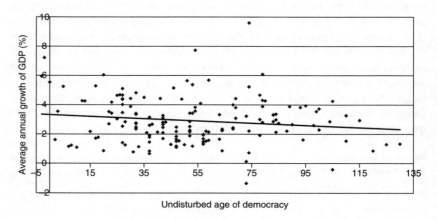

Figure 4.3   Growth of GDP depending on undisturbed age of democracy, OECD countries, 1964–2004 (five-year averages)

consequences for real economic growth, as measured for instance by the real growth rate of GDP per capita. This expectation seems to be supported by empirical evidence (figures 4.2 and 4.3) (Bernholz 1986, 1990; Marlow 1986; Peden and Bradley 1989; Weede 1984, 1990; Tanzi/Schuknecht 1997).

Competitive Forces Counteracting the Growth of Government

Next, it has to be asked, whether there exist forces able to halt or to reverse the consequences of domestic political competition. Let us first mention that there are some institutions, such as referenda and popular initiatives or the influence of public-minded advisers, which can retard the inexorable growth of government expenditures (as a percentage of GDP) and interventions (Frey and Kirchgässner 1994). But apart from perceived crises (see below) they seem unable to stop the growth of government and the erosion of individual rights, as evidenced by empirical developments during the last decades.

Second, if more and more government interventions favouring segments of the population or interest groups occur, the burdens for ordinary voters increase and will finally be perceived by them. In such a situation each voter may benefit from one or more government interventions, but the total burden of all interventions together outweighs the benefits. Such a situation may be perceived as a crisis. But if this is the case it becomes profitable for politicians (especially of the opposition) to propose an election programme which contains an implicit logrolling agreement: namely, each participating group is prepared to forgo its special benefits, if enough other groups are prepared to do the same, so that they together add up to a majority of voters. Indeed, a formal model addressing such relationships has been presented by Dur and Swank (1997). In such a situation public-minded statesmen or advisers may have great influence, if their ideas succeed against competing simplifying ideologies. Examples are the success of the West German (ordo-)liberals after the catastrophe of the Second World War; the reforms by Mrs Thatcher in Britain after it had lagged more and more economically compared to other European countries and even been overtaken by Italy; or the drastic reforms first taken by the labour government in New Zealand after the extended welfare state based on a mainly agricultural economy had led the country into a deep unemployment, budget deficit and foreign exchange crisis.

Third, as has been shown above, a weakening of the relative foreign policy and military position of Great Powers caused by a relatively bad economic performance as a consequence of increasing government activity may be perceived as a crisis and lead to reforms in the direction of re-establishing limited government. Here military and foreign policy competition implies a correction of the results of domestic political competition by furthering institutional reforms.

It is obvious that these relationships have yet to be studied much more carefully and that there are still many gaps in our knowledge. How do we, for example, define a crisis? How deep has it to be? Under what conditions have fundamentalist ideologies a better chance of succeeding in a crisis than sound economic advice?

4.3   LEVELS AND CONSEQUENCES OF INSTITUTIONAL COMPETITION

Institutional Competition between Nations

It has already been mentioned that institutional competition takes place or can take place at different levels: the level of competing nation-states, the level of states, cantons and provinces and the level of communities or their agglomerations. Even private organizations and firms can be involved in institutional competition if the government allows them a free domain for institutional innovation in the form of creating new organizations and private law.

Let us first consider the institutional competition between nations. We have already seen that military and foreign policy competition have caused states to enter into institutional competition. Other factors are international comparisons made by citizens concerning their relative economic affluence or misery, if they can get enough information about the performance of other countries. Third, as we have seen, Max Weber pointed to the growing importance of the free movement of (financial) capital for the rise of institutional competition. Finally, with falling transportation costs the increasing mobility of labour, especially of qualified labour (the so-called brain-drain) has been an important factor in intensifying institutional competition. But these latter causes of institutional competition are not guaranteed by nature. Governments can turn to protectionism and to measures preventing the free flow of capital, labour and even of information. The Soviet Union, China and other communist states did so for decades. But such isolating measures come at a high price: economic efficiency and the rate of innovation (Kornai 1971, pp. 271–9) are miserably low relative to open societies, and this implies for Great Powers the slow erosion of their position in the international system, not to speak of the relatively poor position of their subjects, which is bound to reduce their motivation to work. This means, of course, that in a sense, whatever the government does, it cannot escape the consequences for military and foreign policy competition if it tries to prevent institutional reforms. In this sense it can be asserted that institutional competition between nations is nearly inescapable, barring the creation of a world state.

One might think that institutional competition between nations can proceed without any rules. But this is not necessarily the case. First, it is in the interest of participants in market competition that certain rules are followed. In this way international merchant law and in time some other rudiments of international law have developed (Berman 1983; Bull 1977). Second, politicians may learn that the inherent tendency of domestic political competition towards protectionism hurts their own interests in the long run because of the poorer economic performance experienced by the population. Corresponding experiences with restrictions on the free movement of goods and capital, exchange controls and bilateralism in the wake of the Great Depression have therefore led countries to agree to certain rules allowing relatively free trade, embodied first in the GATT and then in the WTO. Similarly, the Bretton Woods institutions, the IMF and the World Bank, were designed to remove restrictions in the monetary field and led in time (although this was not the original intention) to the widespread liberalization of capital movements.

We have seen that military and foreign policy competition have been and are a decisive cause for the development of institutional competition between nations. War is the dark side of this process. Civil wars within nations are less numerous than wars between nations (Richardson 1960). This means that while empires tended to stagnate they also secured a more peaceful life for their citizens than might have been the case had they been divided into a number of countries. This was one of the reasons for creating the federal system of the USA: 'A man must be far gone in Utopian speculations who can seriously doubt, that if these states should be either be wholly disunited, or only united in partial confederacies, the subdivisions into which they might be thrown would have frequent and violent contests with each other' (Federalist Papers, no. 6 by Hamilton, p. 27). Similarly, the main reason motivating the founding fathers of the European Union was the prevention of further intra-European wars. This has been achieved, though the EU has neither evolved into a federal state nor into a confederation, but is characterized by an innovative institutional structure.

From the perspective of systems competition, federal states, as well as the EU, have been efforts to abolish military competition but to preserve at the same time institutional competition with open borders. In this way they have been an important innovation. But it is also true that all federations until now have shown a distinct tendency towards centralization at the national level in the long run, that is toward a weakening of intra-national institutional competition. This has been true for federal countries like Germany, the USA and even for Switzerland.

The Assignment of Competencies to Different Levels of Government

In a federal or confederate system rules have to be set concerning the assignment of competencies to different levels of government. A first question which arises because of this is who has the right to assign and to reassign such competencies. The federal centre of the system or its members (the states, provinces, *Länder* or cantons)? If we assume, as seems to be warranted by experience, that politicians and bureaucrats aim at increasing their influence, then a location of this right at the centre would imply a strong tendency to reassign ever more competencies to the centre. The opposite might be expected if the right rested with the members of the system, except for tasks which were deemed by politicians to be 'dirty' in the sense that they would cost them (in democracies) votes at the next election or referendum. A way out of this dilemma has been to fix the assignment of rights in a constitution, and to entrust the interpretation of it to independent courts. Though this has worked for some time, historical observation shows that such courts, like the US Supreme Court or the German Verfassungsgericht (the Constitutional Court) have also towards centralization in the long run. By contrast, in the case of Switzerland, where the Bundesgericht (the Supreme Federal Court) does not have the right to interpret the constitution, the Federal Government has violated constitutional rules several times. And popular sovereignty, with the right to change the constitution by simple majorities of the population and of the cantons, has not been able to prevent centralization either. It follows that quite apart from the results of an analysis searching for an optimal assignment of competencies to the different levels of government, there arises the task of designing institutions capable of preventing or at least severely restricting the tendencies towards centralization.

Let us now turn to the question of which competencies should be assigned to which level of government. This is a normative question since it implies value judgements not only about the aims of governments on different levels, but also about the limitation of their domain relative to the private sphere of citizens and their organizations. But before such a normative discussion can be usefully begun, it must first be considered what the economic consequences of different assignments could be. And this is the main task of a scientific exploration, though science can also help in clarifying whether proposed aims are realistic in the sense of actually being attainable or whether they are possibly contradictory.

In discussing the consequences of the assignment of which tasks to which level of government two approaches have been used, the static and the dynamic. The static analysis looks at which tasks are best assigned to which level, given certain characteristics of the political process and taking into account possible externalities, characteristics of public goods and the problems of redistributing income. In doing so, apart from the redistribution problem, it mainly looks to efficiency gains or losses which might be related to different assignments. By contrast, the dynamic approach studies consequences which the assignment of competencies might have for institutional and market innovations and thus for growth, usually measured by that of GDP per capita.

The static approach has been intensively applied by economists and political scientists and it is not the task of the present chapter to pursue it any further. Let us just mention a few points. The better information of citizens about issues, their greater influence because of smaller numbers and the better knowledge of politicians and bureaucrats concerning their problems all speak in favour of as much decentralization as possible. On the other hand, local cartels of interests can be more easily formed and only less specialized expertise may be available at the local or provincial level. Looking at externalities and the provision of public goods it has been agreed that widespread pollution problems, such as general air pollution, or the design of national or even continental road or railway networks should be best assigned to the national level, or even to a higher level like the EU. The same is true for the creation and monitoring of rules securing the free movement of people, goods, services, capital and information. By contrast, zoning rules, the creation of parks or greenbelts or the regulation of local or regional pollution problems should best be left to the community or state level. Finally, many authors argue that redistribution should be located at the centre because otherwise rich people would move to the political units with the lowest degree of redistribution, whereas poor people would emigrate to those which offered them the highest level of support. And it is asserted that this would inevitably lead to a breakdown of the system in the long run. We will return to this question when we discuss the dynamic aspects of the assignment problem.

Before doing so, however, another aspect has to be mentioned. According to the Coase Theorem (for a recent discussion see Mueller 2003, pp. 27–40) all externality problems could be solved if no transaction costs were present. Now it is obvious that the latter condition is not fulfilled. But as Anderson (2004) has argued convincingly and illustrated with several empirical examples, governments today are responsible for a substantial part of such transactions costs. Moreover, because of technological and other developments transaction costs have been and will be further reduced. As a consequence, many problems caused by negative externalities could be solved by private agreements, if only the obstacles created by governments were removed.

Dynamic Aspects of Domestic Institutional Competition

It has already been pointed out that private competition has historically been most successful in innovating new institutions, including law and organizations. However, any such innovation is dependent on an adequate institutional framework. Free markets and safe property rights should be

offered the widest possible scope. A sufficient domain for the free development of institutional innovations in the private sector is of paramount
importance. This implies that as much of the law as possible should be disposable and subsidiary instead of compulsory, and that corporate law
should offer sufficient leeway for new private developments.

A particular aspect of granting a generous domain for legal experimentation to private organizations and firms consists in the possibility of a
gradual development of common business practices, and of private and
possibly international courts of arbitration, as has already been observed
in the past. This unification of law through private action should be
viewed as a fruitful experimental innovation, so long as the aim of the
private parties neither discriminates against the weak nor decisively hinders
competition.

Proceeding from the need to search for better institutions, we have
further to ask, whether and how it is possible to bestow an ability to innovate on government agencies and political decision-makers concerning
governmental organizations, services and the legal framework. The
answer seems to be to introduce as much federalism, in the sense of decentralization, as possible. The competition between different political units
allows the relatively easy introduction of new legal approaches, the organization of government agencies, tax systems, and ways of providing public
goods and coping with externalities. This means that the results of such
innovations can conveniently be compared by the citizens of neighbouring states (cantons, *Länder*) or communities. On the other hand, beneficial
innovations in centralized nation-states are much more difficult to devise
and to introduce, especially since the pressure to reform is solely exerted
by the institutional competition of other countries, which necessarily
works much more slowly. It is interesting in this respect that smaller centralized nations suffer less from the absence of internal institutional competition because they feel the pressure of international competition more
strongly.

Federalism on a regional basis thus prohibits in many ways the
unification of law, either through regulations by the central government
or through cooperation (cartelization) by the member states and
communities of the federation. This enables a certain competition to arise
between the communities or member states, not only over the efficiency of
public output and the size of the fiscal burden but also over appropriate
organizations and legal institutions. Given the right to emigrate, this
competition is sharpened by individuals 'voting with their feet, and, along
with private organizations and firms, choosing the location most
favourable for them.

4.4 HOW FAR SHOULD THE CORRECTION OF THE FORCES OF DOMESTIC POLITICAL COMPETITION BY INSTITUTIONAL COMPETITION GO?

It has been shown that public choice theory predicts an ever increasing activity of the state because of the processes of domestic political competition, and that this corresponds to empirical developments (Figure 4.1). Such a development, however, entails a weakening of efficiency and innovative activities which in time leads to a crisis, especially of the welfare state, which can no longer be financed. On the other hand, it has been stressed that institutional competition constitutes a strong counteracting force to these developments, at least in the long run. And though it is possible to stifle internal institutional competition by growing centralization, this is not true for such competition among nations, at least if borders are relatively open. And as stated above, military and foreign policy competition are working in that direction.

It follows that domestic political competition and institutional competition will enter into conflict as soon as the growth of government has led to a sufficient weakening of one country in comparison to others. Thus, the question arises, how far will the reduction of government activity because of institutional competition go? Will this competition be strong enough finally to erode the desired extent of the welfare state with its 'insurance' by redistribution against the undeserved problems of unemployment, poor health and old age? Or will it undermine government functions in offering an adequate supply of public goods and preventing negative externalities?

The answers given to these questions by scholars are still strongly divergent. Sinn (1999) believes that the 'new' institutional competition, that is one with wide open borders for the movement of products, services, capital and people, will lead to a 'race to the bottom'; this in contrast to the 'old' institutional competition with mainly closed borders. As Sinn sees it, this is especially the case for the old members of the EU, such as Germany, after the breakdown of the communist regimes and the opening of borders of Eastern European countries and of large emerging countries such as China and India with their low wage and tax levels. Even if no free movement of people were still permitted, the free movement of goods, capital and business firms would be sufficient to engender this race to the bottom. Other economists, such as Blankart (1999, 2000), Siebert (1998), Vanberg and Kerber (1994), Berthold and Naumann (2001) and Fehn (2001) come to opposite conclusions. Schaltegger and R.L. Frey (2003) take an intermediate position.

Though it is true that a vast majority of economists insist that the government, even that of the centralized state, has to a certain degree to fulfil the functions mentioned, it is not clear to what degree the centralized state has to play the most important role. For instance, B.S. Frey (2002) points out that citizens are prepared to pay voluntarily a certain amount of taxes, so that essential government tasks can be delivered at a decentralized level. And the empirical studies by Ostrom (1990) have demonstrated that the problem of negative externalities can be solved by private organizations and cooperatives if certain conditions are fulfilled. Also, the tendency of increasing state activity with its negative consequences cannot be denied. It follows that only empirical studies can decide whether institutional competition with open borders leads to an abolishment of essential functions of the government or whether it only limits an excessive extension of the state to tolerable dimensions. Meanwhile quite a number of relevant empirical studies have been undertaken, of which Oates (2002) has written a review. Additionally the papers by Kirchgaessner and Pommerehne (1996) and by Buettner (2001) should be mentioned.

Below I will present some limited empirical evidence, mainly for Switzerland and the USA, since these countries enjoy the most pronounced domestic institutional competition on lower levels of government. Before doing so, however, it is important to point out that the percentage of government expenditures in GDP has massively increased in all OECD countries with the exception of Ireland since 1950 (see also Figure 4.1). Given this evidence it seems unlikely that a race to the bottom will take place, though it will doubtless be argued that this race only began around 1990 with the opening up of the formerly communist Eastern European countries and the reforms taken in China and later India in the direction of free market economies.

To discuss this counter-argument it is helpful to look at the experience of Switzerland and the USA which have known intense institutional competition concerning tax rates, not only at the cantonal or state level but also at the community level for decades. For Switzerland it can at once be seen that a pronounced difference between cantonal and community income and wealth taxes can still be observed (in 1999) after decades of competition (Table 4.1). For instance, inhabitants of Onex in the canton of Geneva with an income of 80 000 Swiss francs had to pay 2.7 times as much in income taxes as the inhabitants of Freienbach in the canton of Schwyz. And for people with an income of 150 000 Swiss francs, those in Onex paid taxes that were twice as high as those in Zug, the capital of the canton of Zug. Even the differences between communities in the same canton are substantial. Again, with a taxable income of 80 000 Swiss francs the taxes in Lauerz are 1.7 times as high as those in Freienbach, both situated in the canton of Schwyz. However, Freienbach increased its communal income taxes by 20 per cent in 2003 in order to maintain services after exhausting its reserves.

Table 4.1   Tax burdens in some municipalities in different Swiss cantons (1998 figures)

Income (Sfr)	Zug		Schwyz		Zürich		St Gallen	
	Zug	Unterägeri	Freienbach	Lauerz	Neerach	Dägerlen	Jona	Degersheim
Cantonal, municipal and church income taxes								
80 000	9500	10 400	8400	14 400	9000	11 100	13 300	15 800
150 000	26 600	28 500	32 600	36 600	28 200	33 600	36 300	42 300
Wealth tax								
Wealth (Sfr)								
300 000	700	1000	900	1600	200	200	1400	1700
1 000 000	3700	4100	2900	5400	1800	2300	5100	6200

Income (Sfr)	Baselland		Basel-Stadt		Wallis		Genf	
	Bielbenken	Duggingen	Bettingen	Basel	Finhaut	Martisberg	Cologny	Onex
Cantonal, municipal and church income taxes								
80 000	12 500	14 100	13 200	16 500	11 200	14 000	20 600	22 700
150 000	35 900	40 000	37 300	43 400	36 400	42 400	48 900	54 400
Wealth tax								
Wealth (Sfr)								
300 000	1300	1500	1500	1500	1200	1500	1300	1500
1 000 000	7300	8400	6500	6500	5000	6300	6300	7000

Note: The municipalities with the highest and the lowest taxes in each canton were selected.

The differences in the wealth tax are even more pronounced. In Switzerland the wealth tax is a prerogative of cantons and communities, not of the federation. Taxes on a taxable wealth of 300 000 Swiss francs are 7.5 times higher in some communities than in others. And for a taxable wealth of 1 million they are higher by a factor of four.

Since these differences have existed for a long time, it seems that institutional competition has not been strong enough to enforce a downward equalization. This is probably related to the different level of services offered and to transaction costs. People may prefer to live in Geneva or Zürich instead of Zug or Schwyz since much more is available there culturally. Moreover, moving also means leaving friends, children's schools and the customary environment. Additionally there are the usual costs of moving. Finally the prices of housing increase if many people move to the places with low taxes, However, the smaller differences in the tax burdens for higher incomes may mean that the relative costs of mobility become smaller with higher incomes and wealth. A development in recent years may point into the same direction. The population in Obwalden decided in a referendum in 2005 to decrease income and wealth taxes especially for the very rich. For very high incomes the tax rates were set even lower than for somewhat smaller incomes (so-called degressive taxes). The canton expected to attract more wealthy people to more than compensate for the lower revenue. Until then the loss of tax revenue will be financed by the share of the canton in the 21 billion gain earned from selling the 'superfluous' part of the gold holdings of the Swiss National Bank. Other cantons, such as Appenzell-Ausserrhoden, followed. It remains to be seen whether this development will in fact lead to a strong general lowering of cantonal taxes because of tax competition. Meanwhile the Bundesgericht (the highest court) has been asked to declare the degressive taxes to be unconstitutional.

Another area in which tax competition has been working during the last years is that of inheritance tax, which is also a prerogative of cantons and their communes. One canton after another has abolished these taxes for direct descendants. The issue was mostly decided by referenda with sizeable majorities of those voting, in favour of the reduction, to the chagrin of left-wing parties.

If we turn to state income and state sales taxes in the USA, a similar picture emerges (Table 4.2). Whereas seven states, including Florida and Texas, have no income taxes, other have income tax rates ranging from 3 per cent for low to 11 per cent for high incomes. Rates for high incomes amount, for instance, in California to 9.3 per cent and in Montana to 11 per cent. The differences in sales taxes are also substantial. They range from zero in five states to 7.25 per cent in California. Moreover, those states with no income

Table 4.2 Income and sales taxes in some states of the USA (%)

	Alabama	California	Illinois	Iowa	Montana	Florida	Pennsylvania	Texas	Rhode Island
Income tax	2–5	1–9.3	3	0.36–8.98	2–11	0	2.80	0	25 of federal tax
Sales tax	4	7.25	6	5	0	6	6	6	7

Notes:
1. New Hampshire and Tennessee have only an income tax on interest and dividend income. Seven states do not have an income tax.
2. The percentage of turnover taken by sales taxes varies. Five states do not charge any sales taxes. The lowest are those of Colorado with 2.9% and the highest of California with 7.25%. From the states without any income tax Alaska has a sales tax of 0%, South Dakota and Wyoming of 4%, Nevada and Washington of 6.5%.

taxes are not necessarily the same ones to have the highest sales taxes. On the contrary, these are reserved for California and Rhode Island (7 per cent).

It may be interesting to note that the value added tax in Switzerland is reserved for the federation, in contrast to the sales tax in the USA. Can this be a consequence of the fact that Switzerland is small whereas distances are much greater in the USA? So that transaction costs to escape high sales or value added taxes are much smaller in Switzerland? Another remarkable point is also that two states in the USA, namely New Hampshire and Tennessee, demand income tax only on capital earnings. This raises some doubts concerning the hypothesis that institutional competition makes it more and more difficult to tax capital because of its high mobility; and that therefore less mobile factors of production have to bear an increasing share of the tax burden (Sinn 2002).

4.5 CONCLUSIONS

We have shown that systems competition comprises rather different kinds of competition which are related by more or less complex relationships. Military and foreign policy competition between countries has exerted a particularly strong influence on institutional competition in the long run, provided that this was not prohibited by ideologies. This led to the rise of the West and to the introduction of institutions favouring economic development in more and more countries, such as Japan, China, India and in South-East Asia. Both kinds of competition are still working. They are in the long run a counter-force to the increasing government activity with its negative influence for economic development and the freedom of citizens caused by domestic political competition in democracies. The expectation by a number of economists of an erosion of necessary government services and of the necessity of a certain redistribution of incomes seems not to be supported by the empirical evidence. Though this question may still be an open issue to a certain degree, it seems that institutional competition is only able to limit the further growth of government activity or to reduce it to a bearable level.

REFERENCES

Anderson, Terry L. (2004), 'Donning Coase-coloured Glasses: A Property Rights View of Natural Resource Economics', *Australian Journal of Agricultural and Resource Economics*, **48** (3), 445–62.
Andreski, Stanislav (1965), *The Uses of Comparative Sociology*, Berkeley and Los Angeles: University of California Press.

Baechler, Jean (1975), *The Origins of Capitalism*, originally published in French in 1971, Oxford: Basil Blackwell.

Berman, Harold J. (1983), *Law and Revolution*, Cambridge, MA and London: Harvard University Press.

Bernholz, Peter (1966), 'Economic Policies in a Democracy', *Kyklos*, **19**, 48–80.

Bernholz, Peter (1969), 'Einige Bemerkungen zur Theorie des Einflusses der Verbaende auf die politische Willensbildung in der Demokratie', *Kyklos*, **22**, 267–78.

Bernholz, Peter (1986), 'Growth of Government, Economic Growth and Individual Freedom', *Journal of Institutional and Theoretical Economics (Zeitschrift für die Gesamte Staats- wissenschaft)*, **142**, 661–83.

Bernholz, Peter and Roland Vaubel (eds) (2004), *Political Competition, Innovation and Growth in the History of Asian Civilisations*, Cheltenham, UK, and Northampton, MA, USA: Edward Elgar.

Bernholz, Peter, Manfred Streit and Roland Vaubel (eds) (1998), *Political Competition, Innovation and Growth. A Historical Analysis*, Berlin, Heidelberg, New York: Springer.

Berthold, N. and M. Naumann (2001), 'Sozialsysteme im Wettbewerb – das Ende der Umverteilung?' Wirtschaftswissenschaftliche Beiträge, Universität Würzburg.

Blankart, Charles B. (1999), 'Die schleichende Zentralisierung der Staatstätigkeit: Eine Fallstudie', *Zeitschrift für Wirtschafts- und Sozialwissenschaften*, **119**, 331–50.

Blankart, Charles B. (2000), *Öffentliche Fiananzen in der Demokratie*, München: Vahlen, 4. Auflage.

Buettner, T. (2001), 'Local Business Taxation and Competition for Capital: The Choice of the Tax Rate', *Regional Science and Urban Economics*, **31**, 215–45.

Bull, Hedley (1977), *The Anarchical Society. A Study of Order in World Politics*, London and Basingstoke: Macmillan.

Dur, Robert A.J. and Otto H. Swank (1997), 'An Explanation of Policy Reversals. Why do Voters Vote for a Smaller Government if They Voted for a Large Government in the Past?' Unpublished manuscript, presented at the 1997 Silvaplana Public Choice Workshop, Pontresina.

Fehn, R. (2001), 'Ist die Globalisierung der Totengräber der nationalen Sozialpolitik?' Wirtschaftswissenschaftliche Beiträge, Universität Würzburg.

Frey, Bruno S. (2002), 'Liliput oder Leviathan? Der Staat in der globalisierten Wirtschaft', *Perspektiven der Wirtschaftspolitik*, **3** (4), 363–75.

Frey, Bruno S. and Gebhard Kirchgässner (1994), *Demokratische Wirtschaftspolitik*, München: Vahlen.

Jones, Eric L. (1981), *The European Miracle*, Cambridge: Cambridge University Press.

Kirchgässner, G. and W. Pommerehne (1996), 'Tax Harmonization and Tax Competition in the European Union: Lessons from Switzerland', *Journal of Public Economics*, **60**, 351–71.

Kornai, Janos (1971), *Anti-equilibrium*, Amsterdam and London: North Holland.

Marlow, Michael L. (1986), 'Private Sector Shrinkage and the Growth of Industrialized Economies', *Public Choice*, **49** (2), 143–54.

Mueller, Dennis C. (2003), *Public Choice III*, Cambridge and New York: Cambridge University Press.

North, Douglass C. (1981), *Structure and Change in Economic History*, New York: W.W. Norton & Co.

North, Douglass C. and Robert P. Thomas (1973), *The Rise of the Western World: A New Economic History*, Cambridge: Cambridge University Press.

Oates, Wallace E. (2002), 'Fiscal and Regulatory Competition: Theory and Evidence', *Perspektiven der Wirtschaftspolitik*, **3** (4), 377–90.

Olson, Mancur (1965), *The Logic of Collective Action*, Cambridge, MA: Harvard University Press.

Olson, Mancur (1982), *The Rise and Decline of Nations: Economic Growth, Stagflation, and Social Rigidities*, New Haven: Yale University Press.

Ostrom, Elinor (1990), *Governing the Commons. The Evolution of Institutions for Collective Action*, Cambridge and New York: Cambridge University Press.

Peden, Edgar A. and Michael D. Bradley (1989), 'Government Size, Productivity, and Economic Growth: The Post-war Experience', *Public Choice*, **61**, 229–45.

Popper, Karl R. (1961), *The Logic of Scientific Discovery*, 1st edn 1939, New York: Basic Books.

Richardson, Lewis F. (1960), *Statistics of Deadly Quarrels*, ed. Quincy Wright and Carl C. Lienau, Pittsburgh: The Boxwood Press, Chicago: Quadrangle Books.

Schaltegger, Christoph A. and René L. Frey (2003), 'Finanzausgleich und Föderalismus: Zur Neugestaltung der föderalen Finanzbeziehungen am Beispiel der Schweiz', *Perspektiven der Wirtschaftspolitik*, **4** (2), 239–58.

Siebert, Horst (1998), 'Disziplinierung der nationalen Wirtschaftspolitik durch internationale Kapitalmobilität', in D. Duwendag (ed.), *Finanzmärkte im Spannungsfeld von Globalisierung, Regulierung und Geldpolitik*, Berlin: Duncker and Humblot, pp. 41–67.

Sinn, Hans-Werner (1999), 'The Subsidiarity Principle and Market Failure in Systems Competition', NBER Working Paper 5411.

Sinn, Hans-Werner (2002), 'Der neue Systemwettbewerb', *Perspektiven der Wirtschaftspolitik*, **3** (4), 391–407.

Vanberg, Viktor and W. Kerber (1994), 'Institutional Competition among Jurisdictions: an Evolutionary Approach', *Constitutional Political Economy*, **5**, 363–86.

Tanzi, Vito and Ludger Schuknecht (1997), 'Reforming Government: An Overview of Recent Experience', *European Journal of Political Economy*, **13** (3), 395–417.

The Federalist (1787/1937), Alexander Hamilton, John Jay and James Madison, with an Introduction by Edward Mead Earle, Indianapolis: National Foundation for Education in American Citizenship.

Tocqueville, Alexis de (1945), *Democracy in America*, New York: Vintage Books.

Weede, Erich (1986), 'Catch-up, Distributional Coalitions and Governments as Determinants of Economic Growth or Decline in Industrialized Societies', *British Journal of Sociology*, **37**, 194–220.

Weede, Erich (1990), *Wirtschaft, Staat, Gesellschaft*, Tuebingen: J.C.B. Mohr.

5. Can competition between governments enhance democracy?

Viktor J. Vanberg

INTRODUCTION

Between the fears that are voiced in the popular as well as in parts of the academic debate on globalization the charge that globalization poses a threat to democracy is particularly prominent (Herman 1999; Bartelson 2004). In globalization, so it is argued, market powers come to dominate politics because democratic governments are forced to compete for internationally mobile capital in ways that hamper their ability to serve the interests of their constituencies whose well-being they are supposed to further.

The purpose of this chapter is to critically examine the conjecture, implied in the above noted fears about globalization, that the kind of competition between governments that globalization induces requires democratic governments to bow to 'market forces' and limits their capacity to act as faithful trustees of the citizens-principals who elected them as their agents. In the sections that follow I will seek to show that contrary to this conjecture competition between governments can very well work as a disciplining force that helps to keep democratic governments in line with their principal duty, namely to advance the common interests of the citizens-principals as whose agents they act.[1]

Before turning to the issue of how competition between governments may or may not interfere with their capacity to act as faithful agents of their citizens, a few comments are in order on the way in which I will use, for the purposes of this paper, the terms 'government' and 'democracy'.

GOVERNMENTS AS 'TERRITORIAL ENTERPRISES'

In the most general sense, governments can be defined as the agencies that are authorized and empowered to define and enforce within the confines of their respective jurisdictions the legal-institutional framework that defines the terms under which natural persons and legal entities (such as business corporations) are allowed to carry out economic and other activities, as well as the terms under which persons and their resources can enter or leave the jurisdiction. In a multi-level political structure such authority may be divided between national governments, supra-national entities (such as the EU), and sub-national governments (such as state and local governments within a federal system). The above definition applies, though, to governments at all levels as long as they command independent authority to define (at least some of) the 'rules of the game' for their respective jurisdictions. For the purpose of analysing the ways in which competition works as a constraint on their ability to act as such agencies, governments may be usefully looked at as 'territorial enterprises', that is as organizations that provide packages of jurisdictional characteristics and services for their citizens as well as for others who, as 'guests', use the respective territorial domains for particular purposes, as investors, workers, inhabitants, tourists, or otherwise. These packages include such things as infrastructure, legal order, environmental regulation, taxation rules, and so on. Just as ordinary enterprises compete for customers by offering their respective price-benefit packages for sale, governments as 'territorial enterprises' find themselves competing with their respective tax-benefit packages for tax-paying citizens and jurisdiction-users.[2]

Many of the attributes that make jurisdictions more or less attractive to citizens and jurisdiction-users, such as, in particular, their geographical and climatic characteristics, are, of course, not subject to wilful change and, therefore, beyond the power of politics. Other such attributes are, however, more or less subject to political choice, in particular the noted legal-institutional framework and other characteristics of a jurisdiction, such as its public infrastructure and various publicly provided facilities or services. Citizens as well as jurisdiction-users can compare different jurisdictions with regard to the relative attractiveness of their politically chosen attributes, and they can make their choices on where to live, work, invest and so on, dependent on such comparison. It is in this sense that governments as 'territorial enterprises' are in competition with each other to the extent that they seek to be attractive to taxpaying citizens and jurisdiction-users. Such competition is, of course, not just a recent phenomenon brought about by 'globalization'. It has always existed where people were able to choose for their business and other activities between alternative jurisdictions. The worldwide extension and integration of markets that we call 'globalization' has only sharply intensified the competition, because of significant reductions in the transaction costs of border-crossing economic activities that have been made possible in recent decades by political-institutional changes and by advancements in communication and transport technologies. The information needed in order to compare different jurisdictions in terms of their attractiveness with regard to various kinds of economic activities has become much more readily available and less costly, and the ability of persons to relocate – based on such information – their economic activities between alternative jurisdictions has markedly improved due to reduced transaction costs.

DEMOCRACIES AS 'CITIZENS' COOPERATIVES'

It is common practice to define democracy in terms of such typical institutional features as, in particular, majority rule or popular elections. Such definitions tend to distract attention, though, from the fact that the institutional features they emphasize are *instruments* that democratic polities use for making political decisions, but do not describe the fundamental and principal character of such polities. The latter must, I suppose, rather be seen in the fact that democracies are *self-governing* polities in the sense that their citizens are the sovereigns with whom all political decision-making authority ultimately resides and from whose consent any governmental decision-making power ultimately derives its legitimacy. In order to capture this fact, democratic polities can best be defined as *citizens' cooperatives*, that is as collective enterprises that are jointly 'owned' and 'operated' by their members, the citizens, for their common benefit. John Rawls emphasizes this defining attribute of democratic polities, an attribute that precedes any of their particular institutional features, when he speaks of democratic society 'as a cooperative venture for mutual advantage' (Rawls 1971, p. 84). It is in reference to the nature of democratic polities as citizens' cooperatives that institutional devices such as majority rule or popular elections need to be, and can be, justified as instruments that citizens may prudently choose for solving practical problems they face in operating their cooperative enterprise.[3]

There are, of course, important differences between democratic polities as citizens' cooperatives and such 'private cooperatives' as member-owned enterprises and voluntary associations or clubs. Yet, just like any private 'cooperative enterprise for mutual advantage', democratic polities are supposed to serve the common interests of their members, the citizens. And just as the *constitutions*, that is, the rules of operation of ordinary, private cooperatives can be judged in terms of their capacity to advance the members' common interests, the constitutions of democratic polities can be examined and compared to each other in terms of how well they enable citizens to realize mutual gains. In other words, the particular institutional provisions adopted in a democratic polity, such as voting or election rules, must be seen as instruments or tools for serving the principal purpose of the enterprise, namely to advance the citizens' common interests. And they are to be judged ultimately in terms of their suitability for serving that purpose.

In any cooperative enterprise, be it a democratic polity or an ordinary, private voluntary association in which individuals participate with the hope of realizing advantages that cannot be had otherwise, they face an unavoidable dilemma. In order to enable the collective enterprise to carry out projects that may benefit its members they must transfer decision-making power, be it by allowing majority decisions to be made or be it by delegating decision-making authority to agents. In doing so they inevitably run the risk that projects may be undertaken that do not serve their interests and that they would veto if they had retained the power to do so. On the other hand, if, in order to be protected against such risk, they limit the extent to which they transfer decision-making power, in the extreme by insisting on a unanimity rule that grants them veto power in each and every collective decision, they inevitably limit the capacity of the cooperative enterprise to carry out mutually beneficial projects. The constitutions on which cooperative enterprises, from voluntary clubs to democratic nation-states, are based reflect the compromise that their respective members are willing to accept in balancing the risk of finding their own interests violated by joint projects against the prospect of benefiting from such projects.

The Western constitutional tradition, not least the contributions of the American Founding Fathers, can be seen as an ongoing effort to design a framework of rules for democratic polities that, on the one hand, enables them to act for the common benefit of their citizens ('enabling constitution'), while, on the other, it subjects them to constraints that serve to protect citizens from political exploitation ('limiting constitution'). In the latter regard it is in particular two kinds of risks that constitutions must account for: first, the risk that the representatives' agents to whom the citizens delegate decision-making power misuse the authority granted to them to serve their own interests at the expense of the principals-citizens and, second, the risk that the political process is misused by subgroups within the citizenry to advance their own special interests at the expense of other members of the polity. Western democratic constitutions have been fairly effective in controlling for the first risk, and, at least in comparison to alternative constitutional regimes, they have been relatively successful in regard to the second risk as well. Yet, in absolute terms the problem of privilege-seeking or rent-seeking on the part of special interests and of privilege-granting or rent-granting on the part of political agents is still a most troublesome feature of democratic politics (Buchanan et al. 1980) and probably the most severe drawback on their capacity to truly operate as 'cooperative ventures for mutual advantage'. It is precisely with regard to this problem that, as I shall argue, competition between governments – in addition to potential further constitutional improvements[4] – may promise to work as a corrective force.

COMPETITION BETWEEN GOVERNMENTS

Governments compete as 'territorial enterprises' in two principal ways. They compete *indirectly* with each other insofar as the ways in which they shape the legal-institutional framework and other characteristics of their jurisdiction impact on the competitiveness of domestic producers in international markets for goods and services. To the extent that legal and other jurisdictional attributes affect the costs of production, domestic producers may have a competitive advantage or disadvantage compared to producers in other jurisdictions, with predictable effects on a jurisdiction's wealth-producing capacity. Governments compete *directly* with each other insofar as the ways in which they shape the legal-institutional and other characteristics of their respective jurisdictions make them more or less attractive to mobile resources that might contribute to the production of wealth. The owners of mobile resources will compare the return they can expect from employing their resources in different jurisdictions and will base their choice between potential alternatives on such assessment.

In both its forms competition will impose constraints on what governments can do in the sense that it 'punishes' policies that make their jurisdictions less attractive for wealth-producing mobile resources and/or that hamper the competitiveness of domestic producers in international markets. And in both its forms competition results from the fact that people, as consumers and resource-owners, are able to choose between alternative options. It is the ability of consumers to choose between the goods and services offered by different producers that puts more costly producers at a disadvantage in the competition for business and, thus, reduces the wealth-producing capacity of jurisdictions with cost-increasing rules, regulations and policies. It is the ability of owners of mobile resources to choose between alternative jurisdictions for the employment of their resources that puts jurisdictions with less attractive properties at a competitive disadvantage and, thus, reduces their wealth-producing capacity. Whatever increases the ability of consumers and resource-owners to choose between alternative options will intensify, indirectly or directly, the competition between jurisdictions. If globalization is rightly seen as a force that puts governments under stronger competitive pressure it is exactly because the worldwide integration of markets that the term 'globalization' describes has significantly increased the choice options for consumers and resource-owners alike.

In regard to the issue of how the improved choice options for consumers and resource-owners affect the ability of democratic governments to serve their constituencies, the distinction, briefly mentioned before, between citizens and jurisdiction-users, deserves a closer look. It is by their choices as consumers and resource-owners that both groups, citizens and jurisdiction-users, can respond to the policies chosen by democratic governments, thereby imposing constraints on what these governments can do. With regard to the issue of democracy, an essential difference between the two groups is, though, that democratic governments are mandated to act as fiduciary agents of their citizens while they have no such obligations with regard to jurisdiction-users.[5] It is their direct fiduciary duty to serve their citizens' interests, and it is only as a derivative of this fiduciary duty that they are required to account for the interests of jurisdiction-users. The difference has to be kept in mind when, in what follows, I turn to the central question of this chapter, namely whether or not competition between governments poses a 'threat to democracy'.

DEMOCRATIC GOVERNMENTS IN COMPETITION

Does the kind of competition that the forces of globalization impose on them impair the capacity of democratic governments to perform their proper function? The answer to this question will surely depend on what one considers the relevant criterion for measuring governments' performance. If one takes the common definition of democracy as majority government to imply that whatever a majority of elected officials approves must be regarded as 'democratically desirable' then, quite obviously, the answer to the above question can only be 'yes', since competition between governments quite obviously imposes constraints on the exercise of 'majority will'. If, however, one looks at democratic polities as citizens' cooperatives and, accordingly, at democratic governments as fiduciary agents whose foremost duty lies in serving the common interests of their citizens, the answer may be quite different. As unquestionable as it is that competition imposes constraints on governments, no less unquestionable is the fact that, from the citizens' perspective, constraints on government are by no means necessarily a bad thing. As noted before, besides enabling a citizens' cooperative to operate as an organized entity, the very purpose of democratic constitutions is to impose constraints on governmental powers in order to prevent them from being misused against citizens' interests. Before concluding that competition between governments, because of the constraints that it imposes, is inimical to democracy one should, therefore, examine first whether these constraints do in fact interfere with the capacity of democratic governments to serve the common interests of their citizens or whether they may not work, instead, as a force that protects citizens' common interests by limiting the extent to which delegated power can be misused by political agents to further their own interests or to grant privileges to rent-seeking special interests at the expense of the citizenry at large.

The kind of competition between governments that is under investigation here has its roots in nothing other than the widened choice-options that are available to citizens and jurisdiction-users in their capacities as consumers and resource-owners. What needs to be examined are, therefore, the ways in which citizens and jurisdiction-users by taking advantage of these choice-options may affect the operation of democratic governments. There are, in particular, two questions that require examination.

1. Is there a conflict between the common interests that citizens share as members of a citizens' cooperative and their interests as consumers and resource-owners such that in their separate pursuit of the latter interests they interfere with their governments' ability to serve the former?
2. And do jurisdiction-users, in taking advantage of their ability to choose between alternative jurisdictions as places for investment, work and so on, interfere with the ability of democratic governments to serve the common interests of their citizens?

The following two sections will discuss these questions, starting with the second.

COMPETITION FOR JURISDICTION-USERS

According to an argument one often encounters in the debate on globalization, competition between governments leads to a 'race to the bottom' in the sense that in their efforts to attract mobile resources democratic governments are forced to reduce ever more the regulatory and tax burden on jurisdiction-users, in particular the investors of mobile capital; thus being increasingly unable to maintain regulatory standards and to carry out public projects that serve the interests of their citizens. As plausible as it may appear on first glance, upon closer examination this argument turns out to be ill-founded, at least if it is meant to imply that the need to compete for mobile resources forces democratic governments to act against their fiduciary duties as agents of their citizens.

The relation between governments as territorial enterprises and noncitizens who wish to use the jurisdiction for particular purposes is comparable to that between commercial hosts and paying guests. It is an exchange relation that both sides rationally enter if they expect to benefit from it. Democratic governments that act as faithful agents of their constituencies should only admit jurisdiction-users, such as investors of mobile capital, if the contribution they can be expected to make to the well-being of the citizenry exceeds the costs they cause. Conversely, rational jurisdiction-users will opt for a particular jurisdiction only if they expect the benefits from doing so to exceed the costs they will incur, in particular the costs of meeting regulatory requirements and the taxes or other contributions they have to pay. They will, naturally, prefer to take advantage of the benefits that a jurisdiction offers at the lowest possible price and, faced with the choice between potential alternative jurisdictions, they will opt for the one that offers the most attractive cost–benefits package.

This implies, of course, that in their competition for mobile resources governments are under pressure to limit the regulatory and tax burden they impose on jurisdiction-users. It does not mean, however, that democratic governments are thereby prevented from providing their citizens with the kind of regulatory framework and the supply of public amenities they desire, *if* they are willing to pay the price. The benefits citizens receive from such regulations and public amenities can be regarded as a kind of 'public consumption', and the members of a citizens' cooperative can choose whatever level of such public consumption they wish as long as they are prepared to make the sacrifices that this requires in terms of reduced wealth and private consumption. All that competition between governments does is limit their government's capacity to shift the cost burden of such public consumption to third parties, such as jurisdiction-users, who do not benefit in any way from the regulations and public amenities in question.

To the extent that a jurisdiction's regulatory standards make it a more attractive place for the kinds of uses that the owners of mobile resources are interested in, rational jurisdiction-users should be willing to accept the burden a regulation imposes on them as a price to be paid for the opportunity to take advantage of the jurisdictional benefits that it produces. The same argument applies to taxes or other financial burdens that can be imposed on jurisdiction-users. To the extent that they are matched by advantages that a jurisdiction has to offer to its 'paying guests', governments can count on their willingness to pay. They cannot count, however, on the willingness of jurisdiction-users to fund projects that are to the exclusive benefit of citizens.

The fear that competition between governments leads to a race to the bottom seems to be based on the tacit assumption that jurisdiction-users consider in their choice between jurisdictions only the price they have to pay in terms of regulatory or tax burdens without regard to other jurisdictional attributes. This is, however, an assumption no more realistic than the assumption that people choose the restaurant they visit for dinner only in light of the prices they find on the menu, disregarding the quality of the food and the décor of the place. Prudent jurisdiction-users, such as investors of mobile capital, will surely compare the prices they have to pay with the advantages that jurisdictions have to offer in regard to the kind of uses they are interested in, and they will be willing to pay the price that these advantages are worth to them. Governments that charge jurisdiction-users a price that is either too low or too high, relative to the benefits they offer, will either drive away – to the detriment of their citizens – potentially wealth-contributing jurisdiction-users, or they will subsidize jurisdiction users at their citizens' expense. In either case, it is not competition that is to be blamed for the damage done but, rather, the defective 'pricing scheme' that such governments apply. And the appropriate remedy should not be sought in futile efforts to escape the forces of competition but, instead, in the correction of the faulty pricing schemes.

CITIZENS' INTERESTS, CONSUMER INTERESTS AND PRODUCER INTERESTS

Democratic politics would be much easier if the interests that individuals harbour in their capacities as citizens, as consumers and as resource-owners or producers were always in perfect harmony with each other, but they are not. As consumers, people have good reasons to prefer open markets and unrestricted access to potential sources of supply. As citizens they may well prefer to maintain particular characteristics of their accustomed socio-cultural environment and they may, therefore, want their governments to restrict access to the jurisdiction for certain kinds of goods, services, investments or persons. And as resource-owners who are engaged in specific production activities within their home jurisdictions, be it as employees, as investors or otherwise, they may wish their governments to adopt protectionist policies that shield them from the pressure of foreign competition. How should democratic governments respond to the various demands arising from these different and partly conflicting interests, and how is their ability to cater to these interests affected by competition between governments?

The general answer to the first part of the question is that, if democratic governments are there to serve the common interests of their citizens, the various demands on them must be critically examined with regard to the extent to which they can justly be assumed to reflect such common interests rather than interests that are shared only by a particular sub-group, and that can be served only at the expense of other citizens. In the case of consumer interests, the result of such examination is unambiguous and straightforward. In their capacity as consumers, citizens' interests are best served by open markets that allow them unimpeded access to their most attractive sources of supply. Citizens may well differ in their particular patterns of consumption preferences and, therefore, may care more about the accessibility of certain sources of supply than others. But their respective interests in no way come into conflict with each other. As consumers they are not hurt by open access to goods and services they are not interested in, nor can they benefit from impediments on the accessibility of such goods and services. As consumers they share a common interest in open markets.

The situation is markedly different with the interests in protectionist provisions that citizens may harbour in their capacity as producers who wish to be shielded from foreign competition. With their protectionist interests as producers citizens are by no means in agreement with each other. Protection is always sought by, and for, particular groups of producers, not as a general rule to be applied indiscriminately to all domestic production. Protection is advantageous only when granted as a privilege to particular categories of producers, not if it were practised as a general rule. And the protection benefits it provides to the privileged group come necessarily at the expense of others in the jurisdiction who have to pay higher prices for the products in question than would otherwise be the case – whether the 'others' are end-consumers of these products or other producers who use them as inputs in their own production. With their protectionist interests as producers, citizens are, therefore, inevitably in conflict with each other, such that democratic governments cannot grant a protectionist privilege to any particular group without acting against the interests of other citizens, thus violating their fiduciary duty to serve the common interests of their citizenries.

The issue is more complicated in the case of protectionist interests that people share *as citizens* who want their government to safeguard certain socio-cultural attributes of their polity that they see threatened in the absence of adequate protectionist provisions. To be sure, no less than the protectionist interests they harbor as producers, protectionist interests motivated by their preferences as citizens come into conflict with people's interests as consumers.[6] The critical difference between the two kinds of protectionist interests is, however, that the interests of producers are, as a rule, about *privileges* and do not, therefore, reflect citizens' common interests, while there may well be certain protectionist interests that the members of a democratic polity have in common as citizens who care about the socio-cultural attributes of the jurisdiction they live in. Where this is the case they may value the benefits to be gained from protectionist provisions more highly than the sacrifices they have to make on the side of their consumer interests, and in such a case a democratic government would fulfil its fiduciary duty in serving such protectionist interests. A democratic government, confronted with a variety of protectionist demands, must take care, though, to sort out the demands that reflect commonly shared interests from those that only serve special interests. And from among the commonly shared protectionist interests it should only serve those that weigh more heavily than the sacrifices they require on the side of citizens' consumer interests.

COMPETITION BETWEEN GOVERNMENTS AND CITIZENS' COMMON INTERESTS

So far, I have only described the different kinds of interests that the members of a citizens' cooperative may harbour and that their governments need to account for. In light of the distinctions drawn the issue of how competition between governments affects democratic polities can now be specified as the issue of how such competition affects the ability of democratic governments to account for the various interests they confront in ways that result in mutual benefits for all citizens and do not just serve the interests of some at the expense of others.

As was noted above, one of the major weaknesses of democratic constitutionalism has been, and still is, its limited effectiveness in controlling the problem of privilege-seeking or rent-seeking. This problem is usually analysed in regard to what may be called its 'incentive aspect', namely the incentives for political agents (governments and legislators) to resist or to give in to the demands of special interests. The problem has a 'knowledge aspect' too, separate from and in addition to any distorting incentives that lobbying special interests may provide, namely the difficulty for citizens as well as for their political agents to *know* which among potential alternative policy projects actually serve citizens' common interests best. As I shall argue, in both regards – in regard to the incentive as well as to the knowledge aspect – competition between governments, rather than being a threat to democracy, can actually assist democratic governments in fulfilling their fiduciary duty.

As far as the 'knowledge aspect' is concerned, competition between governments reveals information about the effects of alternative rule-regimes and governmental practices and, thereby, facilitates a comparison between alternative regimes and policies. It provides citizens-principals as well as their political agents with information about which public projects or policy measures may be more or less likely to advance citizens' common interests. In a complex world in which anticipating the actual effects of potential policy alternatives is by no means always easy, the 'parallel experiments' that competing governments undertake generate relevant information on this issue.

With regard to the 'incentive aspect' the major effect of competition between governments surely is that it limits the scope for privilege-*granting* and, as a consequence, reduces the incentives for interest groups to invest in rent-*seeking* activities. With every privilege that a democratic government grants to a particular interest group – be it a subsidy, protection from competitors, a tax privilege or any other preferential treatment – there are always other parties in the citizenry who are discriminated against and on whom the costs of the privilege are imposed, be it in terms of higher prices, higher taxes or in other forms. To the extent that these negatively affected parties have choice options that allow them to shed the burdens that are imposed on them for the mere benefit of others, they will use these options, thereby drying up the source from which governments must feed the privileges they grant. It is exactly the scope of such choice options that has been significantly enlarged by the forces that are behind the intensified competition between governments, namely the worldwide expansion and integration of markets, called globalization. To the extent that these forces make it easier to shift one's economic activities from less hospitable to more hospitable jurisdictions, citizens' willingness to bear the costs of privileges granted to others is diminished.

The granting of privileges inevitably has, and always has had, wealth-reducing effects for the citizenry at large, and these negative effects have always been a cost of privilege-granting that democratic governments had to take into account. Yet, in the competition for votes the short-term gains that politicians could expect from serving special interests typically carried greater weight than the much more distant and less visible costs they thereby imposed on the citizenry at large. What has changed with the intensified competition between governments is that these costs have become more transparent and that the feedback link through which the negative effects of privilege-granting translate back into damages to the granting government has become shorter.

While it may help citizens' cooperatives to reduce the risks posed by rent-seeking interest groups and privilege-granting governments, competition between governments need not interfere with their ability to realize public projects that are to the mutual advantage of their members. All it does is to make the costs of such projects more clearly visible, forcing citizens to face the true trade-off between the public consumption benefits they expect from such projects and the sacrifices that this may require.

CONCLUSION

If the measuring rod by which we judge the performance of democratic governments is their ability to serve their citizens' common interests and to resist the lures of rent-seeking special interests, then the question posed in the title of this paper can be clearly answered in the positive. This is the argument I have sought to support in the preceding sections, at least for the kind of competition between governments that is induced and intensified by the extension and integration of markets that is the hallmark of globalization.

To be sure, the argument I have presented here is definitely not meant to support the claim that competition per se enhances democracy, irrespective of the ways in which it is carried out. The history of mankind has witnessed a multitude of forms in which governments may compete with each other, between which warfare has been particularly prominent, and many of them are extremely unlikely to serve the common interests of the respective citizenries. What is true for any kind of competition applies no less to competition between governments: how it works out for the persons affected by it will depend on the rules under which it is carried out. For totally unconstrained competition, that is, a competition in which 'everything goes', one could hardly predict what it will produce, and it would be extremely naive to hope that it might work out to the common benefit of the persons involved. It is, for instance, the purpose of the rules of competitive sports to limit the scope of admissible strategies so as to ensure that contests work out in ways desired, such that, for example, the fastest runners have the best chances to win a race rather then those who are most skilled in impeding their competitors, using steroids, or bribing the referees. Similarly, market competition is by no means an 'everything goes' event. It is competition within a framework of rules that are supposed to ensure that voluntary contracting, in the absence of coercion and fraud, is the principal mode by which people coordinate their economic activities (Vanberg 2001). And the beneficial working properties that we may expect from market competition are contingent on the suitability of the rules under which it is carried out; rules that are to ensure, for example, that market success should be achieved by those who serve consumer interests best rather than those who are most skilled in impeding competitors or lobbying government for special privileges.

The kind of competition between governments that this chapter has been concerned with is induced by the enhanced ability of individuals to choose, in their capacities as consumers and resource-owners, between alternative options for their respective economic interests, and its principal effect is that it forces governments to be more responsive to these interests. My aim has been to show that the intensified pressure to respond to these interests does not interfere with democratic governments' ability to act as fiduciary agents of their citizens but only tends to make more transparent the true costs of the public consumption projects they adopt. Governments may, of course, respond to the noted competitive pressure in different ways, not all of which may work out to the mutual benefit of their citizens, and some of which may impose costs on citizens in other jurisdictions. In this regard, the rules that constrain the strategies that governments may adopt in their competition with each other are of critical importance (Vanberg and Kerber 1994).

To adequately constrain governments' choice of strategies in their competition with each other is, in the first instance, the task of national constitutions. Yet, international rule-regimes can play an important role as well, and there is little reason to assume that the existing framework of factually observed, implicit and explicit 'rules of intergovernmental competition' could not be improved. The rules that governments submit to as members of the WTO, for instance, clearly help to constrain them in ways that benefit citizens' common interests by limiting the scope for granting protectionist privileges. But in several regards, not least in the area of agricultural policy, the WTO could surely be made a more effective weapon in fighting the protectionist misuses of governmental powers. In similar ways, rules of competition between governments may be adopted in other areas as well, to the common benefit of their citizens. There are, for instance, good reasons to expect that citizens would benefit from rules that prohibit governments from competing for mobile capital by granting discretionary tax privileges to individual investors and that allow them to compete only in terms of the general tax rates that they apply in a non-discriminatory manner to investors in general, domestic as well as foreign.

To be sure, intergovernmental agreements and international rule-regimes may be, and often enough have been, used to serve interests other than citizens' common interests. They can, for instance, be used by governments to form cartels that harmonize taxes and coordinate their activities in other regards with the purpose of abolishing intergovernmental competition rather than submitting them to rules that benefit their citizens. This insight is important and should be kept in mind as a warning that international agreements must always be carefully examined with regard to their prospective effects, in particular in terms of whether they help to strengthen citizens' rights or only enlarge the power of governments to control their citizens. As relevant as this warning is, it should, however, not distract attention from the important role that a suitable framework of rules of competition can play in the case of competition between governments no less than in the case of ordinary market competition.

NOTES

1. The discussion of this issue in the present chapter is a follow-up to my earlier discussion in Vanberg (2000).
2. Tiebout (1956) is, of course, the classic exposition of this view of jurisdictions as competing 'territorial enterprises'.
3. The classic treatise on why the members of a citizens' cooperative may for prudential reasons choose to decide common matters by majority rule is Buchanan and Tullock (1962). The logic of their argument can also be applied to the question of why it may be prudent for members of a citizens' cooperative to delegate decision-making authority to agents who are subject to periodical elections.
4. On this issue see for instance F.A. Hayek's proposal for the reform of democratic institutions (Hayek 1979, pp. 105ff.).
5. The term 'jurisdiction-user' is to be understood here in the narrow sense in which it refers only to non-citizens who use a jurisdiction for certain limited purposes. Understood in a broader sense it would, of course, include citizens as well insofar as their status as members of a citizens' cooperative can be distinguished from their roles as consumers and resource-owners who may or may not choose to use their home jurisdiction for such purposes as investment, work, residence and so on.
6. In this sense there may exist genuine conflicts between people's interests as citizens and as consumers, a conflict that Kincaid (1993) has discussed under the label 'consumership versus citizenship'.

REFERENCES

Bartelson, Jens (2004), 'Facing Europe: Is Globalization a Threat to Democracy?' *Distinktion, Scandinavian Journal of Social Theory*, **8**, 47–60.
Buchanan, James M. and Gordon Tullock (1962), *The Calculus of Consent – Logical Foundations of Constitutional Democracy*, Ann Arbor: Michigan University Press.
Buchanan, James M. et al. (eds) (1980), *Toward a Theory of the Rent-seeking Society*, College Station: Texas A&M University Press.
Hayek, F.A. (1979), *Law, Legislation and Liberty*, Vol. 3, *The Political Order of a Free People*, London and Henley: Routledge and Kegan Paul.
Herman, Edward S. (1999), 'The Threat of Globalization', *New Politics*, **7** (2) (new series), http://www.wpunj.edu/newpol/issue26/herman26.htm.
Kincaid, John (1993), 'Consumership Versus Citizenship: Is There Wiggle Room for Local Regulation in the Global Economy?' in B. Hocking (ed.), *Foreign Relations and Federal States*, London and New York: Leicester University Press, pp. 27–47.
Rawls, John (1971), *A Theory of Justice*, Cambridge, MA: Harvard University Press.
Tiebout, Charles M. (1956), 'A Pure Theory of Local Expenditures', *Journal of Political Economy*, **64**, 416–24.
Vanberg, Viktor J. (2000), 'Globalization, Democracy and Citizens' Sovereignty: Can Competition among Governments Enhance Democracy?' *Constitutional Political Economy*, **11**, 87–112.

Vanberg, Viktor J. (2001), 'Markets and the Law', in Neil J. Smelser and Paul B. Baltes (eds), *International Encyclopedia of the Social and Behavioral Sciences*, Vol. 14, Amsterdam: Elsevier 2001, pp. 9221–7.
Vanberg, Viktor J. and Wolfgang Kerber (1994), 'Competition among Jurisdictions: An Evolutionary Approach', *Constitutional Political Economy*, **5**, 193–219.

6. Tax competition and tax cartels

Rolf Höijer

6.1 INTRODUCTION

Those who fear tax competition usually argue that some measures of tax harmonization must be employed to limit the extent of tax competition. To mention some examples the French President Jacques Chirac argued that '[we need] genuine fiscal harmonisation in Europe . . .'[1] Similarly EU Trade Commissioner Pascal Lamy argued that 'A natural first step would be to harmonise the tax bases and to adopt minimum tax rates but the ultimate goal should be the creation of a European Corporate income tax.'[2] Policy measures have also been introduced. At a meeting in Verona in 1996 the ECOFIN also introduced a reflection document, which broadened the discussion of 'harmful tax competition' and placed it at the heart of the EU agenda.[3] This resulted in an EU tax agreement in 1997.[4] Within the European Union VAT has also been harmonized, (as have a few other taxes). In May 1996 the OECD also ordered a report with recommendations to be drafted, which resulted in the OECD's famous 1998 report on 'Harmful Tax Competition', and subsequent OECD work to inhibit the activities of 'tax havens' and so on.[5] As these examples show tax harmonization is often suggested as a remedy to tax competition.

This chapter aims briefly to discuss some of the possible dangers and benefits of tax harmonization that are seldom discussed otherwise. Section 6.2 will consider tax harmonization as an attempt to limit competition and also discuss which market failures are usually used to justify replacing competitive markets with government monopolies. In Section 6.3 I briefly review the most important contemporary policy arguments against tax competition. Section 6.4 identifies the most important policy measures for achieving tax harmonization that are presently used (or proposed). Section 6.5 briefly assesses the validity of the arguments for tax harmonization, and Section 6.6 identifies a potential problem with tax harmonization. The chapter does not aim to demonstrate empirically to what extent tax competition actually occurs, or to what extent tax harmonization does alleviate such competition.

Some definitions, I will say that 'tax competition' exists whenever there exists more than one government that can potentially tax a given taxpayer, that is, if a given taxpayer can be taxed by either of two (or more) different governments: if, for a given taxpayer, there exists more than one government by which he can be independently taxed. Such tax competition enables individual taxpayers to evade taxation by a particular government since it enables these taxpayers to become the tax subjects of some alternative (low-tax) government. I will say that 'tax harmonization' exists if the taxing governments cooperate with each other to limit the potential for tax competition, that is, they agree to the removal of some government ability to independently tax the individual taxpayer.

6.2 TAX HARMONIZATION, TAX CARTELS AND MARKET FAILURES

Tax harmonization sounds so . . . *harmonious*. Yet, those who fear tax competition argue that some measures of tax harmonization should be employed to limit tax competition. This suggests specifically that tax harmonization implies the elimination of competition in the field of taxation. In other economic contexts such anti-competitive measures are called things like 'collusion', 'cartelization' or 'monopolism', and are regarded as serious market failures. Otherwise it is always assumed that competitive markets function better than non-competitive markets, and most nations have some antitrust legislation to ensure that markets remain competitive. Yet in fiscal matters tax competition is regarded as harmful and anti-competitive measures are being advocated.

Within the context of VAT harmonization, for example, EU governments get together and set common tax rates that exceed the rates that had been set by them independently. If several private firms were to do the same thing in terms of agreeing to set a high joint price it would be called 'forming a cartel.' When several governments act in this manner tax harmonization should logically be considered equivalent to the formation of tax cartels – the attempt (through collusion) to maintain higher taxes (prices) than would prevail under unregulated competitive conditions.[6]

Yet the OECD and the EU both advocate tax harmonization (see Sections 6.4.1 and 6.4.2), the coordination of tax policies with the objective of removing taxpayers' ability to abstain from paying taxes to particular governments. Competition on ordinary markets puts pressure on prices to reflect relative scarcity, and to be aligned with consumer preferences. Apparently tax-harmonizing governments in these international organizations do not wish to be exposed to these pressures themselves. Instead they form cartels. Until some analysis demonstrates why cartels would not be harmful in this particular context one is left wondering why governments are themselves so eager to form cartels.

Cartels (and monopolism) represent serious market failures. Since competitive markets are always considered superior in other contexts one would need to consider what could justify the elimination of competition in the specific field of taxation. In other markets the introduction of government monopolies are usually considered justified only if these monopolies replace serious market failures of other kinds. What market failures could exist in the market for tax competition which could justify such intervention? To answer this question I will briefly review some important kinds of market failure as these are identified in the literature, and in Section 6.3 I will review the most important arguments that are advanced to justify tax harmonization to see if tax harmonization is indeed introduced to remedy any such market failures.

Externalities are perhaps the most widely discussed market failure. According to Samuelson and Nordhaus's textbook exposition 'Externalities . . . occur when firms or people impose costs or benefits on others without those others receiving the proper payment, or paying the proper price.'[7] In such cases, actor A, who imposes the costs/benefits, will not take the effects on the other party B into account when making his economic decision. Since A has no incentive to take into account the effects his decisions have on B the classical argument is that A will impose too many negative externalities on B, and provide too few positive externalities to him. This is the market failure that governments might intervene to remedy.

Insufficient provision of *public goods* is often regarded as another market failure. A 'public good' may be defined as a good such that if it is made available for consumption to any member of a group of consumers, no member of that group can be excluded from consuming it.[8] It is difficult to provide public goods, because any person who may contribute towards the provision of such a good may rationally be a free-rider, that is, s/he may withhold his/her own contributions and (attempt to) rely on the contributions of others to provide the public good (which s/he can still consume).[9] Public goods and (positive) externalities involve particular failures of markets to clear in the sense that supply is not as high as subjectively estimated demand. The insufficient provision of public goods is widely considered to constitute a market failure and a popular argument is that governments should finance the provision of public goods, since they collect tax revenues that individual taxpayers cannot abstain from paying.[10]

Recent literature has also discussed *information asymmetries* as sources of market failure. Akerlof, for example, considered the market for used cars. To illustrate, assume that on a market only two kinds of used cars exist: high and low-quality cars, and that sellers want £6000 for high-quality cars and

£2000 for low-quality cars. Buyers will pay £6000 for high-quality cars, and £2000 for low-quality cars. The market problem arises because the quality of individual cars is well known to the seller but not to the buyers, and sellers may therefore attempt to sell low-quality cars for more than £2000. Expected utility theory suggests that the price level should then become £4000, if there would be an equal probability that a buyer would be able to purchase a car worth £6000 as that he would acquire a car worth £2000. However, since sellers demand £6000 for high-quality cars buyers will assume that any car offered for sale at £4000 will not be a high-quality car. Buyers will rationally assume that for £4000 they would only be sold lemons (worth £2000), and such buyers would refuse to pay anything more than £2000.[11] As such buyers would offer no more than £2000 for used cars, sellers would only sell cars valued at £2000 or less. The market would not clear for high-quality cars – not all mutually beneficial exchanges would be made.

More generally one can also argue that 'When prices are used to signal or guarantee quality, however, they cannot also clear the market and will not properly measure the relative scarcity of goods and services.'[12] Stiglitz has argued that with regard to credit ratings and labour markets the price (wage/interest) might be used to signal quality, and in such instances prices may not be set such that they clear markets.[13] Stiglitz also emphasizes that 'asymmetries of information greatly limit the opportunities to trade'[14] and maintains that these 'market failures are pervasive in the economy'.[15]

The above presentation of market failures is both inexhaustive and brief, but at least sufficient to draw attention to some common characteristics among market failures. Externalities, public goods and information problems all emphasize that:

1. Markets do not clear adequately.
2. All mutually beneficial gains from trade are not captured.
3. Prices do not adequately convey information about the relative scarcity and subjective valuation of economic resources.
4. As a consequence of point (2) Pareto improvements are possible if the relevant market failures are remedied.

These are important characteristics of market failures that are invoked to justify the introduction of government regulation and government monopolies on other markets. Limiting (tax) competition means introducing serious market failures (cartels), so presumably there must exist strong reasons for doing so. It is therefore worth considering whether tax harmonization is indeed intended to remedy any market failures of the type presented above?

6.3   TAX COMPETITION: A RACE TO THE BOTTOM?

In certain nations, including Sweden, tax competition has been intensively debated in recent years. In January 1997 the *Financial Times* accordingly wrote that international 'fiscal policy has emerged from a long spell of hibernation'.[16] According to Radaelli a narrative about 'harmful tax competition' has emerged in the EU, including claims that tax competition erodes tax bases and shifts the tax burden onto workers.[17] It has been argued that in a globalized world, capital will move away from high-tax nations, towards low-tax nations, thus eroding the tax bases necessary to sustain costly welfare states that are desired domestically. Thus 'a race to the bottom' would allegedly be induced, leading to a world where minimal (and suboptimal) tax rates are adopted in each nation.

In this section I will identify the three most important arguments against tax competition as they feature in policy discussions (primarily in the EU and the OECD),[18] namely that:

6.3.1   Tax competition distorts investments and violates capital export neutrality.
6.3.2   Tax competition undermines the financing of ambitious welfare states.
6.3.3   Tax competition will shift the tax burden from capital to labour.

These arguments will be presented in turn below.

6.3.1   Tax Competition Distorts Investments and Trade

A first argument concerns whether or not tax competition distorts investments and trade and destroys the possibility of having level playing fields for competitors. A basic desideratum for a tax system is that it should not provide incentives that distort trade or investment decisions. In a well-functioning market economy prices send a signal as to where resources are relatively scarce, and investors use this signal to detect in which sectors of the economy they should invest their resources. Accordingly resources are normally allocated to those sectors of the economy where their rates of return are highest. A tax system should not distort such investment decisions, so as to drive investments towards sectors of the economy where the value added from these investments would be lower.[19] A tax system should therefore not distort the relative prices between different sectors of an economy; instead the ideal is to have a *lump sum tax* – that is, collecting a given sum of tax revenue without having any allocative consequences arise from this tax collection.

In international taxation this suggests the doctrine of capital export neutrality, (CEN).[20] This doctrine suggests that for an individual investor I the tax systems in nations A and B should not influence I's decision as to whether to invest in country A instead of investing in nation B. If two companies are equally productive and efficient, but located in two different nations, then they should stand equal chances of attracting I's investment, regardless of the tax regime of the country in which they are located. The objective is that invested resources should be put to their highest use, and earn the largest return. Analogous arguments apply to trade. In effect, if the availability of good and cheap factor inputs in a country A are better than in country B, this should increase the productivity of any investment I makes in A and enable I to earn higher unit returns – regardless of the levels of taxation in the respective countries.

This could suggest that a resident of a given country should pay the same rate of taxation whether the investment is made at home or abroad. In one report the Nordic Council accordingly objects to harmful tax competition on the basis that it is comparable to 'dumping'.[21] The doctrine of capital export neutrality would seem to suggest that different governments should adopt the same tax rates (for mobile capital) so that investment decisions do not reflect differences in tax levels, but instead only reflect the productivity of given production factors in individual countries.[22] This would create a 'level playing field' and promote 'fair competition for real economic activities'.[23] This argument will be assessed in Section 6.5.1.

6.3.2 Tax Competition Undermines the Finances of Welfare States

Probably the most important argument for tax harmonization is that tax competition allegedly means that mobile capital will gravitate towards those tax jurisdictions where taxation is lowest, and away from high-tax countries. Welfare state governments need to impose high taxes to finance their ambitious programmes of welfare provision and redistribution. In a situation of competitive taxation this would mean that taxable capital will gravitate away from such welfare states, and this will erode the tax bases required to finance their welfare programmes. According to this fear, welfare states will not survive in a competitive environment where they are not able to retain sufficient tax bases to finance their welfare provision programmes.

A similar argument would allege that tax competition specifically erodes governments' ability to provide public goods, because tax competition means that individual taxpayers could abstain from paying taxes to one government by instead choosing to become the tax subject of some other (low-tax) state. In other words, free-riders could abstain from contributing towards the provision of public goods.

Obviously these arguments represent no problem for low-tax nations, which do not sustain costly welfare states (or provide public goods). These nations will instead attract investments and tax bases, and presumably fare better.

What levels of taxation should be chosen by a state, and what levels of welfare programmes it should provide, has clearly been debated at great length, without reaching any clear consensus. It can therefore not credibly maintained that it is an absolutely bad – or good – thing in itself if welfare states are maintained – or eroded – due to tax competition. What proponents of welfare states can credibly argue, however, is that if it has been decided in a democratic process that a government should adopt high taxes in order to finance high levels of welfare provision, then tax competition can possibly inhibit the implementation and satisfaction of the subjectively perceived desires that its citizens have given expression to. This argument will be assessed in Section 6.5.2.

6.3.3 Tax Competition Shifts the Tax Burden from Capital to Labour

Another important argument against tax competition is that it might redistribute the tax burden from capital to labour.[24] According to this argument there basically exist two categories of production factors: capital and labour. Each of these may be taxed, and may be regarded as a separate tax base. Tax competition means that mobile tax bases will escape from high-tax jurisdictions and gravitate towards low-tax jurisdictions. Capital is regarded as a more mobile production factor than labour, thus it is assumed that it is primarily capital that will leave high-tax jurisdictions and gravitate towards low-tax jurisdictions. Immobile labour – that is, workers – will not move, they stay in the high-tax nations. If a given government desires to maintain a given level of tax revenues, and it has less capital to tax, then this presumably also means that it must instead increase the taxation of the labour that remains within its jurisdiction. Such a government may also decrease tax rates for capital to attract capital investments back to the nation.

Some economists argue that there is indeed a general trend away from capital taxation towards labour taxation.[25] Sweden, the OECD country with highest levels of taxation, provides an interesting example since it should be most sensitive to tax competition. In this case the taxation of workers is indeed the highest in the OECD (in 2002), while its company and capital taxes are much lower. The low levels of capital taxation are regarded (by a high level expert commission) as one reason why Sweden is not currently exposed to severe pressures from tax competition.[26] Possibly this design of the Swedish tax system is consistent with the proposition that tax competition redistributes tax burdens from capital to labour.[27]

If this argument is correct tax competition would mean that the tax burden would shift from capital to labour.[28] Capitalists – as owners of the production factor capital – would be less taxed. Workers – as owners of the production factor labour – would be more highly taxed. (Possibly the higher costs of labour might also lead to unemployment.[29]) This argument will be assessed in Section 6.5.3.

6.4   METHODS FOR IMPLEMENTING TAX HARMONIZATION

Tax harmonization is not only concerned with arguing against tax competition, however. It also involves methods for coordination or 'harmonizing' tax policies. In this section I briefly outline methods for implementing tax harmonization.

Those who subscribe to the arguments in Sections 6.3.1–6.3.3 above will usually argue that some form of tax harmonization is needed to reduce or eliminate tax competition. Lionel Jospin, former French Prime Minister, for example argued that 'The co-ordination of economic policies should be considerably increased . . . I propose, in terms of corporate tax, that the tax base should first be harmonized and that a minimum rate should be fixed.'[30] In the EU, harmonization of corporate taxes have been discussed since the 1962 Neumark report. On 1 December 1997 ECOFIN reached a comprehensive agreement on taxation.[31] This included (a) work towards a voluntary code of conduct on taxation, (b) work towards a 'savings directive', (c) reconsideration of state aid policy, and (d) ambitions to forward proposals for a corporate tax on international interest and royalty payments.[32] The 1998 OECD report also introduced some 15 specific recommendations to combat tax competition.

In this section I will identify the most important methods for implementing tax harmonization:

6.4.1   Harmonizing taxation by setting unitary minimum tax rates.
6.4.2   Harmonizing taxation through information exchanges between tax authorities.

In this chapter I will regard *tax harmonization* as attempts to coordinate tax policies and tax collection policies between different governments, with the objective of eliminating or reducing tax competition. The important feature of tax competition is that it enables individual taxpayers to avoid taxation by a particular government by becoming the tax subjects of some alternative (low-tax) government. Tax harmonization may accordingly be regarded as the coordination of tax policies with the objective of removing taxpayers' ability to abstain from paying taxes to particular governments.

6.4.1 Harmonizing Taxation by Setting Unitary Minimum Tax Rates

The most obvious way for a group of governments to introduce tax harmonization is by agreeing to set a common and unitary tax rate that applies to all of their taxpayers. This clearly eliminates tax competition. If an individual taxpayer confronts the choice of whether to pay taxes in either country A or country B there is no way he can reduce the amount of taxes he must pay if both countries have the same rate of taxation for the income being taxed. The taxpayer can no longer evade tax payments, and the two countries are no longer engaged in tax competition vis-à-vis one another. Presumably this addresses problems 6.3.1–6.3.3.

Tax harmonization through setting common tax rates does occur. The most important example is probably the EU's common standard on VAT. The EU member states have all agreed to adopt a common minimum VAT rate of 15 per cent.[33] (Individual member states are allowed to introduce VAT rates above this level, however; 15 per cent represents the minimum rate.[34]) This harmonization was introduced largely to ensure that VAT did not distort trade, that is, argument 6.3.1. This minimum rate clearly reduces the scope for tax competition since no country is able to 'outbid' other governments by offering lower rates than 15 per cent when attempting to attract consumption expenditures. As such this appears analogous to price fixing in a cartel on other markets. Inside the EU some taxes on alcohol, tobacco, and mineral oils have also been harmonized in a similar manner.[35]

It is important to note that for the harmonization of tax rates to be fully effective, however, it is also necessary to harmonize tax bases, that is, the rules that determine which transactions are taxed. If two countries, for example, nominally tax incomes at the same rate, but one country allows many kinds of income to be exempted from this taxation then the effective rate of taxation will be lower in that country. The harmonization of tax rates therefore effectively requires the harmonization of tax bases as well. (The EU commission has, for example, harmonized the VAT base, and in 2004 established a 'Common Consolidated Corporate Tax Base Working Group' to develop a model for a harmonized corporate tax base.)

In this context there has been considerable debate regarding the way in which the EU reaches decisions about tax rates. Currently EU statutes demand that (direct) tax policy is determined through unanimous decisions, which allows individual countries to veto any proposal of tax harmonization that they dislike. Individuals in favour of tax harmonization – including Romano Prodi, while President of the European Commission – have emphasized the need to introduce majority voting rules for taxation matters, so that the EU could more easily reach decisions about such harmonized taxes. If majority voting rules were introduced the scope for tax harmonization would increase greatly in the EU.

6.4.2   Harmonizing Taxation through Information Exchange between Tax Authorities

Tax competition can also be impeded through different forms of information exchange. Tax competition effectively offers taxpayers an opportunity to choose to become tax subjects of a tax jurisdiction that offers to tax them at a lower rate. A citizen of high-tax country *A* might therefore move to low tax country *B*, in order to achieve a reduction of the taxation to which s/he is exposed.

A government that claims the right to tax an individual, or company, can try to enforce that claim even if the individual (or company) no longer regards himself (itself) as subject to their taxation. In other words: government A may try to collect tax revenues from a taxpayer even if that person resides, or earns his income, in country B. The US government, for example, taxes the incomes of US subjects even when these incomes are earned abroad, and many other governments do the same to some extent.[36]

There are different kinds of grounds that governments invoke to claim the right to tax particular individuals. With regard to income taxation the *residence principle* means that a government claims the right to tax individuals residing within its borders; according to the alternative *source principle* a government claims the right to tax individuals when their incomes have been earned within the borders of that country. Produced goods and services may alternatively be taxed according to the *origin principle* (in which case the state where the goods/service has been produced claims the right to tax the goods/services); or else according to the *destination principle* (in which case the state where the goods/services end up being consumed claims the right to tax these goods/services).[37] Different states apply different principles.

If governments can tax individuals or companies even when these persons would regard themselves as tax subjects of some other government then this clearly impedes tax competition. (The problems discussed here often concern states adhering to the residence principle.) If high-tax government A can enforce tax revenue claims from a taxpayer even when that taxpayer has relocated his/her economic activities to low-tax country B, then there is no sense in which the individual taxpayer can evade the tax claims advanced by government A.[38] The taxpayer will be subject to government A's high rates of taxation wherever s/he chooses to live or to exercise his/her economic activities. (Americans, for example, cannot escape US taxation of their overseas incomes if the US taxes incomes earned in other countries.)

There are two preconditions for a government A to be able to tax an individual (or company) who would instead prefer to regard him/herself as the tax subject of country B: that government A can gain information about what taxable transactions the individual is engaged in, and that government A can enforce its demands for tax payments. As long as the individual is engaged in some activities (residence, owning property and so on) in country A that government can normally enforce its demands for tax payments by threatening to penalize the individual's activities inside country A. There also exist bilateral agreements by which governments help collect each other's tax revenues in relevant cases.[39]

Before a government can collect tax payments, however, government A also needs information about what taxable economic activities the individual is engaged in inside country B. According to the OECD any 'lack of effective exchange of information is one of the key factors . . . since it limits the access by tax authorities to the information required for the correct and timely application of tax laws'.[40] A second method of tax harmonization is therefore to engage in information exchanges between the tax authorities of different nations. In this case two (or more) governments enter into agreements that they will mutually provide economic information about the foreigners who reside/work in their territories. Once such information is provided the relevant government can collect tax payments even on assets or incomes that are held/earned outside the country, which impedes tax competition.

Many countries have bilateral agreements about this form of information exchange. In terms of multilateral measures the EU, for example, in 2003 passed a 'savings directive'. The aim of this directive is 'to enable savings income in the form of interest payments made in one Member State to beneficial owners who are individuals resident in another Member State to be made subject to effective taxation in accordance with the laws of the latter Member State.'[41] The directive came into effect in 2005, and it is as yet too early to analyse its consequences.

In 1998 the OECD published a famous report, *Harmful Tax Competition: An Emerging Global Issue*, which focused on information exchange. This report states that 'Governments cannot stand back while their tax bases are eroded through the actions of countries which offer taxpayers ways to exploit tax havens and preferential tax regimes to reduce the tax that would otherwise be payable to them.'[42] The report especially focuses on 'tax havens' and 'preferential tax regimes', which it identifies as having a number of particular characteristics[43] (see Table 6.1).

Table 6.1   OECD (1998), characteristics of tax havens and preferential tax regimes

Tax havens	Preferential tax regimes
Have no or low effective tax rates	Have no or low effective tax rates
Suffer from a lack of transparency	Suffer from a lack of transparency
Suffer from a lack of effective exchange of information	Suffer from a lack of effective exchange of information
No substantial economic activities	Ring-fencing of low-tax regimes

That these jurisdictions 'suffer from a lack of transparency' means that the application of their tax laws is not easily understandable to outsiders. That 'no substantial activities' are required means that in tax havens companies can book paper profits or hold passive investments without otherwise engaging in value-adding activities in that nation. 'Ring-fencing' means that in preferential tax regimes foreign companies may operate under more favourable tax rules than the companies that are domestic to that nation, or may not compete with such companies.[44]

Based on this characterization the OECD has identified various states (and dominions) as 'tax havens' and 'preferential tax regimes'. The report makes 15 recommendations as to how to combat harmful tax competition, and most of these recommendations focus on implementing information exchange. The OECD has subsequently put pressure on the relevant tax havens to adopt the information exchange mechanisms that it recommends. In a similar manner the EU has agreed on a 'code of conduct' and within that remit the Primarolo report (1999) worked on roughly the same issues as the OECD report.[45] (Countries such as Switzerland, which has a strong tradition of bank secrecy, have objected to demands for such information exchanges.[46])

6.5   ASSESSING THE ARGUMENTS AGAINST TAX COMPETITION

The main arguments against tax competition, and the main methods for achieving tax harmonization, have been introduced very briefly above. In fact an individual paper could be written about each of these topics, but within this section of this chapter I will only assess the validity of each of the arguments very briefly. I will especially consider to what extent tax harmonization aims at addressing market failures that are serious enough to motivate the introduction of tax cartels.

6.5.1 Does Tax Competition Distort Investments and Trade?

It sounds appealing that the productivity of production factors, rather than arbitrary tax rates, should determine the allocation of investments and trade. In international taxation the doctrine of capital export neutrality (CEN) does not stand alone, however; it is rivalled by another doctrine, that of capital import neutrality (CIN).[47] This 'posits that investments in a particular country should face the same tax rate no matter where the investor resides.'[48] The EU Commission, and the EU Court of Justice, for example, both favour the principle of capital import neutrality.[49] Capital import neutrality could be violated if tax harmonization was accomplished along the lines of residence-based taxation combined with effective information exchange. In such a case a resident of high-tax country A might not pay the same tax rate as a resident in low-tax country B, if both considered making an investment in some country C. Since competing doctrines exist, capital export neutrality should not simply be accepted at face value as a standard for evaluating tax competition.

Market failures must be serious if they are going to justify the introduction of tax cartels, however, and even if CEN is accepted it is not clear that it entails a critical assessment of tax competition. In fact it can be argued that the CEN doctrine only provides a valid argument against tax competition if it is assumed that governments provide no valuable outputs.

The CEN doctrine suggests that for an individual investor I the tax systems in nations A and B should not influence I's decision as to whether to invest in country A instead of investing in nation B. If the availability of good and cheap factor inputs in country A are better than in country B, this should increase the productivity of any investment I makes in A and enable him/her to earn higher unit returns. This way it is ensured that resources are invested where they are put to their highest use.

Prima facie it appears appealing that tax-induced distortions should not determine investment decisions, but that the productivity of underlying input factors should do so. It does not necessarily follow that this is a valid argument against tax competition, however.

Presumably governments offer their taxpayers something in return for the tax payments they make.[50] Governments provide different kinds of infrastructure, most importantly social infrastructure, in terms of defining and enforcing a set of rules (a legal framework) that coordinate how different actors may interact in their society.[51] They also provide systems of transport and communication, and education, medical services, social insurances and so on. When an investor considers whether to invest in country A or country B s/he rationally considers the total bundle of production factors offered by both private actors and governmental actors in the relevant nation. An investor does not only consider the rate of taxes in each nation, but also which such infrastructural production factors each relevant government offers.[52] From the investor's point of view it is rational to regard the tax rate as the 'price' that he needs to pay in order to gain access to the infrastructural facilities that a particular government offers inside its borders.[53] A government that provides good infrastructure at low tax rates clearly is in a good position to attract investment, but a high-tax government that offers high-quality infrastructure can conceivably still attract capital away from a low-tax nation that offers poor infrastructure.

If we accept that governments offer some important production factor(s), and that the tax rates to some extent reflect the monetary sacrifices that investors must make in exchange for gaining access to these production factors, then it is no longer clear that tax competition distorts investments. If the availability of good and cheap factor inputs in country A are better than in country B, this should increase the productivity of any investment I makes in A (regardless of whether the government or the private sector supply them). This holds even if we take tax rates into account, because if the tax rates were not competitive, then (government provided) factor inputs would simply not be cheap in the relevant nation.

In fact, the best way to ensure that tax rates reflect the relative value of the production factors that governments make available is presumably to expose them to competition, since non-competitive markets are notorious for producing market outcomes where prices do not equal marginal costs. Since the tax rate is comparable to the 'price' on ordinary markets it seems perfectly natural that tax competition should be the preferred outcome. In fact, one might well say that the CEN doctrine should more or less automatically imply tax competition as the recommended outcome. Tax competition would ensure that governments offered production factors at the correct tax/price levels. The argument presented in Section 6.3.1 therefore appears as less than convincing.

Furthermore, the argument that tax competition distorts investments does not concern any market failure in the ordinary sense of markets that fail to clear and so on. It is not clear how any Pareto improvement could be effected by reducing tax competition for this particular reason. Instead it could be argued that, if anything, tax competition could help facilitate the capture of more mutual gains from trade since tax competition facilitates the pricing of public services, and thus make a more comprehensive market trading system possible. Removing tax competition will probably not reduce any market failure, but rather worsen it.

CEN does not appear as a natural premise for arguing against tax competition if one accepts the assumption that governments offer important production factors in return for the tax revenues they collect. It is, of course possible to reject this assumption, but this represents a cynical view of government that would hardly be accepted by most persons who oppose tax competition. Especially, it would undermine argument 6.3.2 because if it is assumed that governments do not provide any useful goods/services in return for tax revenues then it is not clear why it would be any problem if tax bases were eroded and governments became less able to collect tax revenues.

6.5.2 Eroding the Tax Bases of Welfare States

Perhaps the most important argument against tax competition suggests that it is problematic because it erodes tax bases so that it becomes impossible to maintain ambitious welfare states (and to provide public goods). The underlying problem is that this would inhibit the satisfaction of the expressed desires of a majority of individuals in society.

If it is true that low-tax governments attract capital away from high-tax jurisdictions this would not involve market failures in the sense of Pareto losses, however. What would happen is simply that low-tax governments would be out-competing high-tax governments in their competition for tax revenues and international investments. This is clearly a question about the distribution of benefits between relevant governments and does not involve any obvious scope for Pareto improvements for all actors. Neither does it appear to involve missed opportunities to capture mutual gains from trade. (At most, if country A adopted a low tax rate, which attracted capital away from country B, then one could possible say that A imposed a negative externality on B. However, this would stretch the meaning of 'externalities' to the limits of credibility, because this would amount to saying that all economic competition should be limited, in order to limit the externalities that competitors impose on each other.) This argument therefore does not involve identifying any conventional market failure as a justification for introducing tax cartels.

Furthermore, it is not clear that institutional competition will necessarily result in either lowering government tax rates or tax revenues, or that it will result in decreasing the output of government services. The degree of competition does not alone determine the size of the government; many other variables also influence outcomes, including demography, endogenous and domestic productivity growth, and international migration. More importantly, institutions may not only compete with price, but also with the quality of its outputs (that is, institutions can both price differentiate and product differentiate). An institution that offers good outputs at high prices might out-compete an institution which offers poor services at low prices. The primary effect of competition is not necessarily to drive down tax rates (or prices charged by other institutions). The important point is that competition allows prices to reflect relative scarcity, and, as such, institutional competition would enable institutions to align their supply of services with the preferences of the relevant consumers.

To understand this argument it is useful to consider Tiebout's classic model of fiscal competition.[54] A classic problem is how to establish a demand function for public goods. For private goods an aggregate demand function is derived by adding each individual's demand for a good (at a given price) to every other individual's demand. This does not work for public goods, however. The demand functions of different individuals may not be added to each other, because once one consumer has bought some units of the public good other individuals may free-ride on this provision, and themselves fail to buy further units of the good.

Tiebout's model addressed this issue by turning the attention towards 'local public goods'. In contrast to a 'pure public good' we may define a local public good as 'a good that must be supplied to all possible consumers within a group – but none outside that group – if it is supplied to any consumer within that group'. A classic example is the swimming club that provides a swimming pool – all members of the club have access to the pool, but non-members do not. In fact, the provision of such local public goods is typical of modern governments. Tiebout models situations in which different governments provide local public goods in competition with each other. Tiebout's model incorporates several assumptions:

1. Within a larger area several (local) governments exist, which supply local public goods and collect taxes.
2. Many local communities, with such local governments, exist.
3. Constituents can move without cost to the community that best satisfies their preferences.
4. Constituents have full information about what public goods are provided by different communities, and what tax rates are charged in different communities.
5. No externalities (spillover effects) exist between the communities.

If these assumptions hold, Tiebout argues that each constituent rationally moves to the community that best satisfies his/her own preferences. Constituents vote with their feet. Each local government is assumed to have set levels of taxation and public goods provision. A constituent's willingness to move into a community indicates that he/she is willing to pay the tax rate imposed there in order to gain access to the bundle of public goods that is provided. As such it can be assumed that each constituent's preferences are satisfied.[55] Each individual's demand for local public goods will be revealed as the amount and mix actually supplied in his/her particular community, and the local tax rates will also reflect different individuals' willingness to pay for the public goods.

Tiebout's model suggests that the argument that tax competition erodes the ability to implement the preferred tax levels is mistaken, because according to Tiebout's model, competition between the local governments reveals the preferences for public goods, and satisfies them. Furthermore, in Tiebout's model there is no implication that tax rates will necessarily be driven down to sub-optimal levels. On the contrary, if there is a high demand for local public goods, then this will be reflected in many constituents moving into communities which charge high tax rates in order to provide high quantities of local public goods. Tax competition might reduce the scope for politicians to allocate resources in ways that would be inefficient from taxpayers' point of view, but it would hardly reduce tax revenues automatically. The tax rates set under competition would instead reveal taxpayers' willingness to pay for the provision of local public goods.

If tax competition makes tax rates reflect the relative scarcity and subjective valuation of government services, then it is not clear how this would represent any market failure that would require 'remedy' through the introduction of tax cartels.

Neither is it clear empirically that tax competition actually erodes the finances of welfare states. One review suggests that tax competition does have some effects on company taxation, but it is unclear what the nature or magnitude of these effects are.[56] Radaelli argues that both theoretically and 'Empirically, the studies conducted so far come to no definite conclusions.'[57] There might be a tendency for tax rates to fall, but no obvious tendency for a fall in government revenues (perhaps because tax bases tend to be broadened). Current empirical findings, including those presented in this volume, seem to lend no clear support to this argument against tax competition.

Although Tiebout's argument overtly concerns local public goods it in fact applies to most welfare state programmes. Most goods and services provided in welfare states are not inherently non-excludable; persons can be excluded from them. To mention some examples: pupils can easily be excluded from public schooling, and patients can easily be denied medical treatment. The relevant authorities can simply deny them access to the relevant premises. But these services are provided to all members of the relevant group, as if they were public goods. It is simply the normative credo of the welfare state that all persons within the state should be able to partake of the same services. Usually such goods and services are denied to persons not living in the relevant state, however. So they are equivalent to local public goods in the relevant sense. Arguments 6.3.2 against tax competition therefore appears inconsistent with Tiebout's model.

Clearly, Tiebout makes strict assumptions and it is easy to disagree with these. Assumptions (2) and (4) resemble ordinary assumptions about perfectly competitive markets with perfect information – as if we were analysing any other market for goods and services. But even if we disagree with these assumptions we would not ordinarily take this as an argument in favour of creating monopolized or cartelized markets, if we were talking of other markets.[58] Yet this is precisely the argument put forward by the proponents of tax harmonization.

Assumption (3) is also easy to dispute – people cannot move easily and costlessly between nations; due to language and cultural barriers they largely prefer to stay in their native countries. This deviation from Tiebout's ideal type does not lend credence to the arguments that tax competition erodes the tax bases of welfare states, however. If there are transaction costs for taxpayers to move to alternative providers of public goods and welfare programmes this in effect means that they will be less sensitive to high taxes/prices for such goods and services. Indeed governments might well be able to charge excessive tax rates for this reason – since constituents prefer to stay in their own land their governments can basically charge a 'land rent' from them. This is, of course, problematic from a preference satisfaction point of view, but it does not mean that governments' ability to charge taxes will be eroded through tax competition – quite the opposite.

More genuine problems might perhaps arise if assumption (5) is violated, in effect, if we are no longer discussing local public goods, but pure public goods – if externalities exist between the communities. In such cases it is quite possible that there will be problems, whether taxation is competitive or harmonized. However, so far the policy literature has not generally concerned itself with externality or public goods problems, or demonstrated that tax harmonization could address such problems. Indeed, in general, the policy arguments have not concerned market failures serious enough to motivate the introduction of cartels on otherwise competitive markets.

6.5.3   Does Tax Competition Shift the Tax Burden from Capital to Labour?

Argument 6.3.3 suggests that tax competition would shift the tax burden from capitalists towards workers since the mobile factor capital could more easily escape taxation than the immobile factor labour.

The distinction between capital and labour is simplistic, however, and need not be co-extensive with the distinction between mobile and immobile tax bases. It is perhaps true that mobile tax bases will more easily escape taxation, but some forms of capital are not mobile. Such capital includes, for example, landed property, buildings, asset-specific investments, and heavy plant investments in factories. Furthermore, labour may itself involve elements of capital, such as human capital or educational capital.[59] Different kinds of workers are also differently mobile – highly educated and highly paid workers are generally more sensitive to tax competition.[60] In addition, tax burdens may also be shifted from taxation of incomes toward taxation of consumption.[61] Even if it is true that tax burdens will shift from immobile towards mobile tax bases it is therefore simplistic to translate this into a Marxist distinction between capital and labour.

Furthermore, there are probably interaction effects between the taxation of capital and labour. An investor considering whether to invest his capital in a factory in a particular country will consider how this capital will interact with other production factors, including labour. In fact, total labour costs are probably one of the most important determinants of average returns to investments in many OECD countries. A rational investor will consider total average costs, including total labour costs. Since the tax on labour heavily determines total labour costs the level of labour taxation will factor into any investor's judgement when considering whether to invest capital in a nation. Thus it is not clear that a government can simply shift tax burdens from capital to labour in order to stem investment flight resulting from tax competition.

If tax competition shifts tax burdens from capital to labour this clearly does not concern any market failure, as discussed in this chapter. The normative question about shifting tax burdens from capital to labour is ultimately a question of redistribution – should costs be redistributed from capitalists to workers, or should costs be redistributed the other way round? Since one party is made worse off in each case there is no room for uncontroversial Pareto improvements or increasing gains from trade. Although everyone can have an opinion on this, it is clear that no uncontroversial argument about whether it is good or bad thing if tax competition results in a shifting of the tax burden can be produced. In the context of this argument, eliminating tax competition will not remove any market failure in the sense that it will represent a Pareto improvement.

In economics literature, there has, however, been a great deal of work on what 'deadweight costs' are imposed by different kinds of taxation, that is, costs that are unnecessary and whose removal would facilitate a Pareto improvement for all parties. Diamond and Mirrless (1971) derived a theoretical result demonstrating that taxes that distort (mobile) production are worse than taxes that distort (immobile) consumption. Chamley (1986) derived another theoretical result suggesting that in order to minimize distortions and excess burdens in the economy there should be no taxation of capital, but only taxation of labour and consumption.[62] How these results can be practically applied is still contested, but in principle they do suggest that if tax competition does result in a shifting of the tax burden from capital towards labour and consumption this might be a good, rather than a bad thing.

6.5.4 Summary of the Arguments for Tax Harmonization

Above I have briefly reviewed the most important policy arguments for tax harmonization, that:

> Tax competition distorts investments and trade.
> Tax competition undermines the Wnancing of welfare states.
> Tax competition will shift the tax burden from capital to labour.

None of these arguments appear to involve clear market failures in the sense described in this chapter; they do not involve strictly Pareto-inferior situations, or problems with clearing markets and so on. Instead it appears that tax competition enables governments to set tax rates that reflect relative scarcity and the subjective valuation of the services that governments provide. As such it remains unclear whether these arguments provide any firm justification for the introduction of tax cartels, since such cartels themselves represent serious market failures and undermine the opportunities for tax rates to reflect relative scarcity.

If, and when, genuine market failures are invoked the argument for tax harmonization would appear stronger. Sinn, for example, has invoked market failures to argue that competition between governments makes it difficult or impossible to sustain welfare states (which he primarily regards as insurances states). According to Sinn welfare states' 'Redistribution of . . . incomes can be seen as insurance' because it can reduce random variations in individuals' incomes.[63] He argues that private markets cannot adequately provide such insurances, due to adverse selection problems and asymmetric information. However, if welfare states compete with each other, then low-risk individuals will arguably migrate to low-insurance states; while high-risk individuals will migrate to welfare states with high insurance cover. Thus institutional competition allegedly results in market failures; due to this adverse selection problem the tax base will be undermined for the high-tax countries that supply high social insurance.[64]

However, it is not clear that this concerns a genuine market failure in the sense that information asymmetries lead to failures of markets to clear. In the EU recently, the failure has not been one of identifying high-risk individuals (several high-tax countries have identified high-risk groups – East European immigrants – and denied them access to these countries), rather it is the EU credo of free movement for all persons that makes it difficult to deny access to high-risk groups and individuals into welfare states. Asymmetric information therefore does not appear as the real problem. Neither does there seem to be a real problem in clearing markets for 'good risks' – these individuals can move into low-insurance nations if they wish, and thereby conclude insurance contracts with those low-tax governments. Markets can thus clear. Possibly Sinn is correct in that this might erode the tax bases of high-tax/high-insurance governments, but this is a distributional concern about the distribution of costs and revenues between high-tax and low-tax governments, not a Pareto-relevant failure of markets to clear, (as in Akerlof's case).

Sinn's argument also appears less convincing because he basically assumes away cases of successful market competition by making heroic assumptions, such as 'governments have [only] taken over all those activities which the private market has proved unable to carry out' (his 'selection principle').[65] And from this premise he infers that if institutional competition between welfare states occur (a market-like provision of insurances), then market failures will occur. Since the important conclusion appears in the premise the argument is not overly convincing. It is also problematic that Sinn assumes this 'selection principle' for heuristic analytical purposes, and admits that it is an open empirical question whether the assumption is actually correct.[66] If the pressures of institutional competition are impeded one wonders what incentives governments would really have to limit themselves to providing only what private markets fail to provide.

I have criticized Sinn above, yet it is because I find Sinn's argument serious and interesting enough to be worth the criticism. Arguably Sinn is on the right track when he criticizes tax competition by attempting to invoke genuine market failures. If serious market failures, like cartels, are to be defended in the field of taxation, then strong arguments are needed.

6.6 UNINTENDED PRESSURE FOR EXCESSIVE TAX INCREASES?

In this section I will briefly outline a finding that suggests that introducing tax harmonization might well produce unintended incentives to raise taxation to excessive levels – levels even higher than those desired by the persons who oppose tax competition.

Sinn (2002) has noted that if tax competition is impeded this might only result in another kind of institutional competition between governments. The argument is that if impeded tax competition means that a government cannot attract investments by offering lower tax rates it might instead attempt to compete by increasing public expenditures and providing better infrastructures for the companies or individuals it hopes to attract.[67] Impeded tax competition might then be replaced by a new competition over public expenditures.

The argument seems compelling, and if correct would suggest that impeded tax competition might soon lead governments to adopt excessive levels of public expenditures that would not have been desired domestically. These expenditures must (in the longer term) be financed through taxation, which will result in increased tax rates. Impeded tax competition would therefore result in unintended incentives to raise taxation to excessive levels. The incentives are there to set tax rates that are even higher than would rationally be desired by any ordinary cartel. It could well be that it is tax harmonization that would provide the incentive for a 'race to the bottom.'

6.7   CONCLUSIONS

This chapter has briefly reviewed arguments for limiting tax competition and methods of implementing tax harmonization. Three main arguments for limiting competition in the field of taxation were considered. None of these arguments clearly involved market failures, as commonly understood, to justify limiting competition. This leaves the question open as to whether it can really be considered justified to create cartels in the area of taxation. But other uncertainties also plagued the three arguments.

Theoretically, the argument that tax competition distorts investments was seen to depend on the assumption that governments do not provide valued goods and services. If they do, then tax rates would – under competitive taxation – presumably reflect the relative value of such services, not distort investments. The argument that tax competition erodes the tax bases of welfare states was similarly seen to be unreliable; in most situations tax competition would allow politicians to align the welfare provided by governments along the lines of the preferences and demands of their constituents, and what quantity is demanded is an open question. The argument that tax competition will redistribute the tax burden from mobile capital towards immobile labour appeared simplistic since the distinction between capital and labour is not necessarily coextensive with the distinction between mobile and immobile tax bases. Furthermore, since these redistributive questions do not involve simple Pareto improvements it is not clear which outcomes should be regarded as either good or bad. Summarized thus, the arguments against tax competition do not appear overly convincing.

The OECD's report, in turn, does not analyse what costs tax competition actually imposes, but only the possible policy measures that may be undertaken to limit such competition. The message seems to be that governments that do not engage in tax information exchange are to be regarded as 'tax havens' and the absence of mechanisms for information exchange in itself represents 'harmful tax competition'. Two OECD members – Switzerland and Luxembourg – thus criticized the report, and refused to ratify it, on the grounds that it was 'partial and unbalanced'.[68]

Meanwhile this chapter has suggested that tax harmonization, in its essentials, should be considered equivalent to the formation of tax cartels – the attempt (through collusion) to maintain higher tax rates (prices) than would prevail under unregulated competitive conditions. On ordinary markets interventions or regulation are not proposed unless some 'market failure', such as externalities, or the presence of monopolies, has been identified. The arguments against tax competition, however, do not concern such Pareto relevant market failures, but seem to focus on cases where one actor is out-competed by another, where it is simply suggested that a form of quasi-monopoly – a cartel – should be introduced. But if there exists no market failure, why introduce a new market failure – a cartel – as a remedy?

Do the OECD and the EU really want to lead the way towards creating new cartels? Radaelli argues that the EU 'Commission does not have much theoretical and empirical evidence at its disposal [regarding tax competition]. But instead of investing in scientific expertise, the Commission has stressed a political determination to act [against tax competition].'[69] It must be asked: *is this wise?*

NOTES

1. Jacques Chirac, *Le Monde*, 7 March 2002.
2. Pascal Lamy, *Financial Times*, 8 March 2002.
3. Radaelli (1999, pp. 668–9).
4. Radaelli (1999, pp. 662, 673, 674).
5. OECD (1998, p. 3 (foreword)).
6. We could theoretically imagine non-competition agreements aiming to *lower* tax rates. However, the main argument (Section 6.3.2) against tax competition points out the need for increasing tax rates through harmonization, and the practice of harmonizing VAT has also increased tax rates. So, for the moment it seems most relevant to consider attempts to use tax harmonization to *increase* tax rates.
7. Samuelson and Nordhaus (1987, p. 48).
8. Olson (1965, p. 14).
9. See Baumol (1952, p. 55). (In this case the contributors provide a positive externality – the opportunity to consume the public good – to the non-contributors.)
10. Baumol (1952, p. 55; see also pp. 56, 180, 182, 191).

11. Rasmusen (1989, pp. 182–4).
12. See Cowen and Crampton (2002, p. 6) who provide an introduction to the subject.
13. Stiglitz (2002a, p. 33).
14. Stiglitz (2002b, p. 50).
15. Stiglitz (2002b, p. 57).
16. Cited in Radaelli (1999, pp. 674–5).
17. Radaelli (1999, p. 669).
18. This chapter does not therefore primarily focus on academic arguments as presented for example by Sinn, 2003 or Oates, 1972.
19. Exceptions to this rule may be when social rates of return deviate from private rates of return.
20. Edwards and de Rugy (2002, p. 14); Radaelli (1999, p. 67).
21. Nordic Council (2002, p. 3).
22. Edwards and de Rugy (2002, p. 3).
23. OECD (1998, articles 8, 29).
24. Radaelli (1999, p. 670); Sinn (2003, Chapter 2).
25. Sinn (2003, p. 24); Persson (2003, p. 39). See also Bergh (Chapter 8 in this volume).
26. SOU (2002: 47, pp. 34, 61, 456, 457); Edwards and de Rugy (2002, p. 11).
27. The reason that mobile tax bases are not highly taxed may be that low tax rates have been set for them precisely as a response to anticipated tax competition. Therefore it is not sufficient to argue that tax competition is relatively unimportant because it only applies to (mobile) capital, and capital taxes account only for a small part of government revenues. Counterfactually, had not tax competition existed, capital taxation could have accounted for a larger proportion of government revenues.
28. OECD (1998, article 30); Radaelli, (1999, p. 670).
29. Radaelli (1999, p. 669); OECD (1998, p. 56).
30. Lionel Jospin, 'Je m'engage', Jospin's Election Manifesto, 22 March 2002.
31. Radaelli (1999, pp. 662, 673).
32. Radaelli (1999, p. 674).
33. SOU (2002: 47, p. 465).
34. Some classes of goods/services are exempted from this rule and may be taxed at lower levels.
35. SOU (2002: 47, pp. 52, 337).
36. Edwards and de Rugy (2002, pp. 10, 15).
37. Persson (2003, pp. 18–21).
38. Sinn (2003, p. 63).
39. SOU (2002: 47, p. 426).
40. OECD (1998, article 54).
41. EU Council Directive 2003/48/EC, article 8.
42. OECD (1998, article 85).
43. OECD (1998, pp. 23, 27).
44. OECD (1998, articles 49, 52, 62); Dahlberg (1999, pp. 211–13).
45. SOU (2002: 47, pp. 168–9).
46. OECD (1998, pp. 73–8).
47. SOU (2002: 47, p. 140); Edwards and de Rugy (2002, p. 15).
48. Edwards and de Rugy (2002, p. 15).
49. SOU (2002: 47, pp. 162–3).
50. To be sure there is no strict connection between the payment of individual tax dollars and receiving particular services in returns – taxes are not fees. Nevertheless, the standard assumption is that taxpayers receive loosely-defined bundles of goods and services in return for the taxes they pay (even if it is not always the bundles that the taxpayers would themselves prefer).
51. See Höijer (Chapter 1).
52. Persson (2003, p. 23).
53. See for example Sinn (2003, pp. 35, 36).
54. Tiebout, reprinted in Cowen (1992, pp. 179–92).

55. If the number of communities is infinite, then constituents' preferences are even perfectly satisfied, because then each constituent can form his own community with his preferred levels of taxation and public goods provision. This is, however, an unrealistic assumption due to scale economies.
56. Persson (2003, p. 25).
57. Radaelli (1999, p. 671).
58. See, however, Section 6.5.4 for Sinn's interesting argument about reducing tax competition in order to alleviate adverse selection problems.
59. Persson (2003, p. 16).
60. Edwards and de Rugy (2002, p. 15); Sinn (2003, p. 28).
61. OECD (1998, p. 56).
62. Persson (2003, pp. 15–16).
63. Sinn (2003, pp. 81–2).
64. Sinn (2003, chapter 3).
65. Sinn (2003, p. 7).
66. Sinn (2003, pp. 13, 49).
67. Sinn (2003, pp. 52–4).
68. OECD (1998, pp. 73–8).
69. Radaelli (1999, p. 671).

REFERENCES

Baumol, J.W. (1952), *Welfare Economics and the Theory of the State*, London: The London School of Economics.

Chamley, Christophe (1986), 'Optimal Taxation of Capital Income in General Equilbrium with Infinite Lives', *Econometrica*, **54**(3), 607–622.

Chirac, Jacques (2002), *Le Monde*, 7 March 2002.

Cowen, T. (ed.) (1992), *Public Goods and Market Failures*, New Brunswick: Transaction Publishers.

Cowen, T. and E. Crampton (eds) (2002), *Market Failure or Success*, Cheltenham, UK and Northampton, MA, USA: Edward Elgar.

Dahlberg, M. (1999), 'Skattekonkurrensprojekten inom EU och OECD', pp. 209–21 in 'Skattenytt' (tidskriftsartikel)

Diamond, Peter and Mirrlees, James (1971), 'Optimal Taxation and Public Production I: Production Efficiency, and II: Tax rules, *American Economic Review*, **61**, 8–27 and 261–278.

Edwards, C. and V. de Rugy (2002), 'International Tax Competition: A 21st Century Restraint on Government', Cato Institute Report No. 431, Washington DC, http://www.cato.org/pub_display.php?pub_id=1290.

EU, Council Directive, 2003/48/EC.

Jospin, Lionel (2002), 'Je m'engage' (Jospin's Election Manifesto), 22 March 2002.

Lamy, Pascal (2002), *Financial Times*, 8 March 2002.

Oates, Wallace (1972), *Fiscal Federalism*, New York: Harcourt Brace Jovanovic.

Nordic Council (2002), *Skadelig skattekonkurrence i nordisk perspektiv*, A Report by the Nordic Council.

OECD (1998), *Harmful Tax Competition, an Emerging Global Issue*, Paris: OECD.

Olson, M. (1965), *The Logic of Collective Action*, Cambridge MA: Harvard University Press.

Persson, M. (2003), *Skatterna – konkurrens eller harmonisering*, Stockholm: SIEPS.

Institutional competition

Radaelli, C. (1999), 'Harmful Policy Competition in the EU: Policy Narratives and Advocacy Coalitions', *Journal of Common Market Studies*, **37** (4), 661–82.
Rasmusen, E. (1989), *Games and Information*, Oxford: Blackwell.
Samuelson, P. and W. Nordhaus (1987), *Economics*, New York: McGraw-Hill.
Sinn, H.W. (2003), *The New Systems Competition*, Oxford: Basil Blackwell. (References in this chapter are to the online version available at www.cesifo-group.de/portal/page/portal/ifoContent/NeueSeiten/publ/einzelschriften/SINNBOOK1/30223F1B959D089FE0440003BA988603.
SOU (2002: 47), Våra Skatter, Stockholm, 2002 (an official report by the Swedish Government).
Stiglitz, J. (2002a), 'Toward a General Theory of Wage and Price Rigidities and Economic Fluctuations', in T. Cowen and E. Crampton (eds), *Market Failure or Success*, Cheltenham, UK and Northampton, MA, USA: Edward Elgar, pp. 31–40.
Stiglitz, J. (2002b), 'Kenyesian Economics and Critique of First Fundamental Theorem of Welfare Economics', in T. Cowen and E. Crampton (eds), *Market Failure or Success*, Cheltenham, UK and Northampton, MA, USA: Edward Elgar, pp. 41–65.
Tiebout, C. (1992), 'A Pure Theory of Local Expenditures', in T. Cowen (ed.), *Public Goods and Market Failures*, New Brunswick: Transaction Publishers, pp. 179–92.

7. Fiscal competition and the optimization of tax revenues for higher growth

Victoria Curzon-Price

Fiscal competition has been in the news ever since the OECD launched a campaign against 'harmful tax competition' in 1996. Nor is it likely to disappear any time soon. Instead, it is likely to intensify, as more and more governments resort to lower taxes to stimulate their economies. Is all tax competition harmful, or is it possible to distinguish between harmful and beneficial tax competition? Is it likely to result in a shifting of the tax burden from internationally mobile to immobile factors of production? And is even beneficial tax competition – supposing that it can be defined – not likely to end in a 'race to the bottom' – a race to cut taxes to such low levels that the very existence of the state as we know it might be threatened? The first part of this chapter will discuss the virtues of competition in general, and what fiscal competition in particular might yield, on both the positive and the negative side. We will suggest that the criterion of sector-specific misallocation of resources should be used to distinguish between harmful and beneficial tax competition. Section 7.2 will look at various tax regimes, which have sometimes been criticized by the OECD and EU, in the light of this criterion. Section 7.3 will discuss the pros and cons of fiscal competition in general, while Section 7.4 will judge the actual extent of fiscal competition today (2006) and its apparent impact on tax revenues and economic growth. Although most tax rates have indeed fallen, we find no 'race to the bottom' in tax revenues which, if anything, have risen. We furthermore find no evidence of a shift of taxation from mobile capital to immobile labour, although there is a slight shift from direct to indirect taxation. As this points in the direction of greater efficiency in tax collection, and in no way precludes income redistribution for the realization of social objectives on the expenditure side, the benefits of fiscal competition appear to outweigh the drawbacks, which for the moment are hypothetical only. We conclude that further fiscal competition is needed in order to encourage governments to optimize, rather than maximize, tax revenue and public expenditure.

7.1　DISTINGUISHING BETWEEN BENEFICIAL AND HARMFUL TAX COMPETITION

Competition is universally hailed as a 'good thing'. It is recognized as being socially superior to its opposite, namely a monopoly or a cartel. The reason is very simple: where there is competition, even among the few, the individual customer or small firm is much better treated. The scope for exploitation disappears. The competing firm must innovate, watch its cost structures, seek to please its market, and sell at market prices which it cannot raise without running the risk of seeing its customers shift to its competitors. A monopoly or cartel does none of these things. It exploits its customers and suppliers, does not care about costs, does not innovate, and prices its product to maximize its own utility function. The rents it extracts from its privileged position are usually dissipated in high salaries, long holidays and short working hours for its employees.

Anyone arguing against competition must bear the burden of proof, for the general presumption is heavily in favour.

Turning now to fiscal competition in particular, is this not also presumably a 'good thing', for the very same reasons that competition in general is to be preferred to monopoly? Fiscal competition is merely a special case of the more general phenomenon of institutional or regulatory competition, which both an Austrian like F.A. Hayek[1] and a neo-classical economist like Douglass C. North[2] have described as being a process whereby 'better' institutions (from a utilitarian standpoint) gradually replace worse ones. Thus fiscal competition could be expected to yield both lower taxes and more care in controlling the costs of raising them; greater attention would be paid to the rational management of public expenditure, and possibly even some institutional and regulatory innovation might occur. The taxpayer could expect to get better value in terms of public goods, per unit of tax effort, and s/he would enjoy more freedom to spend his/her own money as s/he pleases.

A fiscal monopoly, on the other hand, would tend to exploit its taxpayers to the hilt, waste their money, and meet every financial shortfall with higher taxes rather than lower expenditure, for this would be the easy way out, and there would be no restraining influence on its actions.

To the extent that government is not all-wise and benevolent, but rather subject to capture by[3] and of[4] special interest groups, many of the conventional arguments in favour of optimal public goods provision by the state fall by the wayside, for we learn that the state will tend to maximize, rather than optimize its role. If so, the case in favour of fiscal competition is stronger than ever.

What, then, might be its drawbacks? In an increasingly open world economy, where investments flow easily from one country to another, one country's tax system may have a negative impact on another's, and vice versa. One obvious negative spillover effect might occur when a tax-induced misallocation of resources spills over onto a neighbouring country through unfair competition in trade and investment. However, tax-induced misallocations which have no negative external effects must surely be permitted, since countries have no right to interfere in one another's sovereign affairs. A country's own internal misallocations must be considered to be motivated by a public policy agenda which overrides considerations of efficient allocation of resources, and to lie within the normal sovereign sphere of action of a modern state. Therefore, a useful guide to distinguishing between beneficial and harmful tax competition would be to distinguish between taxes which cause a clear *international* misallocation of resources, and which are therefore harmful to others, and those which do not. If fiscal competition were to reinforce harmful tax practices, then it would itself be harmful. On the other hand, if fiscal competition were to reinforce broad-based, non-discriminatory taxes, then it would tend to beneficial. We shall now use this guiding principle to judge various tax measures.

7.2   TESTING VARIOUS TAX MEASURES AGAINST THE EFFICIENCY CRITERION

7.2.1   Discriminatory Tax Regimes for Favoured Industries

When governments offer special tax regimes to the shipbuilding industry, or for oil exploration, or for informatics research, they are really offering a subsidy.[5] Such tax privileges distort the allocation of resources and are indeed harmful – harmful to the country engaging in them, harmful to the firms receiving the tax breaks (they are shielded from economic reality, and will in due course wither away precisely because once support is withdrawn, they will fail, whereas if they had been forced to face reality from the start, they might have had at least a chance of long-term survival) and ruinous for the exchequer if several governments decide to subsidize the same industry at the same time. Sectoral tax privileges are clearly harmful and competition in granting them simply makes things even worse. It is therefore no surprise that the EU and the GATT have strict rules and understandings limiting governments' freedom to act in this domain.

7.2.2   Non-discriminatory Tax Regimes

While sector-specific tax breaks, discussed above, distort the allocation of resources between sectors and are clearly harmful and banned in both the

WTO and the European Union, many governments use the tax code to pursue more general policy objectives, such as investment in general, or, more specifically, foreign direct investment. Clearly, the more 'general' a measure, and the less sector-specific it is, the less it distorts the allocation of resources, and the less harmful it is in economic terms. Competition between countries on matters of general taxation cannot be harmful, because it does not lead to an inter-sectoral misallocation of resources with negative international effects. It must therefore benefit from the general presumption in favour of competition outlined above, and be deemed beneficial. A generally favourable attitude to business, for instance, achieved by low taxes and light labour laws, might make a country prosperous, and might even attract investment from high-tax countries, but according to the above rule would not constitute harmful tax competition, even if it did appear to be 'bidding aggressively for the tax base of other countries'[6] (one of the OECD's definitions of 'harmful tax competition'). A moment's reflection will confirm, however, that this definition of 'harmful tax competition' is either wrong and/or inoperative: wrong, because light tax laws are not *necessarily* harmful, and might be beneficial to some; inoperative, because 'bidding aggressively' is in the eye of the beholder and would be stoutly denied, for instance, by a country like Estonia.[7] It is an unscientific and unverifiable criterion.

7.2.3 'Ring-fenced' Tax Regimes

Under the heading of 'ring-fencing' the OECD/EU identify, and condemn as being harmful, intermediate measures which are neither clearly sector-specific, nor absolutely general. Here, some distortion of resources occurs, and is indeed intended, in the name of public policy objectives of various kinds. By 'ring-fencing' the OECD/EU mean tax measures which distinguish between various potential taxpayers within the same tax jurisdiction, but which are not sector-specific.

For example, governments often offer tax inducements to foreign multinational firms, in the hope of attracting them to their shores. These tax privileges are 'ring-fenced' in that they are not available to local entrepreneurs, in the belief that foreign investments are somehow superior to local investment, or represent net new investment, and therefore need to be encouraged. Sometimes governments further limit such tax privileges to 'green-field' foreign direct investment, in the belief that a 'new' plant in a green field is somehow better for the economy than refurbishing an existing plant in an established industrial area (known as a 'brown-field' investment). Of course it does not matter which form the investment takes, as long as the existing assets (green or brown fields) are put to more productive use by more imaginative entrepreneurs. However, since the foreign entrepreneurs benefit from a tax privilege compared with local firms, we cannot be sure that this is in fact the case. In the meantime, the assets having been bought up by foreigners, the local sellers must then decide what to do with their money: since all countries offer much the same type of inducements, they will probably look abroad for an equivalent tax deal . . . Tax competition of this kind causes an over-stimulation of foreign, as opposed to domestic investment and is clearly harmful in an economic sense. But does it distort *international* competition? The answer is yes, but it is a matter of degree, and only a judicial or diplomatic procedure can identify the cases which deserve redress. For example, when the UK succeeds in attracting a major Japanese car manufacturer to Scotland with a tempting tax package, firms trying to make money from automobile production without tax breaks are clearly discriminated against, and may well complain. International misallocation spillovers occur within a single market like the EU or in global markets under the law of the WTO and give rise to disputes.

This type of competitive behaviour is a good example of 'bidding aggressively for the tax base of other countries'. It is clear that if all governments compete with each other to attract foreign multinationals, resource misallocation will surely occur and much taxpayers' money will be wasted. It certainly does not increase employment overall, even for the country which wins the race, since resources spent attracting foreign investment have to be taken from somewhere else in the economy. Both the OECD and the EU[8] have tried their best to outlaw such wasteful measures, which clearly distort markets in their actual application, even if formally they do not favour one sector over another.

Channelling foreign direct investment into economically backward regions is generally considered to be acceptable, at least in the EU, and will not be condemned as 'illicit state aid' as long as the investment takes place within the designated area and is not 'excessive'. Such policies find their justification in the notion of market failure, and the need for corrective government intervention. However, the aid must not *exceed* the failure, for that would constitute a subsidy. A considerable part of the EU budget and manpower is devoted to supervising and enacting the EU's regional policy. While neither the EU nor the OECD classify these policies as 'harmful tax competition' they do in fact create a distortion between subsidized and non-subsidized regions of a country, and shift employment and investment from one area to another. However, that is indeed their objective, and as long as the distortion exercises no negative competition externalities on other countries, it may generally be considered as non-harmful (but not necessarily beneficial) in terms of our classification system.

7.2.4   Other Forms of 'Ring-fencing'

Most countries tax their residents on the basis of the 'territorial principle': they tax income earned within the country, give tax credits on income earned abroad by their residents and already taxed once by a foreign tax authority, and they tax income earned by non-residents if it arises within their jurisdiction. It is generally agreed that income should not be taxed twice, giving rise to a dense network of double tax agreements which regulate the detailed application of these general rules. The United States is exceptional in that it taxes its citizens wherever they reside, on their worldwide income, but gives tax credits for any prior taxes paid to foreign tax authorities. Exceptions to these general rules exist, and give rise to the (perfectly legal) tax avoidance industry.

Among these exceptions is a policy which gives special tax status to firms or individuals who reside in one country, but who earn all their income abroad. This is perfectly consistent with the territorial principle, but the benefit is 'ring-fenced' since it is not available to other taxpayers in the domestic market and does not 'affect the national tax base'.[9]

The UK, for example, does not tax foreigners residing in the UK as long as all their income arises abroad, and many Swiss cantons negotiate the tax rate with wealthy foreign residents on condition that they earn nothing in Switzerland. So far, these practices have not caused international disputes, because no distortion of markets can be invoked. On the other hand, the United States for many years offered special tax advantages to domestic firms which earned over 95 per cent of their income from exports (the so-called 'Designated International Sales Corporation' or DISC). This was later amended to the 'Foreign Sales Corporation', or FSC, as a result of a successful complaint from the EU that the DISC regime was in effect an export subsidy, forbidden under GATT rules. In 2000 the WTO Dispute Settlement Body judged the FSC regime to be distortionary, also because it offered an effective export subsidy.[10] From an economic point of view, there is a clear distortion in the allocation of resources between products exported and similar products sold on the domestic market by the same firm.

7.2.5   'Ring-fenced' Holding Companies

However, the OECD and EU are not after the Swiss and British schemes to attract wealthy foreign residents (or not yet), and are happy to leave the DISC/FSC problem to the WTO. What they are really concerned about is ring-fenced international holding companies. These are well-known corporate devices which exist in order to hold shares in other companies, or to own patent or other rights which are then leased to 'daughter' companies in return for a fee. Firms operating in many countries find it useful to concentrate their 'holdings' in a single structure, especially if that structure is exempt from normal corporate tax. As far as the holding company's dividend income is concerned, this has usually been taxed at the 'daughter' company level, so it is normal that dividends paid to 'mother' should be tax exempt, or enjoy a lighter tax burden, and when the latter pays out dividends to the ultimate owner, incorporated in a high-tax country, these will be taxed according to the law of that state. However, it is frequently asserted that such holding companies are not transparent and may facilitate tax evasion through international transfer pricing, inflated service charges or exaggerated royalty payments. This may indeed be the case, but it is a long-established principle that one country does not enforce another's tax laws,[11] so it is up to each sovereign state to enforce its own laws. In fact, most countries have very strict laws which allow tax authorities to bring declared inter-firm prices into line with market prices.

This question is, however, different from whether a 'ring-fenced' international holding company, by nature, distorts the international allocation of resources. The answer is not quite the same as that given earlier with regard to encouraging inward foreign direct investment with tax holidays. The international holding company attracts inward capital flows and encourages outward foreign investment. It concentrates capital on the inward flows, and then disperses it again on the outward flows. It provokes, on its own account, no inter-sectoral misallocation of resources, and therefore according to our standard cannot be considered harmful.

7.2.6 No or Low Effective Tax Rates[12]

The OECD, in its first report on 'Harmful tax competition', was unwise enough to claim that general, non-discriminatory, low or zero tax rates could be 'harmful', if used in conjunction with other 'harmful practices', such as ring-fencing, lack of transparency, or lack of information-sharing between tax authorities, if they shifted resources, and hence economic activity, away from high and towards low-tax countries.[13]

This is close enough to saying that low taxes are harmful because they attract mobile productive resources from high-tax countries. But are mobile productive resources not fair game? As long as there is no inter-sectoral misallocation of resources, it cannot be a crime to attract them. Resources move to where their general overall rate of return is the highest, and tax treatment is only part of a long list of variables which will be taken into consideration by investors.

To say that low taxes are harmful because they shift mobile resources in their direction is much the same as saying that low wages in China are harmful because they shift resources, and hence economic activity, away from high-wage Europe to low-wage China. For sure, such things constitute competition, but it is not harmful competition, because it does not distort the allocation of resources. Thus, as far as wage differentials are concerned, China attracts resources into labour-intensive industries, while Europe attracts resources into capital-intensive sectors. Far from being inefficient, this shift of resources is generally considered to be positive and in line with comparative advantage. As for international tax differentials, as long as they are sectorally neutral, any investments which do occur because of them will presumably reflect the host country's underlying pattern of comparative advantage, and cannot be considered harmful or distortionary in any way. Generally low taxes, like market-friendly laws or an incorruptible judiciary, are part of the general factor endowments of a country, and will help to determine the overall level of economic activity. This is sometimes called 'absolute advantage', in contrast to comparative advantage, and intergovernmental competition in shaping absolute advantage is sometimes referred to as institutional competition. Since it does not distort comparative advantage, nowhere is it condemned in international law.

Furthermore, unlike the climate, or natural resources, laws, including tax laws, are man-made and can be changed. Therefore the high-tax country, if it wants to attract economic activity, and even retain such economic activity as it still has, is free to modify its policies, if it so desires. Conversely, it is not at all clear why the low-tax country should alter its laws to suit the high-tax state. Each country remains fully sovereign in this regard.

The OECD's definition of harmful tax competition in these terms is also almost naively transparent. If tax competition is deemed 'harmful' when it is likely to shift resources, and hence economic activity, away from high and towards low-tax countries, the OECD is making the implicit claim that high-tax, big governments are somehow 'better' than low-tax, small ones.

7.2.7 Transparency and Exchange of Information

Many 'tax havens', which make a business of taking in the savings of residents of high-tax countries and investing them in tax-free securities, have strict bank-secrecy laws and do not share any information with foreign tax authorities concerning their clients, unless the latter can show that they suspect criminal activity. They do not make easily available the identity of the beneficial owner of this or that account or shareholding (although they 'know their customer' because they must be able to respond to a request for information from criminal investigations). According to the OECD, such countries 'lack transparency' and are liable to be accused of harmful tax competition.

Thus the OECD supports the idea of information-sharing between tax authorities, on request, while the EU would like to instigate automatic, permanent and comprehensive information flows between tax authorities. Either would put an immediate stop to people accumulating savings in tax havens and omitting to declare them to their own tax authorities. It is of course illegal not to declare assets and income held abroad, but the fact that some people are driven to this extreme suggests that in some countries taxes have reached unacceptably high levels. In exactly the same fashion, people are also driven to hide some of their economic activity from the taxman, giving rise to the well-known phenomenon of the underground economy.[14] In fact, tax evasion is as old as taxes themselves, and the best way to minimize it is to levy reasonable taxes.

International tax evasion and the local underground economy provide the two main escape routes. In modern democratic times, they also set implicit limits to the growth of government. They are both illegal, but the local shadow economy is now so widespread that governments know that they cannot enforce compliance without becoming hugely unpopular (suggesting that high taxes are, in fact, not as widely accepted by the population as some would like to think). Limiting international tax competition looks a much easier bet. However, if high-tax countries are successful in stopping the shift of savings to tax havens by enforcing transparency and information exchange, they will displace, but not halt, tax evasion and fiscal competition. The underground economy, both local and international, will grow. In the meantime, wealthy people and their assets will continue to move from high to low-tax environments. Over time, the economically more attractive places will still enjoy much higher rates of economic growth. So are high-tax countries really better off without fiscal competition?

Since full information sharing would put a stop to all international tax competition, it has become the main focus of both OECD and EU efforts in this area. The question which interests us, however, is whether tax evasion causes a distortion in the allocation of resources. The answer is surely no, for the same reasons outlined above. There is no inter-sectoral misallocation of resources. Savings are channelled to where returns are highest, almost never in the tax haven itself, which is just handling and collecting small streams of savings to form a great river of capital, which goes to whichever industry has successfully competed for it, wherever in the world that might be. In fact, tax havens perform a very useful job in this regard.[15]

7.2.8   Disagreement on the Nature of Tax Evasion/Avoidance

There is a fundamental difference of opinion between high and low-tax jurisdictions with regard to tax evasion (illegal) and tax avoidance (legal).

Apart from the fact that in low-tax jurisdictions most known forms of tax avoidance are perfectly legal, the high-tax jurisdiction will consider tax evasion to be a matter of criminal law, while the low-tax jurisdiction will usually consider it to be a civil offence, except in cases where fraud is involved. Switzerland, in particular, will only furnish information to foreign authorities if the case is deemed criminal in both jurisdictions (the principle of double incrimination). This means that Switzerland is fully compliant in all cases to do with fraud, money laundering, terrorism, corruption charges and criminal gangs' financial activities, but it does not cooperate with other countries in tracking down ordinary people who fail to report their savings. This act of omission is not a crime under Swiss law and they therefore do not consider themselves bound to furnish such information to foreign tax authorities. The difference may cause hollow laughter in high-tax jurisdictions, because here taxes have risen so much that the state must needs resort to threats of criminal proceedings and prison sentences to obtain compliance, whereas in low-tax jurisdictions, most people prefer to pay their taxes rather than risk being fined. When the OECD claims that 'lack of effective exchange of information' constitutes 'harmful tax competition' it shows that it has become the mouthpiece for high-tax jurisdictions. However, we have seen above that no distortion of economic activity is involved, so we ourselves would not cast it into this category.

7.3   INTERNATIONAL TAX COMPETITION: PROS AND CONS

7.3.1   The 'Race to the Bottom'

As mentioned in the introduction, this is often cited as the principal argument against fiscal competition. Clearly, we need the state, so we need taxes. No one is arguing in favour of pure anarchy, nor would it be chosen in any democratic society. However, there is a wide range of choice between the minimal night-watchman state and the all-embracing modern welfare state. In the *absence* of tax competition we would presumably get a 'race to the top'.

The neoclassical approach is to seek the optimum somewhere in between, the point where the marginal benefits of public and private expenditures are equal. However, neoclassical economics does not tell us how we find this point in practice. It tells us that the state is needed to supply pure public goods, like the police, justice, defence of property rights and national security, and simply assumes that a benevolent and just government will supply these goods up to the point where their marginal opportunity cost equals their marginal benefit. But is government really so benevolent and intelligent? More to the point, is it really interested in limiting itself in this way? And even if it were, how can it calculate the marginal benefit of extra spending on this or that public good? Even if it were benevolent, it would err on the side of optimism. Public choice theory warns us to be very careful and not to take government at its word. The mere fact that government expenditure has doubled in advanced societies since the 1960s should serve as a sufficient warning.

In point of fact, modern government is much more involved in supplying *private* goods, such as health, education and insurance, on the grounds that they generate some positive externalities. Here it would be easier to discover the optimal role of government, because a market price for these goods would emerge if free competition were permitted.

In either case, however, tax competition is likely to reveal voter preferences far better than the imperfect political process. Since societies differ in regard to their public vs private goods preference schedule, tax competition is not likely to lead to a 'race to the bottom', but to a wide variety of outcomes. This is consistent with the Austrian approach to competition, which is far more subtle than the neoclassical approach, and which reminds us that competition does not result in a single market price, the lowest possible, but in a wide variety of products at different prices, combining prices and qualities in different ways. So with tax competition, which is likely to produce all sorts of different outcomes, from the minimal night-watchman state to the all-embracing welfare state, depending on democratically expressed preferences. At this point, if we are speaking in a European context, people may wish to move from one tax jurisdiction to another, each offering a different package of services, and sorting themselves out *à la* Tiebout,[16] according to their individual preferences.

All this would be fine if capital were not free to move to the lowest tax jurisdiction, say the pessimists, so that in fact the electorate cannot freely choose a high-tax/high public goods profile, since this economy would suffer a capital outflow and loss of economic dynamism. Indeed, this general loss of democratic sovereignty is one of the main complaints of the anti-globalization movement.

There are two interconnected arguments here. The first relates to internationally mobile resources (including small streams of personal savings, portfolio investments by institutional investors and large concentrations of capital, know-how and intellectual property taking the form of foreign direct investment), where as we shall see in the next section, the 'race to the bottom' in tax rates is already in full swing. However, total tax revenues have been rising since 1990, rather than falling,[17] which suggests that lower tax rates have helped to open up greater opportunities, and increased the total stock of capital available. This is hardly a negative outcome for society as a whole.

The second interconnected argument is that the 'race to the bottom' concerning the taxation of mobile resources will in due course spill-over onto all other forms of taxation as well, threatening the state as we know it. This is speculation for the moment, but the above discussion concerning voters' public/private goods utility function is relevant here. The likely outcome is not zero taxes and zero public goods, but a public/private goods mix in line with voters' preferences. This can hardly be considered an affront to democracy.

It should also not be forgotten that nominally high corporate tax rates (30 per cent or more) yield a very small part of total tax revenue in most countries, usually not exceeding 5 per cent, because tax codes make many allowances for investment, depreciation and business expenses, such that some people maintain that the payment of corporate tax is largely a matter of choice. For the remaining 95 per cent of government revenue, many more general and less costly ways of financing government expenditure can be found.[18]

Finally, concerning the supposed loss of 'democratic sovereignty', it should not be forgotten that no sovereignty is absolute. It must be exercised in the real world. Thus it makes no sense for an assembly to vote by majority on the question of whether the sun circles the earth, or rather, it can vote as much as it likes, but the outcome of the vote will not change the physical reality. Thus also with economic reality. An assembly can vote for higher taxes and more equal income distribution as much as it likes, but it cannot change the laws of economics which tell us that this will slow and ultimately halt the wealth creation process.

7.3.2   Shifting the Burden of Taxation

Reference here is to the notion that international fiscal competition seems to be most prevalent in the areas of corporate taxation, and with regard to high marginal taxes aimed at wealthy taxpayers. In other words, subject to fiscal competition, it is claimed that governments will tend to reduce taxes on corporations and the mobile rich, who therefore benefit from fiscal competition, while they are forced to make up the short-fall in revenues by increasing taxes on the poor (especially in the form of social security contributions taken from wages) and on immobile factors, like housing. This takes the argument onto another plane. We will find it a bit harder here to apply our criterion of allocative efficiency, because this is a question of social justice, which people tend to put at one end of a negative equity/efficiency trade-off curve. However, the needs of social justice are also met by economic growth and an abundance of job opportunities, so we shall not abandon our efficiency criterion completely.

First, we have just seen that although tax competition on mobile resources is indeed intense (see also next section), tax revenues have not declined, so there is no need to shift to other sources of taxation.

Second, were tax revenues to decline because of fiscal competition, governments could first think about reducing expenditure before immediately seeking to 'make up the short-fall' in revenue. We have argued earlier that governments tend to maximize rather than optimize their expenditure, so if fiscal competition were to reduce their propensity to tax and spend, so much the better.

The next points are more technical. Capital and labour are both complements and substitutes. When it is cheap to replace men by machines, even a slight change in wages, interest rates, relative taxes, and dozens of other factors, will produce substitution effects. Reducing taxes on capital while holding taxes on labour steady could therefore be expected to increase capital-intensiveness and, at the margin, put some low-skilled people out of work. However, this is not new. The West has been replacing manpower by machinery for over 250 years, a process known as productivity growth, further accelerated by international trade pressures. Would the 'victims' of this process (the low-skilled, poorly-paid individuals) really like us to revert to the labour-intensive ways of producing things of the 1750s? Of course not! They and their descendants are as much the beneficiaries of productivity improvements as anyone else. They are consumers as well as producers. I would argue that a small, for the moment hypothetical shift from taxing capital to taxing labour would add but a small element to an already very dynamic process.

Most of the time, however, capital and labour are complements. Capital can do nothing without labour, but likewise, labour is nothing without capital. To put them in opposition to each other is simply an unconscious Marxist reflex. It actually does not matter at which point, or on which factor in the production chain taxes are raised, as long as there is no distortion of resource allocation between sectors. Capital and labour being complementary, if I diminish the cost of capital by taxing it less, I raise the demand for labour, and thereby its price. Conversely, the losers in the game of taxing the rich more than the poor, are not only the rich themselves, but also all the modest salaried employees who have never found the varied and well-paid jobs that would have been created for them, because entrepreneurs are operating on only one cylinder.[19] This being so, it would be hard to argue that reducing taxes on capital is somehow harmful to labour – quite the contrary, it is likely to be extremely beneficial.

Neither capital nor labour will ever earn more (but they need not earn less) than their marginal product, minus taxes, on their joint efforts. All taxes in the end will be paid by the owners of factors of production, that is, the general public. VAT and income tax are in fact the same, except that VAT is a flat tax on factor incomes, while income taxes are usually progressive. But they are both taxes on factors.

High marginal personal income taxes are often justified on grounds of social justice: it is thought to be right and proper that the rich should pay for public goods and to support the poor. However, it has become increasingly clear that high marginal taxes are not costless, but have a negative effect on growth and investment,[20] thus lowering the absolute amount of wealth created and reducing the absolute amount available for social policies. This provides the core of the argument why redistribution should be reserved for the expenditure side of public finance, while leaving the revenue side as free of economic distortions as possible.

7.3.3   Dynamic Laffer-curve Effects

In the 1980s Ronald Reagan and Margaret Thatcher started the tax competition game. They were convinced that taxes had reached the point of negative inflection on the Laffer curve, and 'sold' the idea of tax cuts on the grounds – amazing at the time – that they would lead to the growth of public revenue. The argument is familiar by now, but at the time it was highly controversial, for it was believed that if you taxed a high income-earner heavily enough, he would actually *work harder* to maintain his standard of living, and that business enterprises, once established, were sitting ducks for tax authorities and would not change their behaviour. On these assumptions, there was no rising opportunity cost to levying taxes in terms of lost output. In point of fact, as we have just seen, there are good reasons to believe that the opportunity cost of high levels of taxation is well above zero. And we shall see in the next section that while taxes have been steadily lowered over the past 25 years due to international fiscal competition, public revenues have actually grown, just as Arthur Laffer foretold. However, the point of optimal taxation on the Laffer curve is the point of *maximum* tax revenue for the government, which is not necessarily *optimal* from the point of view of society at large, nor compatible with long-term wealth creation for individuals. Indeed, Laffer's argument is static, in the sense that he is only speaking of drawing currently idle resources into economic activity at the margin, by changing the terms of the work/leisure trade-off. As with all marginal calculations, the effects can only be small. However, far more important are the long-term effects, which only develop after a generation or two, and whose impact is far from marginal.

The negative dynamic effects of heavy taxes are numerous. We saw earlier that the tax authorities lose at both ends: the underground economy flourishes at the expense of the official economy, while people and capital flee abroad. Official growth rates stagnate at home, but take off in a spectacular fashion elsewhere. Why is the illegal, untaxed economy so dynamic, while the official one is so anaemic? Why are economic growth rates much higher in the UK, Ireland, the USA, Australia and New Zealand than in France, Germany or Italy? Capital, technology, innovative talent and productive entrepreneurs are gravitating to where their after-tax (or no tax) return is growing, taking their growth potential with them. Some of these productive resources do actually move, but many are new, conjured up out of society by the right institutional mix. In other words, lower taxes both 'poach' existing mobile resources from high-tax countries, and create new ones. The low-tax country wins, while the high-tax country loses, on both counts. This is a difficult challenge for high-tax governments to meet, and so far the only answer they have found is to engage in a concerted international effort to discourage fiscal competition. However, even if high-tax countries could successfully lock up their productive resources, and stop them escaping to lower-tax havens, they still could not prevent such resources from evaporating, or disappearing into the informal economy. So in the long run, lower-tax environments would enjoy higher rates of growth.

Although our leaders are doubtless aware of these challenges to 'big government', they are not anxious to share the bad news with the electorate. Voters, brought up to believe in the welfare state, still have total trust in it and will not hear of any but the most superficial tinkering with its basic structure. As a result, politicians remain bound to social welfare, which today absorbs about 25 per cent of GDP on average (up from 13 per cent in the early 1970s). However, many years of slow growth in 'old Europe' have meant that most European countries are running public sector deficits and burdening themselves with a large and growing national debt. They can hardly continue along this road for much longer, especially as most of them face a demographic crisis: some time between 2020 and 2040, depending on the country, there will be only two people at work for each retiree, as compared with five or six today, and 20 in 1945.[21] Luckily, a solution is perhaps at hand. If fiscal competition lowers tax rates and boosts economic growth, it is possible to generate just as much public revenue in absolute terms as before. Let us now see what two decades of fiscal competition have actually done.

7.4   THE STATE OF FISCAL COMPETITION TODAY

We can see the effects of the Reagan and Thatcher tax revolution in international tax competition on both personal and corporate tax rates.

From 1980 to 2003 top personal marginal income tax rates[22] in the older developed countries fell on average from 71 per cent to 44 per cent. The same trend can also be observed for all other major country groupings (see Table 7.1). Today, the world average top personal marginal tax rate is 37 per cent, as compared to 60 per cent in earlier years. Developing countries have joined the race as well, and among the 101 countries for which sufficient data was available to make these comparisons over time, only six actually raised marginal personal taxes: Hong Kong, Papua New Guinea, Cameroon, Côte d'Ivoire, Senegal and Zimbabwe. All the others lowered their taxes substantially: by 23 per cent in Asia, 22 per cent in Africa and 18 per cent in Latin America. Among the champion tax-cutters were Botswana (from 75 per cent to 25 per cent), Nigeria (from 70 per cent to 25 per cent), Bangladesh (from 60 per cent to 25 per cent) and Egypt (from 80 per cent to 34 per cent). In Latin America we have Bolivia (from 48 per cent to 13 per cent) and Paraguay (from 30 per cent to zero). In old Europe we have the UK (from 83 per cent to 40 per cent) and Portugal (from 84 per cent to 40 per cent) (see Table 7.2). Here not a single country has failed to cut marginal taxes, although some are still feeling their way cautiously: Denmark (from 66 per cent to 59 per cent), France (60 per cent to 48 per cent), and Austria (62 per cent to 50 per cent).

Transition countries have had less time to develop their tax culture, but they too show a keen interest in keeping personal taxes as low as possible. Furthermore, they have pioneered the remarkable flat tax revolution. The

Table 7.1   Weighted average top personal marginal tax rates (%)

	1980*	2003	Change 1980 = 100
Older developed countries	71	44	62
Transition countries	37	23	40
Asia	61	38	73
Mediterranean & Arab world	32	20	53
Latin America	48	30	57
Africa	58	36	64
World average	60	37	67

Note: * Or nearest available.

Source: Fraser Institute (2005) and own calculations.

Table 7.2 *Top marginal personal income tax rates in older developed countries (%)*

	1980	1990	1995	2003	Delta 1980 = 100
Australia	62	49	47	47	76
Austria	62	50	50	50	81
Belgium	76	58	61	52	68
Canada	64	49	49	44	69
Cyprus	60	60	40	30	50
Denmark	66	68	64	59	89
Finland	68	60	56	53	78
France	60	53	51	48	80
Germany	65	53	57	47	72
Greece	60	50	45	40	67
Iceland	63	40	47	44	69
Ireland	60	56	48	42	70
Italy	72	66	67	47	65
Japan	75	65	65	50	67
Luxembourg		56	50	41	73
Malta	65	65	35	35	54
Netherlands	72	60	60	52	72
New Zealand	61.5	33	33	39	63
Norway	75	51	42	48	64
Portugal	84	40	40	40	48
Spain	66	56	56	40	61
Sweden	87	64	49	58	67
Switzerland	37	38	37	35	95
United Kingdom	83	40	40	40	48
United States	72	38	43	38	53
Weighted average, above countries				44	62

Source: Fraser Institute (2005) and own calculations.

most dramatic case is the well-known Russian example, where a highly progressive income tax system (80 per cent in 1990) was replaced by a 13 per cent flat tax in 2001, giving rise to a dramatic increase in tax revenues.[23]

This is a worldwide trend. It shows that the 'soak the rich' mentality is being quietly dropped. Egalitarianism is out, tax-revenue maximization is in.

Corporate taxes have also been cut. Table 7.3 tracks changes in a number of developed countries since 1986, and only Spain, among the countries listed, has failed to enact any changes at all. KPMG International follows over 100 countries and confirms that the worldwide trend is definitely in a

Table 7.3   Corporate tax rates (%)

	1986	1991	1995	2000	2005	Delta 2005/1986
USA	46	34	35	35	35	76
Canada	36	29	29	28	22.1	61
Australia	49	39	33	34	30	61
Japan	43	38	38	27	40.69	95
New Zealand	45	33	33	33	33	73
Austria	30	30	34	34	25	83
Belgium	45	39	39	39	33	73
Denmark	50	38	34	32	28	56
Finland	33	23	25	29	26	79
France	45	42	33	33	33	73
Germany	56	50	45	40	40	71
Ireland	50	43	40	24	12.5	25
Italy	36	36	36	37	33	92
Netherlands	42	35	35	35	31.5	75
Norway	28	27	19	28	28	100
Portugal	47	36	36	32	27.5	59
Spain	35	35	35	35	35	100
Sweden	52	30	28	28	28	54
Switzerland	10	10	10	8	8.5	85
UK	35	34	33	30	30	86

Note: Does not include regional corporate taxes.

Sources: Mitchell (2004, pp. 25–38), for years 1986–2000; KPMG International (2006) for 2005.

downward direction.[24] However corporate taxation is a highly complex area, and 'headline' rates may mean very different things in practice. Furthermore, most of the information refers only to tax rates applied by central government, which may be misleading in the case of federal states, such as Switzerland, where corporate income is taxed at several levels. Table 7.3 should therefore be considered as indicating a trend, rather than providing hard data on actually applied tax rates.

It is clear from tables 7.1, 7.2 and 7.3 that international fiscal competition is progressing in the expected direction for mobile factors – downwards.

In the meantime, and contrary to the hypothesis that fiscal competition will tend to shift the burden of taxation from internationally mobile capital to immobile labour, social security contributions and income tax rates for the low to middle end of the income distribution have also been declining, in order 'to boost the demand for labour, and to foster work incentives'[25]

Table 7.4   Tax wedge: social security contributions and income tax as percentage of gross labour costs*

	1979	1983	1991	1996	2000	2005
Austria	21.9	22.6	22.8	23	24	32.1
Belgium		49.2	53.7	56.4	56	41.9
Canada	23.2	25.6	29	32.1	31	23.8
Denmark	40.6	46.5	46.7	44.8	44	41
Finland	41.6	43.2	44.5	50.3	47	31.3
France				49.7	48	29
Germany	40.8	43.4	46.4	51.2	52	41.7
Ireland	33.9	40.1	39.8	36.1	29	17.7
Italy	45.3	50.5	48.8	50.8	47	27.3
Japan	16.7	17.7	21.5	19.4	24	18.5
Netherlands	48	52	46.5	43.8	45	32.2
New Zealand	26	26.6	23.8	22.3	19	20.5
Norway	43.5	42.3	41.2	37.6	37	29
Portugal	28.1	32.3	33.9	33.8	34	21.1
Spain	36.4	38	36.5	38.8	38	20.3
Sweden	50.7	50.6	46	50.2	50	31
Switzerland	28.2	28.8	27.3	30.4	29	21.7
United Kingdom	36.1	38.2	33.2	32.6	30	25.5
United States	31.9	34.9	31.3	31.1	31	23.6
Weighted average**	48					25.37

Notes:
*   Unmarried average production worker without children.
** Weighted by GDP.
Data up to 1996 include transfer payments received, and are not strictly comparable with 2000 and later data. Without transfer payments, the tax wedge during earlier years would of course be *higher*, so the general decline from 1979 to 2005 is in fact steeper than the figures suggest.

Source: OECD, *Taxing Wages*, annual report, various years.

(see Table 7.4). The weighted average 'tax wedge' on the average production worker's wage in advanced industrial countries has fallen from 48 per cent in 1979 to 25 per cent in 2005. This shows that most governments are fully aware of the complementary nature of capital and labour, and with few exceptions are also competing in this area.

Meanwhile, consumption tax rates (mainly VAT) in the EU have risen by 2 percentage points on average since 1980 (see Table 7.5). Needless to say, VAT and consumption taxes are 'flat' taxes which the rich and the poor pay at the same rate. This finding suggests that if international fiscal competition has had an effect, it has not been to shift direct taxes from mobile

Table 7.5   Standard VAT rates (EU-25)

	1980	1990	2005	Trend 1980 = 100 or 1990 = 100
Austria	18	20	20	111
Belgium	16	19	21	131
Cyprus		5	15	300
Czech R		23	19	83
Denmark	22	25	25	114
Estonia		10	18	180
Finland		22	22	100
France	17.6	18.6	19.6	111
Germany	13	13	16	123
Greece		18	19	106
Hungary		25	20	80
Ireland	25	23	21	84
Italy	14	19	20	143
Latvia		18	18	100
Lithuania		18	18	100
Luxembourg	10	15	15	150
Malta		15	18	120
Netherlands	18	18.5	19	106
Poland		22	22	100
Portugal	16	17	21	124
Slovak R		23	19	83
Slovenia		19	20	105
Spain		12	16	133
Sweden	23.46	25	25	107
United Kingdom	15	17.5	17.5	117
Unweighted average	17.3	18.4	19.4	120

Source: EU Commission (2006).

capital to immobile labour, but rather to shift from a narrow direct tax base to a much broader indirect tax base, at a much lower marginal rate.

Also – and rather surprisingly in view of the fears generated by the 'race to the bottom' school – real tax revenues have risen everywhere except for Italy, where they fell by 8 per cent in real terms from 1990 to 2003 (see Table 7.6). This is not just because of a hypothetical Laffer-curve effect, but also as a result of generally buoyant economic conditions due to the IT revolution during the 1990s. I doubt that the two effects can easily be separated, because it could be argued that the extent of the IT revolution was greatly helped by generally lower taxes. However, it would be difficult to conclude, on the basis of the evidence in Table 7.6, that the

Table 7.6   Tax revenues compared (bn local currency*)

	1990	2003	Change 1990 = 100	GDP deflators	Real growth tax revenues (%)
USA	1890.9	3495.0	185	134	51
Canada	291.4	495.1	170	130	40
Australia	139.5	286.7	206	129	77
Japan		na			na
New Zealand	30.9	45.6	148	125	23
Austria	61.5	110.8	180	128	52
Belgium	70.3	131.4	187	128	59
Denmark	464.5	828.8	178	128	50
Finland	48.3	75.8	157	116	41
France	441.7	784.9	178	124	54
Germany	454.0	959.2	211	126	85
Ireland	14.2	32.6	230	159	71
Italy	356.0	537.7	151	159	−8
Netherlands	112.4	207.2	184	136	48
Norway	397.8	895.8	225	153	72
Portugal	19.5	51.4	263	188	75
Spain	135.0	277.8	206	168	38
Sweden	854.5	1362.0	159	136	23
Switzerland	98.9	158.7	160	122	38
UK	229.6	441.0	192	147	45

Note: * Converted to € at current ECU exchange rate at the time.

Sources: IMF (1997/2006); IMF (1994/2004).

state is being starved of resources as a result of international fiscal competition.

Even more surprising is the fact that, in many countries, total government revenues have actually grown as a *proportion* of GDP (see columns 1, 2 and 3 of Table 7.7), while most direct tax *rates* have been falling, as we have seen. This is may be due to the shift towards broadly-based indirect taxation noted above. It will be noted that Japan is absent from Table 7.7, not because we wish to ignore this important country, but because it has not supplied the IMF with any data concerning tax revenues since 1993. The IMF is in the process of changing and much improving its presentation of government finance data, but this unfortunately makes intertemporal comparisons difficult. One of the great improvements in data presentation is the new 'General Government' category, which consolidates central, provincial and local data into a single table. For some countries this does not change

Table 7.7   Tax revenues and economic growth

	1990 tax (%GDP)	2003 tax (%GDP)	Delta tax (%GDP)	Real GDP growth 1990 = 100 (%)
USA	34	32	−2.5	149
Canada	43.6	40.8	−2.8	149
Australia	37	37	−0.2	160
New Zealand	42	34	−8.0	153
Austria	49	51	1.4	132
Belgium	46	49	2.7	128
Denmark	58	59	1.1	131
Finland	46	53	7.3	138
France	47	50	3.5	128
Germany	38	45	6.7	124
Ireland	32	25	−6.6	236
Italy	41	46	4.8	121
Netherlands	51	46	−5.2	135
Norway	55	57	2.2	149
Portugal	37	42	4.8	133
Spain	35	43	7.6	145
Sweden	63	58	−4.8	132
Switzerland	31	38	6.8	115
UK	42	40	−1.6	142
Weighted average GDP growth rate (1990–2003)				141

Source: As Table 7.6.

much – provincial and local government being a minor matter. For federations it can make a very big change indeed, and we have recalculated data from 1990 to ensure comparability with 2003.

What is the effect of lower direct taxes on economic growth? This question cannot be answered with any degree of accuracy, because countries are always at different stages in the business cycle; they have introduced various structural reforms (and not just fiscal reforms) at different times; and they have each grasped the exogenous technological IT revolution of the 1990s in different ways.

However, for what it is worth, it is possible to show the existence of a negative correlation between economic growth and the evolution of total government revenues as a proportion of GDP. Table 7.8 divides our sample of countries into those which experienced an increase in the share of tax as a proportion of GDP from 1990 to 2003, and those which experienced a decline. Ireland and Switzerland represent extremes at either end

Table 7.8   Growth and taxes (1990–2003)

	Real GDP growth (1990 = 100)	Change in tax ratio (%)
Group I		
New Zealand	152.9	−8.0
Ireland	235.9	−6.6
Netherlands	135.1	−5.2
Sweden	131.9	−4.8
Canada	148.8	−2.8
USA	149.0	−2.5
UK	141.7	−1.6
Australia	160.0	−0.2
Unweighted average	170.0	−2.6
Group II		
Spain	145.2	7.6
Switzerland	115.2	6.8
Germany	124.4	6.7
Finland	138.3	7.3
Italy	121.3	4.8
Portugal	133.4	4.8
France	128.4	3.5
Belgium	128.2	2.7
Norway	148.9	2.2
Austria	132.5	1.4
Denmark	131.2	1.1
Unweighted average	127.0	5.2

Source: As Table 7.5.

of the spectrum: Ireland cut the tax ratio by 7 percentage points, and experienced spectacular growth. Switzerland raised its tax ratio by 7 percentage points, and grew very slowly. More ambiguously, Spain (for example) increased its tax ratio by 7.6 percentage points, and grew by a middling 45 per cent, while Australia reduced its tax ratio by a marginal 0.2 percentage point, and grew most handsomely. The (negative) correction is therefore not perfect, but comes out at –0.5. On average, countries which raised the tax ratio grew by 27 per cent, much less than half the rate of those which reduced it (70 per cent) during the time under consideration. I justify taking an unweighted average here on the grounds that each 'experience' is of equal value. More work with a larger sample and different time intervals would have to be done in order to confirm this relationship.

7.5   CONCLUSIONS

We hope to have established that most international fiscal competition is beneficial rather than harmful, especially that type which is most severely criticized by the OECD and the EU, namely lower direct taxes. This is because most tax regimes do not distort the international allocation of resources.

However, international fiscal competition is still in full swing and we have yet to see its long-term effects. For the moment, there is no 'race to the bottom'.[26] Although direct taxes have fallen dramatically over the past 20 years, they are still well above zero (see tables 7.1, 7.2 and 7.3). Furthermore, there has been no shift in the tax burden from capital to labour, but rather a shift from direct to indirect taxation. To the extent that this distinction can in fact be maintained (all taxes are, in the end, taxes on factor incomes), this trend is probably to be welcomed, because broad-based taxes applying a single standard rate to all economic activity would be among the least distorting taxes one could imagine.

Total government revenues have increased, not fallen (as expected by the 'race to the bottom' school), and in some cases have even increased as a proportion of GDP (though with expected negative side-effects on the rate of growth). This is a somewhat surprising result, given all the fuss about harmful tax competition. However, it suggests that fiscal competition may still have some way to go.

Fiscal reform forced upon sometimes reluctant governments is in fact likely to prove extremely productive, because current tax structures are so inefficient and tax rates probably exceed the Laffer optimum. However, the Laffer optimum, which is the point of maximum public revenue, is not necessarily the optimum for society at large. The case of Ireland illustrates this point. Here the government both reduced tax rates substantially as a proportion of GDP, and also cut public expenditure in the early 1980s, unleashing an astonishing period of economic growth. As a result, the Irish today enjoy one of the highest per capita incomes in the developed world: $50 100 per capita (2005 $ and exchange rates), well above Germany ($33 577) or Spain ($26 810).[27] Government revenue as a proportion of GDP has fallen from 32 per cent to 25 per cent, but absolute levels of real public revenue have risen by 70 per cent, allowing the Irish to enjoy both better public services and much higher personal incomes. Only a few years ago, in 1990, the picture was quite different. Ireland's per capita income then stood at $9 550 (1990 $ and exchange rates), well below Germany ($22 320) and even Spain ($11 020). Even allowing for the usual measurement and comparability problems, it is difficult to avoid the conclusion that other countries could also achieve far higher rates of economic growth if tax reform were sufficiently bold. Indeed, unleashing growth potential is surely a priority, given the demographic challenges facing advanced industrial economies. The latter probably cannot hope to emulate Ireland's growth experience, because a lot of this had to do with 'catching-up'. But Ireland has not just caught up – it has since forged ahead, showing that the rest of 'old Europe' should set itself far more ambitious wealth targets. It is in order to return to wealth, growth and full employment that we still need international fiscal competition to do its work. Then governments can look forward to presiding over really impressive rates of economic growth and, if they can resist raising taxes once prosperity returns, to rising public revenues in real terms as well. The question then becomes how to keep public taxation and expenditure permanently at more modest levels, while the rest of the economy forges ahead. This will indeed prove difficult, unless international fiscal competition continues to exercise its disciplinary effects.

NOTES

The author has drawn on research sponsored by IREF (Institute for Research in Economics and Fiscal Affairs) for parts of this chapter.

1. Hayek (1960). See especially Chapter 3 'The Common Sense of Progress', pp. 39–53.
2. North (1981).
3. Buchanan and Tullock (1962). The publication of this book launched the public choice school and revolutionized the way economists judged state intervention.
4. North (1978).
5. One should not forget that different rates of customs tariffs are also disguised subsidies for particular industries, which in an open world economy could also result in the artificial shifting of investment from one country to another. This form of subsidization and 'poaching' other countries' investments is however absent from the OECD's definition of harmful tax practices and will not be further alluded to.
6. OECD (1998, p. 16).
7. Estonia is currently attracting much foreign direct investment, possibly as a consequence of a zero corporate tax rate on retained earnings.
8. See Curzon Price (2004) for an account of forbidden state aids to industry in the European Union.
9. ECOFIN (1998).
10. WTO (2000).
11. Teather (2005, p. 83).
12. OECD (1998).
13. Switzerland and Luxembourg refused to endorse the OECD's report, *inter alia*, on the grounds that it described their laws allowing for 'ring-fenced' low taxes and client confidentiality as being 'harmful'.
14. Council of the European Union, Joint Report on Employment 2004–2005, Brussels, 9 March 2005.
15. Teather (2005, Chapter 6).
16. Tiebout (1956).
17. EU Commission (2003, p. 109 and next section).
18. We shall address the question of the 'over-taxation' of immobile productive resources shortly.

19. What is the value of anecdote? I have in mind a first-rate entrepreneur who by the age of 40 decided that he had 'enough' and was not going to take risks and work the skin off his back just to pay ever higher taxes. He runs nice cars, several houses, a small aeroplane, but employs no one anymore.
20. Feldstein (1999) calculates that for every dollar of extra tax revenue, the US economy loses two dollars of additional output.
21. OECD (1996).
22. Data is from Fraser Institute (2005), but weighted averages (by population) are my own.
23. Rabushka (2003), cited in Mitchell (2004, pp. 25–38).
24. KPMG International (2006).
25. EU Commission (2003, pp. 12, 41).
26. Germany was raising the VAT rate from 16 to 19 per cent on 1 January 2007, but is most unwisely also raising taxes on corporations and wealthy individuals. No race to the bottom here!
27. OECD (2006).

REFERENCES

Buchanan, James M. and Gordon Tullock (1962), *The Calculus of Consent*, Ann Arbor, Michigan: University of Michigan Press.
Curzon Price, Victoria (2004), 'Industrial Policy', in El-Agraa (ed.), *The European Union, Economics and Policies*, 7th edn, London: Financial Times and Prentice Hall.
ECOFIN (1998), *Conclusions of the ECOFIN Council Meeting on 1 December 1997 concerning taxation policy (98/C, OJ C 2/1 of 6 January 1998)*, Annex 1 'Code of conduct for business taxation'.
EU Commission (2003), *Structures of the Taxation Systems in the European Union*, Luxembourg: EU.
EU Commission (2006), *VAT Rates Applied in Member States of the European Community*, DOC/1829/2006.
Feldstein, Martin (1999), 'Tax Avoidance and the Deadwight Loss of the Income Tax', *Review of Economics and Statistics*, November.
Fraser Institute (2005), *Economic Freedom of the World: 2005*, Fraser Institute, Vancouver.
Hayek, F.A. (1960), *The Constitution of Liberty*, Chicago: The University of Chicago Press.
IMF (1997/2006), *International Financial Statistics, 1997 & 2006 Yearbooks*.
IMF (1994/2004), *Government Finance Statistics, 1994 & 2004 Yearbooks*.
KPMG International (2006), *Corporate Tax Trade Survey 2006*, website.
Mitchell, Daniel J. (2004), 'The Economics of Tax Competition: Harmonzation vs. Liberalization', Heritage Foundation, 2004 Index of Economic Freedom, Washington.
North, Douglass C. (1981), *Structure and Change in Economic History*, New York and London: W.W. Norton & Co.
North, Gary (1978), 'Walking into a Trap', *The Freeman*, May 1978.
OECD (1998), *Harmful Tax Competition: An Emerging Global Issue*, Paris: OECD.
OECD (2006), *Main economic indicators (2006)*, Paris: OECD.
OECD, *Taxing Wages*, annual report, various issues.
OECD (1996), 'Ageing Populations, Pension Systems and Government Budget: Simulations for 20 OECD Countries', WP 168.

Rabushka, Alvin (2003), 'The Flat Tax at Work in Russia: Year Three, January–June 2003', *The Russian Economy*, 13 August 2003.

Teather, Richard (2005), *The Benefits of Tax Competition*, London: IEA.

Tiebout, C. (1956), 'A Pure Theory of Local Expenditure', *Journal of Political Economy*, **64**, 416–24.

WTO Appellate Body Report (2000), *United States: Tax Treatment for 'Foreign Sales Corporations'*, adopted by Disputes Settlement Body, 20 March 2000.

8.   A race to the bottom for the big welfare states?

Andreas Bergh

INTRODUCTION

During the 1990s, economic integration in Western Europe was high paced: the introduction of the single European market 1993, stage two of the European Monetary Union 1994, and the launch of the euro in 1999. And in 1995, the big welfare states Finland and Sweden, with total tax revenues around 50 per cent of GDP, were accepted as members of the EU.

This development has contributed to a debate around the central questions analysed in this chapter: how are big, high-tax welfare states affected by institutional competition and increased international mobility of labour and capital? Are there any signs that we will see a race to the bottom among European welfare states in the near future? What is likely to happen in the future with the high-tax European welfare states?

This chapter focuses on institutional competition between big welfare states, in the sense that most EU countries have big welfare states: the average tax rate in the EU-15 is around 42 per cent, and in the Nordic welfare states the figure is around 50 per cent.[1] By institutional competition, I mean the fact that these welfare states compete for attractive production factors (such as highly educated labour), and also the fact that they may wish to avoid bad risks that may strain the welfare state (such as labour with high risks for being unable to work).[2]

Recently, empirical evidence points against the view that a race to the bottom has occurred or is likely in the near future.[3] The main part of this chapter aims to explain this and to make some predictions regarding the future of high-tax societies.

EXISTING THEORIES AND EMPIRICAL EVIDENCE: SO FAR, NO RACE TO THE BOTTOM

The idea of a race to the bottom triggered by institutional competition can be traced back at least to Gramlich (1982). Following Peterson and Rom (1990), the term 'welfare magnets' has been used to describe the mechanism by which states with higher welfare benefits than their neighbours will experience increasing poverty because of immigration.

The view that institutional competition is harmful for welfare states is probably most clearly stated by Hans-Werner Sinn. For example, note the following passage in Sinn (2004, p. 23):[4]

> The new systems competition will likely imply the erosion of the European welfare state, induce a race to the bottom in the sense that capital will not even pay for the infrastructure it uses and erode national regulatory systems.

Sinn's argument is that state interventions are motivated by adverse selection on national private insurance markets: mandatory social insurance can handle this by forcing high-risk people (net recipients) and low-risk people (net payers) to stay within the same insurance scheme. Competition between nation-states is harmful, according to Sinn, because of the free migration of net payers and net recipients:

> every state would have the incentive to treat the net recipients a bit worse and the net payers a bit better than their neighbors do in order to ward off the latter and attract the former and in doing so create a budget surplus. (pp. 13–14)

Sinn's main point is the *selection principle*, according to which analogies between competition in the private sphere and competition between states are 'completely inadmissible' (p. 12). In other words, Sinn holds that while competition between firms will have positive effects for consumers, this does not imply that competition between nation-states will be positive for citizens. In Sinn's model, this is a consequence of states dealing mainly with correcting for so-called market failures. In reality, however, states do not only deal with market failure, and thus it may well be the case that competition between states is positive for citizens. The selection principle is theoretically described in Sinn (1997).[5]

A different take on the race to the bottom is provided by Mendoza and Tesar (2005). They point to 'The Package to Tackle Harmful Tax Competition' by ECOFIN in 1997, and note that as early as 2001, the EU commissioner for the internal market expressed the view that a 'reasonable degree' of tax competition would not be harmful at all, but rather lead to a market-driven convergence towards lower tax rates.[6]

Early empirical studies did seem to support the race to the bottom hypothesis, see for example Gramlich (1982) and Peterson and Rom (1990). More recent research, however, has identified problems with the early studies. Volden (2002) suggests that the methods of the early studies are flawed, among other things because they neglect the fact that the real value of welfare benefits can be lowered by not adjusting them for inflation. Volden studies Aid to Families with Dependent Children (AFDC) in the US and concludes that 'a more careful assessment of the data shows little support for a strict interpretation of the [race to the bottom] story' (p. 360). Volden's study indicates clustering of states with similar benefit levels, rather than a race to the bottom.

Berry et al. (2003) share Volden's view that the study by Peterson and Rom is problematic, and that the support for the welfare magnet hypothesis is very weak: '[t]he poor do not migrate in large numbers for more generous welfare assistance' (p. 329). They do find that states without a residency requirement for AFDC-recipients will in fact experience higher poverty when neighbouring states decrease their benefits. But they also note that '[t]he magnetic effect of welfare is substantially weaker than the magnetic effect of high wages for low-skill workers and a low unemployment rate' (p. 344). Thus, migration within the US seems to be more about seeking higher wages and employment than it is about seeking welfare benefits.

Translating this conclusion to the European setting is not straightforward. Granted, labour mobility between EU member states is lower than between US states. This suggests that if welfare migration is not a problem in the US, it is hardly a problem in Europe. However, the difference between the generosity of welfare benefits between the richest and the poorest EU countries is much bigger than the difference within the US.

There is, however, some European evidence available as well. Mendoza and Tesar (2005) study taxes on capital, labour income and consumption in France, Germany, Italy and the UK between 1965 and 1996, and find no evidence of a race to the bottom: taxes on labour income seem to increase and diverge, whereas consumption taxes seem to converge. The trend for capital taxation is unclear – but compared to taxes on labour and consumption, capital taxes are unimportant for the financing of the welfare state. Consequently, high-tax countries can easily lower their taxation of capital and corporate taxes without jeopardizing the financial basis of the welfare state.[7]

The most relevant tax measure for the welfare state is the amount of total tax revenue collected, regardless of source. This is shown in Figure 8.1 for the three countries with the highest and the lowest total taxes in the EU in 1995. The figure suggests that what we have seen so far does not much

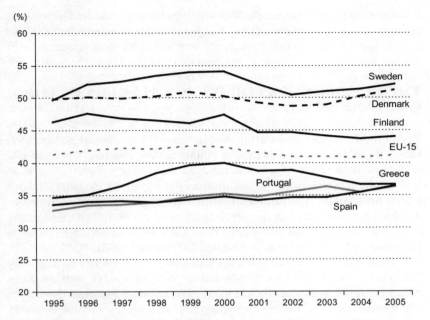

Figure 8.1 *Taxes as share of GDP in high and low-tax EU nations*
1995–2005

resemble a race to the bottom: the two countries with the highest taxes in 1995 both had higher taxes in 2005. Furthermore, while there seems to be a trend towards increasing taxes in the low-tax countries, the average in EU-15 seems very steady. If anything the decade of economic integration may have produced some small degree of convergence towards the EU average: the average standard deviation was 4.6 for the years 1995–2000 and 4.3 for 2001–05.

Finally, several case studies confirm that the high-tax welfare states did survive the economic crisis of the 1990s and show remarkable resilience, see for example Castles (2004), Bergh (2004), Lindbom (2001), Timonen (2001), Kvist (1999) and Kautto (1999). As a consequence, political scientists are now devoting themselves to explaining 'the mysterious survival of the Scandinavian Welfare States' – see Rothstein and Lindbom (2004).

At this point, it is important to note that the fact that we have not witnessed a race to the bottom for the European welfare states does not imply that nothing has happened with the way welfare states are organized and structured, nor that nothing will change in the future. On the contrary, it may well be the case that big universal welfare states have survived precisely because they have undergone sufficiently big changes to adapt to changing circumstances. In the next section, I argue that this is indeed the case, and that further changes in the same direction are very likely to occur.

THE CHALLENGES FOR POLICY-MAKERS IN THE WELFARE STATE

Currently, European integration has increased institutional competition between the world's most advanced welfare states. This has happened at a time when the welfare state would have faced a number of challenges even without such competition: in addition to the increased mobility of both labour and capital, the European welfare states face a substantial demographic challenge: the old age dependency ratio in the EU (defined as the population aged 65 and above relative to the population aged 15 to 64) is projected to double between 2000 and 2040 (Disney 2003).

A third challenge comes from the fact that people are richer than they have ever been. This poses a substantial problem for big welfare states because of the substantially changed consumption patterns caused by rising incomes. Fogel (1999) estimates that the long-run income elasticity for health care services is 1.6, and equally large for education. Thus higher incomes mean that people want to spend an increasing share of their budget on these areas. This poses a challenge because these areas are mainly publicly financed in the welfare states.

Throughout this chapter, I will make the simplifying but perhaps justifiable assumption that policy-makers in the welfare states are reluctant to adapt by drastically lowering taxes and expenditure. Besides ideology, there are several other reasons why such reluctance can be expected. As pointed out by, for example, Pierson (1994), and also a central theme in the literature on rent-seeking and interest groups, public administration and bureaucracy is politically easier to create than to terminate. Facing a threat of economic cutbacks, public bureaucracy has resources that can be used to motivate public opinion against such cutbacks.

Another reason why we do not expect welfare states to give in without a fight is noted for example by Rothstein and Lindbom (2004): in high-tax societies, a large part of the population works for the public sector or is supported by public transfers. Because a smaller state would imply less politics, politicians also have some degree of self-interest in maintaining big government. Even right-wing politicians might have trouble finding jobs in the private sector after having spent their entire life in politics.

To understand how policy-makers can maintain support for the big welfare state despite institutional competition and other challenges, we first need to understand welfare state support and how it is affected by institutional competition.

Understanding Welfare State Support

To understand welfare state support, we depart from a simplified model of a universal welfare state suggested by among others Rothstein (1998), shown in Figure 8.2. The idea is that approximately proportional taxes are used to finance benefits (both cash and in-kind) to which people are entitled regardless of their income. As shown by Bergh (2004), this simplified model is actually a good approximation of the tax-side of the Swedish welfare state, whereas the distribution of benefits is highly sensitive to the way in which different benefits are defined.

To account for the fact that incomes vary over the life cycle, think of taxes and benefits in a lifetime perspective. As indicated in Figure 8.2, this creates net-receivers and net-payers ex post. A naive approach to explaining welfare state support in a democracy would be simply to note whether net-gainers represent a majority. However, for several reasons, explaining welfare state support is more complicated than simply identifying net-receivers and net-payers.

First of all, welfare state support can be explained by, for example, ideology and altruism towards net-gainers. If there are positive externalities to

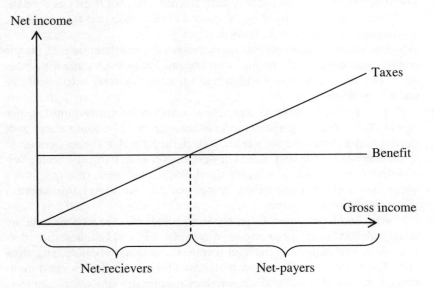

Figure 8.2   A simplified model of a universal welfare state

redistribution, such as lower social tension and lower crime rates, supporting the welfare state may be virtuous even for net-payers.[8] Of course, such
positive externalities should be weighed against negative externalities, for
example growth impeding incentive effects or effects on possibly desirable
values such as dignity – see Karlson (2004).

There is, however, substantial empirical evidence that big welfare states
survive simply because they are supported by the broad middle class – see
for example Goodin and Le Grand (1987), Rothstein (1998) and Korpi and
Palme (1998). There is also evidence that the historical expansion of the
welfare state can be explained by political factors based on voters' self-
interest (see Lindert 2004).

Thus, the idea that voters are self-interested is not a bad assumption to
make when it comes to analysing the future development of the welfare state.
It would, however, be a crucial mistake to assume that it is in the self-interest
of all net-receivers to support the welfare state. Similarly, it would be wrong
to assume that all net-payers are non-supporters. There are at least four
reasons why these assumptions are incorrect, and these reasons are important for understanding how welfare states adapt to institutional competition.

First, and perhaps most importantly, people's support for the welfare
state depends on what they perceive to be the relevant alternative. More
important than being a net-gainer or a net-payer is whether people perceive
that they are better off under current welfare state institutions than they
would be under the most likely counterfactual scenario. It may also be the
case that people suffer from fiscal illusion in the sense that they misjudge
the amount of taxes they actually pay.

Second, there may be an insurance motive for redistribution. If people
are risk-averse and worry about future income losses, even some who even-
tually end up as net-payers will support the welfare state because of the
safety it provides.

Third, receiving public consumption worth a certain amount is not
equivalent to receiving the same amount in cash. For this reason, net-
gainers may still oppose the welfare state if they feel that the services given
to them are not what they would choose to consume had they been given
cash transfers instead. The bigger the difference between what the citizen
would buy and what the welfare state provides, the bigger this negative
effect on welfare state support is.

Fourth, and finally, even if the services provided by the welfare state are
exactly what citizens would buy anyway, there may still be a negative effect
on welfare state support if the level spent is lower than the desired spending
level. For example, in the absence of a welfare state, both low- and high-
income earners would spend some money on primary education. But low-
income earners would spend less and high-income earners more than the

equal amount provided by the welfare state. Thus, high-income earners may feel that the consumption level provided by the welfare state is insufficient.

While these four qualifications are important on the margin, it is clear that the broad patterns of welfare state support follow the predictions of self-interest. For example, since 1980, surveys have confirmed that socio-economic groups with higher incomes report lower welfare state support – see for example Svallfors (2004). Thus, other things being equal, bigger net-recipients are more likely to support the welfare state.

This is important, because it gives some clear theoretical predictions for successful adaptation strategies: policy-makers trying to maintain majority support for a welfare state like the one illustrated in Figure 8.2, need not worry very much about the poorest, who are the biggest net-recipients: these are most likely to support the welfare state anyway. Much more important are the voters on the margin, somewhere in the broad middle class, who currently support the welfare state but might easily change. Furthermore, the biggest net-payers are most likely lost in terms of polit-ical support under all circumstances. They are however needed in the country because of the tax revenue they deliver.

In the next section we shall see that these considerations are important to understanding how the policy-makers in the welfare state handle the challenges they are facing.

How Welfare States Adapt

In short, welfare states adapt by avoiding a situation where net-payers, capital and corporations leave the country, while at the same time avoiding a situation in which the strategic middle-class voters turn their back on the welfare state and start demanding substantial tax cuts. On top of this, welfare states must handle the fact that people live longer and are richer than ever before.

In the following, I show that welfare states have already begun tackling this challenge using at least some of the following measures:

- Restructuring the tax system
- Tying benefits closer to taxation
- Increasing work incentives
- Increasing reliance on private topping-up of public consumption and social insurance
- Increasing freedom of choice through voucher systems
- Increasing efficiency through competition-enhancing reforms

This development is described in more detail below.

Restructuring the tax system to handle increased tax mobility

For policy-makers trying to maintain high tax revenues, increased tax mobility causes problems if important tax bases move out of the country. Policy-makers in the big welfare states can handle the situation in different ways. They can ignore the threat, and potentially run deficits – but in the long run this is not economically feasible. Instead, welfare states have employed two strategies to cope with increased tax mobility:

1. Shifting the tax burden to relatively less mobile production factors.
2. Counteracting increased mobility by offering compensating benefits to the production factors that would otherwise move.

Boadway (2005) argues that the system which best combines the objectives of a good tax system in an internationally competitive environment is the dual income tax system used in the Nordic countries where capital is taxed at a low flat rate and non-capital income is taxed progressively. Lindert (2004) points outs that the Swedish tax level is substantially higher than, for example, US taxes on all areas except capital taxes.

The argument applies not only to the difference between taxation of labour and capital, it also concerns labour taxation. The Nordic welfare states have much higher average taxes, but compared to the US and the UK, they collect a relatively larger share of taxes from low and middle-income earners, and a smaller relative share from high-income earners – see Table 8.1.

In the early 1990s, both Sweden and Norway conducted reforms that reduced tax distortions by lowering the statutory tax rates and broadening

Table 8.1   *Proportion of taxes paid by the lowest 30%, the middle 40% and the highest 30% of the population (based on final disposable adjusted income)**

	Low	Mid	High
US	6%	28%	65%
UK	6%	32%	62%
Finland	10%	33%	57%
Norway	10%	36%	54%
Sweden	11%	36%	53%
Denmark	14%	37%	49%

Note: * Taxes include all direct income taxes including employee social security contributions.

Source: Förster (2000).

the tax bases – see, for example, Agell et al. (1996) and Aarbu and Thoresen (1997). Lazar and Stoyko (1998) show that the number of tax brackets and the top marginal tax rates have decreased markedly between 1975 and 1990 in almost all modern welfare states.

In addition to broad structural measures like those described above, welfare states also use more selective measures to cope with increased mobility. Sweden, Denmark and Finland have all introduced exceptions in income taxation, according to which, for example, foreign experts are given substantially lower marginal income tax rates.

In Sweden, the so-called 'expert tax' means that 25 per cent of the gross wage is exempt from taxation for a maximum of three years. In Denmark, the highest marginal tax rate is roughly 60 per cent, but foreign researchers staying for a maximum of three years pay only a proportional tax at 25 per cent. Sweden also has an exception in the wealth tax for those who own at least 25 per cent of the shares in a company, if these were bought before 1990. For further details regarding selective exceptions in income taxation, see ITPS (2005). While marginal for total tax revenue, exceptions like these may be important for recruitment possibilities in certain companies, and thereby indirectly important for tax revenue in the longer run.

Tying benefits more closely to taxation
Changes in the tax structure are not enough to explain welfare state adaptation. As pointed out by, for example, Steinmo (2003), it would be wrong to ignore tax-financed benefits when analysing the sustainability of high-tax systems. High taxes increase costs for employers, but there may be compensatory benefits associated with the high-tax society, such as low poverty, low crime rates and a healthier work force. Furthermore, employers in welfare states may spend less resources on for example pension schemes and health care plans for their employees.

In many cases, however, these benefits have public good properties: those who avoid paying high taxes can still enjoy the benefits of low poverty or universal health care. But in many cases, welfare states can handle the problem by tying benefits closely to individual labour market participation. For example, the biggest social transfer, the pension system, is typically designed specifically to avoid this problem. In Sweden, income-related pension rights are earned only for incomes in Sweden, and the full flat rate pension is granted only to citizens who lived in Sweden for at least 40 years between the ages of 16 and 64 (with an exception for refugees).

Nevertheless, increased labour mobility means that strategic welfare migration cannot be ruled out: if people enjoy publicly financed education until the age of 25, work abroad for most of their adult life, and move back to take advantage of publicly financed care for elderly, this will cause problems for the welfare state. While migration levels are currently very low, there are some trends worth noting: Pedersen et al. (2003) report that there was a marked increase in emigration from Sweden during the 1990s, especially among the highly educated.

There have also been worries that increased immigration from poorer European countries will put the Nordic welfare states under pressure. As noted above, however, empirical research does not support the idea of strategic welfare migration, even between states in the US.

Very tentatively, these American findings seem to apply to Sweden as well. A study conducted by the Swedish National Social Insurance Board found that the EU expansion to include 10 new and substantially poorer countries, only marginally affected expenditure on family benefits – see Försäkringskassan (2005) and EUbusiness.com (2004). However, the fact that, for example, Latvian construction workers can now compete for work in Sweden, has triggered some spectacular conflicts on the Swedish labour market (see, for example, EIRO 2005). This suggests that, at least for Sweden, increased labour mobility is problematic not mainly because of the social transfer system, but because of the highly unionized and regulated labour market.

Work incentives: some progress in the long run, big problems in the short run

In addition to the potential problems caused by higher mobility of capital and labour, the big welfare states need to improve employment in order to maintain a balance between the number of people who work and the number who do not.

Increased work incentives can be achieved in different ways. In the long run, welfare states can encourage people to work longer before retiring. In the short run, reforms can increase incentives to work longer hours per day and more days per year. The Nordic welfare states are currently struggling with both types of reform, and not without success.

Increasing the age at which people retire can be achieved through rules or incentives (or, of course, a combination of these). The latter is the option best suited to maintain welfare state support as it lets each individual trade leisure against consumption according to preference. Disney (2003) reports that pension reforms in this direction have already been undertaken in many countries. In particular, the Swedish reform undertaken in 1998 means that pension benefits are adjusted actuarially to the (within some limits) freely chosen retirement age, resulting in substantially higher monthly pension benefits if retirement is postponed. Pension reforms aimed at increasing the retirement age have also been undertaken in high-tax countries like Belgium and Finland.

Especially Sweden, but also Denmark and Finland, still have substantial problems caused by weak work incentives in the short run: the combination of high taxes on labour, generous unemployment benefits with no clear time limit and income-tested benefits create high marginal net tax rates – see Lindbeck (1994) and Bergh (2006). Since Sweden drastically lowered tax progressivity in the early 1990s, the work disincentives now typically appear for low-income earners, mainly due to the means-tested nature of social assistance (see Bergh 2004).

Furthermore, employment protection laws tend to benefit well-established groups (so-called insiders) on the labour market. This protection, however, comes at the expense of higher barriers to labour market entry for outsiders on the labour market, typically young people and immigrants. One consequence was that Sweden operated at full employment for most of the 1970s and 1980s – but after the crises of the early 1990s, it has been very difficult for these outsider groups to return to employment.

In general, one can expect that increased focus on work incentives will favour Bismarckian benefits (where income losses are replaced proportionally) over flat-rate (Beveridge-style) benefits, which cause big, negative labour supply responses for low-income earners.

To sum up: by reforming pension systems, many welfare states have begun to handle problems caused by low work incentives in the long run. Reforms aiming to increase short-run work incentives are currently at the heart of the political debate in the welfare states.

Topping up of public consumption

Increasing incomes and the rapid development of modern medical technology means that it will be difficult to provide quality public health care at a level sufficient for all. In a recent Swedish survey, Rosén and Karlberg (2002) found that 59 per cent of citizens and only 12 per cent of physicians agreed fully with the statement that the public health services should always offer the best possible care, irrespectively of cost.[9]

As already noted, health care services and education are normal goods with income elasticity higher than one. This means that as the population in a welfare state grows richer, the demand for these services will increase, and more so among those who are relatively richer. Thus the difference in the absolute spending level desired by high-income earners and low-income earners will increase over time.

The gap between the publicly provided level and the level desired by high-income earners, can actually be used by the policy-makers of the welfare state to decrease labour mobility. The choice for policy-makers is between allowing topping up, which means that citizens may add private money to publicly financed services, and having citizens pay twice in order to attain the level of services they prefer – once through taxation, and again to a private provider when topping up is not allowed.

A fundamental insight of our analysis is that political support for the welfare state is greater under the topping up strategy than under the paying twice strategy. If topping up is allowed, the reasons for moving to another country are much weaker because those who desire to do so can add private money on top of the public funding in order to achieve a more desired quantity or quality of welfare services. Compared to the paying twice alternative, this means that a smaller share of the taxes paid by the higher income earners is redirected to consumption by other groups.[10]

Thus, by allowing topping up, welfare states will enjoy higher political support and lower labour mobility compared to a scenario when the publicly provided services are merely a take it or leave it offer.

Empirically, the effect on political support has been verified by Hall and Preston (1998) who showed that people who opt out from publicly provided health care and pay for private health insurance support less spending on the public system.

Topping up of social insurance
Topping up is possible not only to complement publicly provided services, it can also complement monetary social insurance transfers of the Bismarckian type where incomes are replaced proportionally. In this context, topping up means increasing the effective replacement rate from the publicly provided level towards full insurance. Topping up alleviates the negative level effect on welfare state support for the following reason. Mandatory social insurance with replacement rates close to 100 per cent means that people who have low demand for insurance (because they have low risk-aversion or low risk for income losses) are forced to consume more income protection than they otherwise would. If the mandatory replacement rate is lowered, people may complement protection up to the desired level, either individually through market insurance or group-wise through occupationally negotiated insurance schemes. Ståhlberg (2003) shows that the latter solution is indeed already well established: occupational contracts cover almost the entire working population, and as expected the details and conditions vary between groups.

Because they are mandatory, social insurance schemes can avoid costs of advertisement and also the costs associated with identifying risk groups. Empirically it has also been shown that social insurance typically has lower administration costs than private insurance – see for example Gouyette and Pestieau (1999). For this reason, it may well be the case that the most preferred alternative for many voters is the combination of social insurance and private topping up, and this alternative may be strictly preferred to a system based only on market insurance, as well as to a system based only on social insurance. In fact, Bergh (2003) shows that topping up contracts can induce high income earners to support social insurance in situations when they would otherwise favour a pure market insurance over social insurance without topping up.

Vouchers

Vouchers are a well-known way to maintain public financing while giving the citizens of the welfare state more influence over the service provided. Blomqvist (2004) describes the so-called 'choice revolution' in the provision of public welfare services in Sweden, which in addition to vouchers also contained the use of quasi-markets such as purchaser/provider arrangements.

An increased use of vouchers can be seen as a way to dampen the negative effects on welfare state support caused by the in-kind effect, by giving people more freedom to choose what services to consume. Note that the opportunity to choose more freely may be appreciated and used only by a small part of the population – but if these are the voters who would otherwise stop supporting the welfare state, the use of vouchers may well be the policy that secures majority support on the margin.

Indeed, the standard result from studies of voucher systems in practice is that the freedom to choose is used initially by very few, but that this share is constantly growing over time (see, for example, Edebalk and Svensson 2005). Also, for education, child care and health care, user satisfaction is higher among those who have chosen private providers compared to those who have chosen public providers.[11]

The pattern that private providers initially play only a small role, but that their share is slowly growing, is confirmed in Sweden by Blomqvist (2004), relying mainly on data from a public expert commission report (Socialdepartementet 2002):

- The share of privately employed health care staff increased from 5 to 7 per cent between 1993 and 2000.
- The share of privately employed workers in the elder care sector grew from 2 to 13 per cent between 1993 and 2000.
- The share of children in publicly funded private day care facilities grew from 5 to 15 per cent between 1990 and 1999.
- In 2002, ten years after the introduction of school vouchers, the share of students attending publicly financed private schools had grown from 0 to 5 per cent for primary schools and 6 per cent for secondary schools.

Furthermore, the share of private providers is typically higher in urban areas and in high-income municipalities. Also, parents with high income and education are more likely to take the opportunity to send their children to a privately provided school (Blomqvist and Rothstein 2000). Importantly, this shows that the increased freedom of choice is used more by citizens whose welfare state support is negatively affected by the the in-kind effect and the level effect described above. Also, as reported above, the highly educated are an increasingly mobile group of taxpayers. This leads to the conclusion that vouchers and similar reforms change the way the welfare state has traditionally been organized, but at the same time they alleviate some problems related to tax mobility and political support.

Again, these trends are not limited to Sweden. For example, Edebalk and Svensson (2005) analyse customer choice for elderly people and persons with functional disabilities recently implemented in all of the Nordic countries. In some Swedish municipalities the process started in the early 1990s, but currently Denmark, which has employed a nationally regulated customer-choice system since 2003, is the most progressive of the Nordic countries.

When the public service is privately provided through a voucher system, it is much harder to avoid topping up for political reasons. For example, when health care is privately provided and partially tax financed, there is nothing that stops private providers from selling other services as well. If a particular private provider is highly efficient, it is possible to cross-subsidize other offers using tax money from the voucher.

Topping up of publicly financed private consumption will look different depending on how the provision is organized. In a system based on vouchers, topping up means that individuals are allowed to take their publicly financed voucher to any supplier, add private funding and buy a higher quality service. In a system with only public providers, topping up means selling higher quality services to those with higher willingness to pay.

Increased efficiency
Vouchers and quasi-markets may actually lead to increasing support for publicly provided welfare services. Competition and organizational experimentation speeds up the learning process, so that efficient ways of producing welfare services are spread more rapidly. Theoretically there should be positive effects of competition not only for private providers, but also in public units which have incentives to increase quality in order not to lose funding because people choose private providers instead. Studying the Swedish school voucher reform, Sandstrom and Bergstrom (2005) found empirical support for this hypothesis, and conclude that competition has had a positive effect on school results in public schools. Similar findings

appear in other countries, see for example Hoxby (2000) for the case of the USA.

Domberger and Jensen (1997) summarize the theory and evidence of contracting out by the public sector, and conclude that lower costs are the result of improved management, more flexible work methods, more efficient use of capital and higher-paced innovation. Thus, market reforms such as vouchers and quasi-markets impose strong efficiency incentives for the whole public sector, which may dampen discontent with high taxes in marginally important groups of voters.

IS GRADUAL ADAPTATION THE PATH TOWARDS FULL PRIVATIZATION?

An interesting question is whether vouchers, quasi-markets and similar reforms will lead the way towards a full privatization of many welfare services. There are mechanisms working in both directions. For example, Blomqvist (2004) notes that further privatization may be accelerated by the dynamics set in motion by consumer choice, and that private provision of welfare services may lead to increased pressure for private financing as well. This argument is not new. In fact, an old article in the *Cato Journal* describes exactly such an incrementalistic strategy for social security privatization (see Butler and Germanis 1983).

Another important factor pointing towards full privatization is that increasing reliance on private providers and quasi-markets will likely imply changes in people's perception of what society would be like without the big welfare state. If partial privatization works well, the long-run effect may be that people become more positive towards full privatization as well.

However, as noted above, competition through vouchers and similar reforms has the effect of forcing the public sector to become more efficient, providing the median voter with better value for taxes paid. If this effect is sufficiently strong, partial privatization has put the welfare state on a path where high taxes can persist despite increasing institutional competition.

CONCLUSIONS

We have seen that welfare states have responded – more or less successfully – to the challenges through a series of measures:

- Tying benefits more closely to being a taxpayer.

- Offering selective exemptions in the tax system for strategic groups.
- Modifying major benefit programmes to make them more beneficial for the middle class, and less beneficial for the poorest and the richest.
- Increasing the efficiency of the public sector.
- Increasing the freedom of choice in publicly financed benefits.
- Allowing citizens to top up publicly financed benefits with private money.
- Increased long-run work incentives to keep the proportion of the life cycle spent working constant despite increasing longevity.

A possible conclusion is that institutional competition between welfare states does not lead to a race to the bottom, it leads to improvements of the tax–benefit package for those groups that would otherwise move or demand drastically lower taxes. In one way, the development is a case study of how increased competition leads to increased efficiency. But this is efficiency in the sense of giving marginal voters what they want.

The preferences of voters who are unlikely to move and unlikely to demand drastically lower taxes are less important. On the other hand, the preferences of an increasingly mobile, increasingly rich and demanding middle class are of high importance for policy-makers who wish to preserve majority support for big government in the future.

NOTES

1. These, as well as following, data on tax rates are from Eurostat, and refer to general government's total receipts from taxes and social contributions (including imputed social contributions) after deduction of amounts assessed but unlikely to be collected.
2. Thus, the main issue here is not the competition Europe is facing from less developed countries, but rather competition between welfare states.
3. As also noted by for example Curzon Prize in this volume.
4. Available as a working paper in 2001.
5. Another limitation in Sinn's model worth mentioning is that it contains no migration costs.
6. *The Economist*, 10 February 2000, p. 52, citing Frits Bolkenstein.
7. As noted and discussed by, among many others, Lindert (2004).
8. For example, Nelson and Greene (2003) argue that some political positions can be interpreted as ways of signalling goodness.
9. Similar 'expensive expectations' may exist in other publicly financed areas, such as schooling.
10. Recently, public policy documents show that the Nordic welfare states are indeed facing exactly the strategic choice described here – see for example the Swedish Långtidsutredningen 2003/04, SOU2004:19.
11. For elder care, the difference is insignificant – see www.kvalitetsindex.se, used by the Swedish government in Långtidsutredningen 2003/04.

REFERENCES

Aarbu, Karl Ove and Thor Olav Thoresen (1997), 'The Norwegian Tax Reform; Distributional Effects and the High-income Response', Discussion Papers No. 207, December 1997, Statistics Norway, Research Department.

Agell, Jonas, Peter Englund and Jan Södersten (1996), 'Tax Reform of the Century – the Swedish Experiment, *National Tax Journal*, **49**, 643–65.

Bergh, Andreas (2003), 'Distributive Justice and the Welfare State', Lund Economic Studies 115, Department of Economics, Lund University.

Bergh, Andreas (2004), 'The Universal Welfare State: Theory and the Case of Sweden', *Political Studies*, **52**, 745–66.

Bergh, Andreas (2006), 'Is the Swedish Welfare State a Free Lunch? A Comment on Peter H. Lindert's Book *Growing Public*', Econ Journal Watch, **3**, 210–35.

Berry, William D., Richard C. Fording and Russel L. Hanson (2003), 'Reassessing the "Race to the Bottom" in State Welfare Policy', *Journal of Politics*, **65**, 327–49.

Blomqvist, Paula (2004), 'The Choice Revolution: Privatization of Swedish Welfare Services in the 1990s', *Social Policy and Administration*, **38**, 139–55.

Blomqvist, Paula and Bo Rothstein (2000), *Välfärdsstatens Nya Ansikte: Demokrati och Marknadsreformer inom den Offentliga Sektorn*, Stockholm: Agora.

Boadway, Robin (2005), 'Income Tax Reform for a Globalized World: The Case for a Dual Income Tax', presented at the International Symposium of Tax Policy and Reform in Asian Countries, Hitotsubashi University, Tokyo, Japan, 1–2 July.

Butler, Stuart and Peter Germanis (1983), 'Achieving a "Leninist" strategy', *Cato Journal*, **3**, 547–56.

Castles, Francis G. (2004), *The Future of the Welfare State: Crisis Myths and Crisis Realities*, Oxford Scholarship Online, Oxford University Press.

Disney, Richard (2003), 'Public Pension Reform in Europe: Policies, Prospects and Evaluation', *The world Economy*, **26**, 1425–45.

Domberger, S. and P. Jensen (1997), 'Contracting Out by the Public Sector: Theory, Evidence, Prospects', *Oxford Review of Economic Policy*, **13**, 67–78.

Edebalk, Per Gunnar and Marianne Svensson (2005), 'Kundval för äldre och funktionshindrade i Norden', TemaNord 2005:507, Nordiska ministerrådet, Köpenhamn, available with English summary at www.norden.org.

EIRO (2005), 'Dispute Over Pay of Latvian Building Workers in Sweden', European Industrial Relations Observatory online, http://www.eiro.eurofound.eu.int/2005/01/feature/lv0501101f.html.

EUbusiness.com (2004), 'No "Social Tourism" to Sweden Following EU Expansion: Study', http://www.eubusiness.com/East_Europe/040825093559.y65bxren.

Fogel, Robert W. (1999), 'Catching Up With the Economy', *American Economic Review*, **89**, 1–21.

Förster, Michael F. (2000), 'Trends and Driving Factors in Income Distribution and Poverty in the OECD Area', OECD Labour Market and Social Policy Occasional Paper 42.

Försäkringskassan (2005), Utbetalning av familjeförmåner med stöd av EG-lagstiftningen under 2004, Försäkringskassan Analyserar 2005:3.

Goodin, Robert E. and Julian Le Grand (1987), *Not Only the Poor: The Middle Classes and the Welfare State*, London: Allen & Unwin.

Gouyette, Claudine and Pierre Pestieau (1999), 'Efficiency of the Welfare State', *Kyklos*, **52**, 537–54.

Gramlich, Edward M. (1982), 'An Econometric Examination of the New Federalism', *Brookings Papers on Economic Activity*, **2**, 327–60.

Hall, J. and I. Preston (1998), 'Public and Private Choice in UK Health Insurance', Institute for Fiscal Studies Working Paper Series W98/19.

Hoxby, C. (2000), 'Does Competition among Public Schools Benefit Students and Taxpayers?' *American Economic Review*, **90**, 1209–38.

ITPS (2005), 'Utvärdering av expertskatten', Stockholm: Institutet för tillväxtpolitiska studier.

Karlson, Nils (2004), 'Dignity and the Burden of the Welfare State', Ratio Working Papers No 34.

Kautto, Mikko (1999), *Nordic Social Policy*, London: Routledge.

Korpi, Walter and Joakim Palme (1998), 'The Paradox of Redistribution and Strategies of Equality: Welfare State Institutions, Inequality, and Poverty in the Western Countries', *American Sociological Review*, **63**, 661–87.

Kvist, Jon (1999), 'Welfare Reform in the Nordic Countries in the 1990s: Using fuzzy-set Theory to Assess Conformity to Ideal Types', *Journal of European Social Policy*, **9**, 231–52.

Lazar, Harvey and Peter Stoyko (1998), 'The Future of the Welfare State', *International Social Security Review*, **51**, 3–36.

Lindbeck, Assar (1994), 'The Welfare State and the Employment Problem', *American Economic Review*, **84**, 71–6.

Lindbom, Anders (2001), 'Dismantling the Social Democratic Welfare Model?' *Scandinavian Political Studies*, **24**(3), 171–93.

Lindert, Peter H. (2004), *Growing Public*, Cambridge: Cambridge University Press.

Mendoza, Enrique G. and Linda L. Tesar (2005), 'Why Hasn't Tax Competition Triggered a Race to the Bottom? Some Quantitative Lessons from the EU', *Journal of Monetary Economics*, **52**, 163–204.

Nelson, Phillip J. and Kenneth V. Greene (2003), *Signaling Goodness: Social Rules and Public Choice*, Ann Arbor: University of Michigan Press.

Pedersen, Peder J., Marianne Røed and Lena Schrøder (2003), 'Emigration from the Scandinavian Welfare States', in T.M. Andersen and P. Molander (eds), *Alternatives for Welfare Policy. Coping with Internationalisation and Demographic Change*, Cambridge: Cambridge University Press, pp. 76–104.

Peterson, Paul E. and Mark C. Rom (1990), *Welfare Magnets: A New Case for a National Standard*, Washington, DC: The Brookings Institution.

Pierson, P. (1994), *Dismantling the Welfare State? Reagan, Thatcher, and the Politics of Retrenchment*, New York: Cambridge University Press.

Rosén, Per and Ingvar Karlberg (2002), 'Opinions of Swedish Citizens, Health-care Politicians, Administrators and Doctors on Rationing and Health-care Financing', *Health Expectations*, **5**, 148–55.

Rothstein, Bo (1998), *Just Institutions Matter: The Moral and Political Logic of the Universal Welfare State*, Cambridge: Cambridge University Press.

Rothstein, Bo and Anders Lindbom (2004), 'The Mysterious Survival of the Scandinavian Welfare States', paper presented at the annual meeting of the American Political Science Association 2004, Chicago.

Sandstrom, F. Mikael and Fredrik Bergstrom (2005), 'School Vouchers in Practice: Competition will not Hurt You', *Journal of Public Economics*, **89**, 351–81.

Sinn, Hans-Werner (1997), 'The Selection Principle and Market Failure in Systems Competition', *Journal of Public Economics*, **66**, 247–74.

Sinn, Hans-Werner (2004), 'The New Systems Competition', *Perspectiven der Wirtschaftspolitik*, **5**, 23–38.
Socialdepartementet (2002), *Welfare in Sweden: The Balance Sheet for the 1990s* (Ds 2000: 32), Stockholm: Socialdepartementet.
Ståhlberg, Ann-Charlotte (2003), 'Occupational Welfare', in T.M. Andersen and P. Molander (eds), *Alternatives for Welfare Policy. Coping with Internationalisation and Demographic Change*, Cambridge: Cambridge University Press, pp. 189–206.
Steinmo, Sven (2003), 'Bucking the Trend? The Welfare State and the Global Economy: The Swedish Case Up Close', *New Political Economy*, **8**, 31–49.
Svallfors, Stefan (2004), 'Class, Attitudes and the Welfare State: Sweden in Comparative Perspective', *Social Policy and Administration*, **38**, 119–38.
Timonen, Virpi (2001), 'Earning Welfare Citizenship: Welfare State Reform in Finland and Sweden', in P. Taylor-Gooby (ed.), *Welfare States under Pressure*, London: Sage Publications, pp. 29–51.
Volden, Craig (2002), 'The Politics of Competitive Federalism: A Race to Bottom Welfare Benefits', *American Journal of Political Science*, **46**, 352–63.

9. Fiscal federalism and economic growth in OECD countries

Lars P. Feld

9.1 INTRODUCTION

In recent years, there has been a broad discussion as to the proper vertical organization of government in highly-developed and less-developed countries, in unitary states and federations alike. For instance, in the discussion of reforming German federalism, it is widely recognized that the inability to make reform decisions in Germany is partly the result of the 'joint decision trap' (Scharpf 1988) emerging from cooperative federalism, German style. Many observers propose the introduction of elements of competition to German federalism, in particular to give the states (Länder) the competence to levy a surcharge on personal and corporate income taxes (Feld 2004). The proponents of fiscal competition between sub-federal jurisdictions in Germany emphasize the beneficial impact this may have on the efficiency of public goods' provision while opponents point to the undesired effects of fiscal competition on personal and regional income redistribution. Such arguments are not specific to Germany, but were also brought forward in the reform of Swiss fiscal federalism adopted in a referendum on 28 November 2004. Apart from the discussions in federations, decentralization processes continue in unitary states where similar arguments are rehearsed. Moreover, the benefits and costs of decentralization are also focused in studies on less-developed countries. While some authors argue that federalism or decentralization of state activity favour individual initiatives and serve as a market-preserving device (Weingast 1995), others emphasize the dangers arising from increasing corruption and local capture due to decentralization (Rodden and Rose-Ackerman 1997; Brueckner 2000; Bardhan 2002).

The advantages and disadvantages of fiscal federalism or decentralization are widely discussed in economics and political science today. The assessment of competitive and cooperative forms of fiscal federalism is however ambiguous from a theoretical point of view (Wilson 1999; Wilson and Wildasin 2004). Equally reasonable theoretical arguments do not offer clear-cut economic policy advice. On the one hand, some authors evaluate fiscal competition positively by emphasizing that it induces high variability and quality of goods and services and enforces individual preferences in the provision of these. Tiebout's metaphor (1956) of 'voting by feet' implies that fiscal competition leads to an efficient supply of public services. On the other hand, Gordon (1983) and Sinn (2003) have extensively criticized this result, supporting the critiques of fiscal competition for allocative and redistributive reasons. Finally, from a political economy perspective (Brennan and Buchanan 1980), fiscal competition is interpreted as a chance to reduce the size of government and thus to maintain the efficiency of a market system. Because of enhanced migration opportunities for mobile investors, governments of sub-federal jurisdictions tailor their fiscal policies to the needs of investors and thus find policy solutions favourable to market economies.

Another aspect of fiscal competition has only recently gained attention. In a system of competitive federalism, sub-federal jurisdictions can experiment with new economic policies in a decentralized fashion, and efficient solutions can successfully be copied by other jurisdictions. Competition between jurisdictions results in a discovery procedure which contributes to progress in the public sector. Federalism and decentralization lead to a higher innovative capacity of the political system. This argument appears to be tailored to the political discussion in Germany where the lack of competition between states is supposed to inhibit reform of the German welfare state. Oates (1999) speaks of 'laboratory federalism' and points out that the reform of welfare in the USA in 1996 followed these considerations (see Inman and Rubinfeld 1997). The higher innovative capacity of competitive as compared to cooperative federalism is however also questioned. In a decentralized system, citizens use the quality and prices of public services in other jurisdictions as yardsticks in elections of representatives in their own jurisdiction (for 'yardstick competition' see Salmon 1987; Besley and Case 1995). If the government of a state faces uncertainty of re-election, it has an incentive, however, to act as free-rider with respect to the policy innovations of other jurisdictions reducing the absolute amount of policy innovations in a federal country (Rose-Ackerman 1980; Strumpf 2002).

Obviously, the implied hypotheses from this discussion need to be tested empirically in order to provide confidence in specific policy proposals. However, the empirical results are inconclusive. In cross-country studies as well as studies for the USA, Germany and China, a positive or negative impact of fiscal decentralization on economic growth can be found. Methodological problems aside, one reason for the ambiguity of these results may be seen in the fact that fiscal decentralization is mainly measured in terms of the share of sub-federal spending from total spending.

This measure does not reflect actual fiscal autonomy of sub-federal jurisdictions because they may largely depend on federal grants, or participate in a system of joint taxation, or are restricted by federal mandates on either the revenue or expenditure sides of their budgets (Ebel and Yilmaz 2002). This critique particularly holds for less-developed countries in which the fiscal autonomy of sub-central jurisdictions cannot be easily assessed.

In this chapter, I empirically study the impact of fiscal federalism on economic growth only for high-income countries using panel data for 19 OECD states from 1973 to 1998. As a measure for fiscal decentralization, I use new data collected by Stegarescu (2005) following an OECD (1999) method. These data differentiate the revenue of state and local jurisdictions according to the degree of determining the different revenue sources autonomously, such that the revenue from taxes is calculated according to (1) which sub-central governments decide on tax rates or bases or both, (2) which sub-central governments co-determine tax rates or bases or both in systems of joint taxation, or (3) negligible sub-central tax autonomy. This distinction of revenue sources according to the decision-making autonomy of states and local jurisdictions allows for a test of the impact of sub-central tax autonomy on economic growth.

The remainder of the chapter is organized as follows: the different transmission channels by which fiscal federalism affects economic growth are discussed in Section 9.2. Section 9.3 surveys the empirical literature on the impact of fiscal federalism on growth. In Section 9.4, the data on revenue decentralization are introduced in more detail. The econometric model appears in Section 9.5 while Section 9.6 discusses the obtained results. Finally, Section 9.7 provides some concluding remarks.

9.2   TRANSMISSION CHANNELS OF FISCAL FEDERALISM ON ECONOMIC GROWTH[1]

Given the political controversy, the theoretical question emerges as to how the different institutional arrangements of federalism could influence the economic development of a country and its regions. What are the transmission channels of fiscal federalism on economic growth? Figure 9.1 summarizes the theoretical channels by which the vertical organization of a state possibly affects economic development. Three different sources of an impact of fiscal federalism on economic growth are distinguished. The first channel captures the standard economic argument that fiscal competition affects economic efficiency. It could be hypothesized that a system which is relatively more efficient than another will induce higher total factor productivity such that, at least temporarily, higher economic growth would

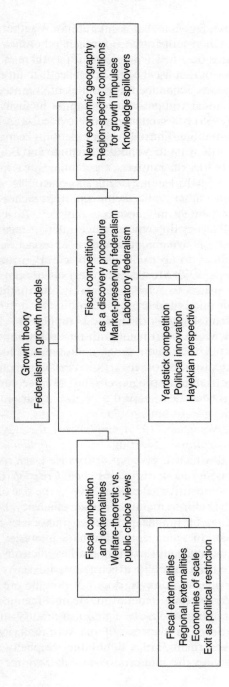

Figure 9.1 Fiscal federalism and economic development

result (Brueckner 2005; Sato and Yamashige 2005). Whether fiscal competition is more efficient than cooperative federalism is however strongly contested in the literature on fiscal federalism. First, there is the standard Tiebout (1956) argument that fiscal competition leads to an efficient provision of local public goods. Second, a whole bunch of potential externalities might obtain under fiscal competition leading to inefficiencies (Wilson 1999). As Wildasin (1989) has shown, grants provide for an instrument to internalize these externalities. Third, fiscal competition keeps governments in check if they do not do what they should (Brennan and Buchanan 1980). Facilitated exit possibilities offer citizens a potential threat if governments capture political rents, finally leading to efficient outcomes.

In contrast to these rather static theoretical approaches according to which fiscal federalism might influence economic growth only indirectly because of relative efficiency differences under different regimes, the other two channels consist of dynamic theoretical approaches. The second channel interprets fiscal competition as a discovery procedure in the Hayekian sense (Hayek 1939). Most economists evaluate competition positively because it is a means to achieve variability and quality of product supply, and to provide goods and services according to individuals' preferences. By drawing an analogy to private goods supply, fiscal decentralization allows governments to experiment with new solutions for economic problems in a decentralized fashion. Better solutions succeed in a process of imitation and adaptation by other jurisdictions. Competition between jurisdictions thus contributes to progress in the public sector. Such a 'laboratory federalism' (Oates 1999) served as a role model for US welfare reform in 1996 (Inman and Rubinfeld 1997).

In a similar way, Weingast (1995) emphasizes the advantages of a *'market-preserving federalism'*. Starting from a *'fundamental political dilemma'*, according to which *'a government strong enough to protect property rights and enforce contracts is also strong enough to confiscate the wealth of its citizens'* (p. 1), competitive federalism reduces the size of government interventions and thus helps to maintain market efficiency. Because of the increased opportunities of mobile production factors to migrate, sub-federal jurisdictions conduct policies that are in the interest of these mobile factors and thus create solutions favouring market efficiency. Similar conclusions can be drawn from the political economy analysis by Brennan and Buchanan (1980). Weingast, however, does not provide precise considerations as to the growth effects of federalism. He only mentions the advantageous development in England in the eighteenth century and in the USA in the nineteenth century as evidence of market-preserving federalism. Rodden and Rose-Ackerman (1997) doubt the simplicity of the argument. Instead of serving the interests of mobile investors, sub-federal jurisdictions may be captured by local interest groups and introduce protectionist measures in order to shelter them from external competition. Whether federalism produces market-preserving or protectionist policies thus depends on additional institutional safeguards.

The higher innovative capacity of a federal as compared to a unitary system as explanations of differences in the economic development of countries is therefore contested. In a decentralized system the citizens use the services provided by governments of other jurisdictions as a yardstick to evaluate the policy of their government in elections (Salmon 1987; Besley and Case 1995; Feld et al. 2003; Reulier 2004). A government is re-elected if it provides services that are at least not worse than those in other jurisdictions or the tax prices of which are not higher. Thus, each government initially has incentives to wait in order to imitate only those policies of other jurisdictions that have turned out to be relatively successful. If the government of a state is uncertain about re-election, it has an incentive to act as a free-rider with respect to the policy innovations of other jurisdictions, finally reducing the absolute amount of policy innovations in a federation (Rose-Ackerman 1980).[2] Schnellenbach (2004) studies the incentives for policy innovations in a decentralized setting by focusing on the incentives of voters. As voters' incentives to be politically informed before elections are small, policy innovations are mainly possible in times of crisis. Citizens' incentives to become informed on policy innovations are however improved by high mobility and elements of direct democracy in political decision-making processes. Political rents of governments can hence be reduced by competition, and politicians can be offered incentives to innovate.

This second line of thought offers a dynamic view of fiscal federalism. The link between federalism and growth is however still indirect and mainly stems from more favourable public policy conditions under competitive than under cooperative federalism. The third channel consists of a direct influence of decentralized policy decisions on regional or national economic growth. It is often hypothesized in political discussions on advantages and disadvantages of fiscal federalism that far-reaching competencies of the subnational levels to decide on revenue and spending leads to unfavourable regional income distribution, such that poor regions become poorer and rich regions become richer (Feld 2004). The more affluent taxpayers sort themselves into regions where the tax burden is lower. Poor regions, however, supposedly need to levy high taxes to finance the 'necessary' infrastructure for catching up with richer regions. If these jurisdictions enter fiscal competition, the economic differences between regions are exacerbated. Instead of having a regional convergence, divergence of regional incomes results. The policy conclusion from this reasoning is clear:

fiscal competition should be eliminated by harmonization or centralization and it should be supplemented by grants that equalize regional fiscal capacity. Cooperative federalism would be the policy conclusion.

Ludema and Wooton (2000), Kind et al. (2000), Anderson and Forslid (2003), Baldwin and Krugman (2004), Brakman et al. (2003) and Borck and Pflüger (2006) challenge this view from the perspective of the new economic geography by analysing the impact of fiscal competition on the economic development of central and peripheral regions. The advantages of agglomerations in the economic centres permit the governments of central regions to raise higher taxes than the peripheral regions. The agglomeration rent obtained by the mobile factor in the core region can be taxed. An example from the EU may illustrate this. Northern Italy offers firms an excellent infrastructure, well-established relations with customers and suppliers, and a highly qualified workforce such that it can afford the relatively high Italian tax burden. Peripheral regions, like Ireland, have hardly any options for balancing their locational disadvantages other than tax policy and public investment in infrastructure. They need to attract economic activity through an appropriate mix of taxes and public services. Harmonization or centralization of fiscal competencies would take from peripheral regions the few instruments available to compensate for their locational disadvantages vis-à-vis the central regions, and it would therefore be harmful for regional development. It is nevertheless questionable whether government policies are sufficiently powerful to compensate for the strong locational advantages of central regions. These theoretical studies necessarily cast serious doubts as to the success of grants in fostering regional development.

Given these arguments, fiscal federalism might influence economic development in several ways that also depend on the perspective adopted. According to the first perspective, it could be asked whether fiscal competition or fiscal cooperation between sub-federal jurisdictions affects regional economic growth. In that case, fiscal competition theoretically has ambiguous effects because, while on the one hand it might induce higher efficiency of public goods provision and higher political innovation and hence a better economic performance of the regions or states, on the other hand it might lead to a migration of mobile production factors to centres of economic activity where agglomeration economies can be realized such that they are sufficiently affluent to afford excellent infrastructure. Single poorer regions might suffer from that competition. They may however equally likely gain from fiscal competition when they can credibly commit to a low tax policy which compensates for locational disadvantages.

Similarly, grants, as the main fiscal instrument of cooperative federalism have ambiguous effects on economic performance. On the one hand, grants may help poorer regions to provide more attractive conditions to potential investors than they could otherwise afford such that investors do not emigrate from the region (or additional investors can be attracted). The payment of fiscal transfers as such is an income increase for the recipient regions and may be reflected in a higher GDP per capita. On the other hand, grants provide adverse incentives to the poorer regions such that structural change is postponed and promising new technologies are not adopted. The status quo is hence preserved and declining industries are artificially kept alive – ensuring that future restructuring will face worse conditions. Specific problems emerge for regions in excessive debt because grants as a bail-out payment provide incentives to stay indebted (Feld and Goodspeed 2005).

The second perspective is connected to the first: it could be asked whether fiscal competition or fiscal coordination accelerate or decelerate regional convergence. The same reasoning as before with respect to regional economic development applies here with the exception that the catching up process is more focused.

The third perspective, however, is different, because a national point of view is adopted. Fiscal competition or cooperation could lead to better economic performance of the whole country by exploiting efficiency reserves in the provision of public goods. Again there is an ambiguous assessment of the relation between economic development and fiscal federalism. On the one hand, and quite simply, fiscal competition might lead to a more efficient allocation of labour and capital in the central regions that are the main growth poles of the economy. In addition, the incentives from fiscal competition to innovate and provide public services more efficiently reduces the waste of resources in the economy as a whole. From that perspective, grants mainly provide negative incentives to successful regions in exploiting their economic potential because the payment of transfers in a horizontal fiscal equalization system is perceived by them as a tax on the additional revenue they could capture by the location of new taxpayers. On the other hand, fiscal competition may deprive poorer regions of structural change which could lead to higher overall growth rates when completed. In this case, the positive impact of grants to induce structural change in recipient regions needs to compensate for the negative incentives to donor regions in order to have an overall positive impact on economic development of a country.

9.3   A SURVEY OF THE EMPIRICAL EVIDENCE

As the theoretical results on the relation between fiscal federalism and economic development are ambiguous, empirical studies might shed some light on the relation between federalism and economic growth. The empirical studies testing this hypothesis do not, however, provide consistent results. This holds for cross-country studies as well as for studies on single countries. In the area of cross-country studies, Davoodi and Zou (1998) find a weakly significant negative relation between the degree of fiscal federalism and the average growth rate of GDP per capita for a sample of 46 countries from 1970 to 1989.[3] For the sub-sample of industrial countries this effect is not significant. The negative influence for developing countries, however, is robust though only weakly significant. Woller and Philipps (1998) also do not find a robust relation between economic growth and decentralization, using a sample of 23 developing countries and the period 1974 to 1991. In a more recent analysis, Iimi (2005) finds a robust positive effect of fiscal decentralization on (average) economic growth for a cross-section of 51 countries from 1997 to 2001 by endogenizing fiscal decentralization.

In an analysis for average economic growth of the past 25 years in a cross-section of 91 countries, Enikolopov and Zhuravskaya (2003) show that the effects of fiscal decentralization depend to a large extent on the structure of the party system as well as on the degree of 'subordination' of subnational levels. According to them, especially in developing and transition countries, the age of the most important political parties is favourable to the positive effects of decentralization on economic growth. In countries with what is in this respect a weaker party system, a 10 per cent higher decentralization of revenue decreases real per capita GDP growth in developing countries by 0.14 percentage points. These results are in contrast to those of Martinez-Vazquez and McNab (2002) who observe that the decentralization of revenue significantly reduces the growth of real GDP per capita of developed countries, but not of the developing and transition countries. Yilmaz (2000) analyses the different effects of fiscal decentralization in 17 unitary and 13 federal countries for the period 1971–90 with annual data. Decentralization of expenditures to the local level increases the growth of real GDP per capita in unitary states more strongly than in federal states. However, the decentralization to the intermediate level in federations is not significant.

Thießen (2003) analyses the average growth rates of real GDP per capita for a cross-section of 21 developed countries in the period 1973–98 and in a parallel study (Thießen 2003a) for a panel of 26 countries between 1981 and 1995. According to his estimates a 10 per cent stronger decentralization of expenditures increases the growth of real GDP per capita by 0.12–0.15 percentage points in high-income countries. However, the relation between federalism and economic growth might be non-linear, because the quadratic term of expenditure decentralization is significantly negative.

For a sample of 22 OECD countries between 1972 and 1996, Eller (2004) finds that high income and high to middle income OECD countries show a positive growth performance when they converge to a medium degree of expenditure decentralization while revenue decentralization does not have any significant effect on economic growth. His analysis thus corroborates Thießen's findings at least indirectly.

The impact of decentralization on economic growth has also been analysed for China, India, Russia, the US, Germany and Switzerland. Zhang and Zou (1998, 2001) note a significantly negative effect of expenditure decentralization on economic growth in 28 (29) Chinese provinces, using annual data between 1987 and 1993 (1980 and 1992) respectively. Jin et al. (1999), however, report a weakly significant positive effect of expenditure decentralization on economic growth of Chinese provinces over time. The most important difference between the studies is the use of time dummies that are not included by Zhang and Zou. Consequently, symmetric shocks are not adequately controlled for. Lin and Liu (2000) strengthen the result of a positive relation between decentralization and economic growth in Chinese provinces for the period 1970 to 1993, also for the revenue side. In addition, higher responsibility of public budgets at the provincial level is connected with increased economic growth. These authors also use time dummies in addition to fixed cross-section effects.

The relevance for the estimates of using time dummies points to the strong economic dynamics in China. The sometimes enormously high Chinese growth rates apparently cannot be captured by structural variables alone so that auxiliary variables for the individual years are necessary for correctly specifying the econometric model. The fact that Zhang and Zou neglect them must be interpreted as mis-specification of the model. Thus, for China, there might well exist a positive relation between decentralization of governmental activity and economic growth. Such a positive relationship between fiscal decentralization and economic growth has also been found by Zhang and Zou (2001) for a panel of 16 Indian states in the period 1970 to 1994. In addition, Desai et al. (2003) report a significant positive effect of tax retention as a measure of sub-national fiscal autonomy on the cumulative output recovery of 80 Russian regions between 1996 and 1999.

In a time-series analysis for the US from 1951 to 1992, Xie et al. (1999) claim that the US finds itself in a decentralization equilibrium. They ascribe this to the fact that differences in decentralization at the state or local level do not exert statistically significant effects on total real GDP growth. Akai and Sakata (2002) offer evidence for the US states. Considering additional explanatory factors and various indicators for the degree of fiscal federalism, they find a positive influence on economic growth. However, decentralization on the revenue side and indicators for fiscal autonomy of sub-national levels, measured by the share of own revenue in total revenue, do not show significant effects. In addition, Akai and Sakata (2004) find that local autonomy reduces regional inequality for 50 US states between 1993 and 2000. Finally, Stansel (2005) reports a positive effect of local decentralization on local economic growth. These studies might not necessarily contradict each other because of the different perspectives adopted. While the first study starts from a national perspective, the other three adopt the perspective of the single states and local jurisdictions. As mentioned in Section 9.2, these perspectives might well coincide.

The same argument might hold for Germany. Berthold et al. (2001) analyse the effects of horizontal fiscal equalization between states and supplementary federal grants on economic development of the 16 Länder in a panel analysis with annual data from 1991 to 1998. According to their estimates, higher grants in horizontal and vertical fiscal relations significantly reduce the growth of nominal GDP per capita of the Länder. Their study might be flawed by the reversed causality running from growth to grants. Behnisch et al. (2002), indeed, find a positive effect of increasing federal activities – measured by the share of expenditure at the federal level – on total German productivity growth in a time series analysis from 1950 to 1990.

In a recent study of Swiss cantons, Feld et al. (2004) focus on the different instruments of competitive and cooperative fiscal federalism instead of solely looking at decentralization ratios. For a sample of 26 Swiss cantons between 1980 and 1998, they find evidence that tax competition positively affects cantonal economic performance. The fragmentation of a canton in its communities does not have any robust impact on economic performance, such that arguments for a merger of local jurisdictions are not supported. Finally, no reasonable evidence on federal government grants is obtained because of the reversed causation problem that cannot be easily coped with econometrically. At least, this study emphasizes the importance of sub-central tax autonomy more strongly than any other surveyed in this section. It is thus worth looking more closely on tax autonomy in OECD countries.

9.4   NEW DATA ON THE DECENTRALIZATION OF TAX REVENUE

The tax autonomy of state and local jurisdictions in OECD countries was first measured by the OECD (1999). In a cross-section of the 18 OECD countries – Austria, Belgium, the Czech Republic, Denmark, Finland, Germany, Hungary, Iceland, Japan, Mexico, the Netherlands, New Zealand, Poland, Portugal, Spain, Sweden, Switzerland and the United Kingdom – the OECD calculates the revenue from different tax sources, fees and user charges, privatization and grants and determines to what extent sub-central jurisdictions have an impact on the outcome of taxation decisions. This involves the possibility that they can determine tax rates, tax bases or both of certain tax types autonomously, or that states or local jurisdictions have a decision-making power on tax rates, tax bases or both in the higher level political process which determines joint taxation systems. In fact, the OECD even differentiates tax sharing agreements further by assessing whether the revenue split can only be changed by consent of state or local governments, whether the revenue split can be unilaterally changed by the central government but is fixed in the legislation, or whether the revenue split can be unilaterally changed by the central government in the annual budgetary process. On the basis of these data, the share of revenue of sub-central jurisdictions with different degrees of autonomous decision-making can be assessed for each country. The advantage of the data consists in the assessment of the relative importance of the different revenue sources in addition to a differentiated perspective on the assignment of revenues to levels of government.

Stegarescu (2005) follows the OECD approach, but extends the data, first, to 23 OECD countries and, second, to the period 1970 to 2001. From the 18 countries mentioned above, the Czech Republic, Hungary and Poland are not covered by his data, while Australia, Canada, France, Greece, Ireland, Italy, Luxembourg, Norway, and the US are additionally included. Though the quality of the data is outstanding, there remains a minor problem: the main variation in the data stems from the cross-section domain and the variation in time series domain is reduced. This characteristic of the data is illustrated by Figures 9.2 to 9.7.

Germany and Spain are taken as examples. Figure 9.2 shows the share of state and local spending from total spending from 1973 to 1999. The share of spending of the sub-federal jurisdictions in Germany fell from slightly above 50 per cent in 1973 to less than 45 per cent in 1999. The level of this decentralization indicator reflects that Germany is a federation with a non-negligible role of the states and local jurisdictions. Although the reduction of the weight of the states and local jurisdictions in government spending across time is remarkable, they nevertheless play an important role in government policy. Moreover, and despite this reduction across time, the time variation is not very strong. The figure reflects a relatively stable distribution of competencies between the German states and local jurisdictions on the one hand and the federal government on the other hand.

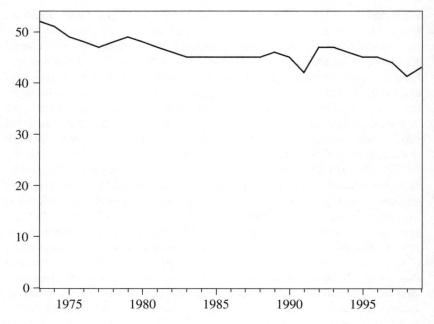

Source: Stegarescu (2005).

*Figure 9.2   Share of state and local government expenditure from total
           expenditure in Germany (%)*

Considering Germany as a very decentralized country is however
obscured by the fact that neither the states nor the local jurisdictions
possess a similarly strong autonomy on the revenue side as they do on the
expenditure side of the budget. This is illustrated by Figure 9.3 which
shows the share of state and local government revenue from total revenue
that is autonomously decided by the states and local jurisdictions.
Autonomy is meant in the sense outlined above, as autonomy over tax
rates, tax bases or both. These figures are much lower than those reported
for spending decentralization. They vary between 6.5 and 8 per cent. In
Germany, the states do not have the power to determine tax rates or bases
autonomously. Only the local jurisdictions can fix the tax rates of a local
business tax and of property taxes. The numbers in Figure 9.3 reflect the
low weight these taxes have in the whole system of taxation, although
they are important revenue sources for the local jurisdictions. It can
also be easily realized that the time variation of these tax revenues is
higher than that of spending decentralization owing to the fact that local
business tax revenue is highly affected by business cycle developments

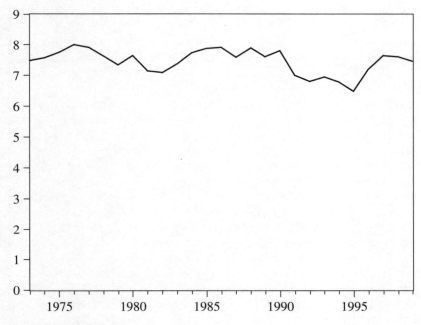

Source: Stegarescu (2005).

Figure 9.3 Share of state and local government revenue from total revenue of which states and local jurisdictions autonomously decide on tax rates or tax bases in Germany (%)

and has also undergone significant legal changes during the last thirty years.

The German states can however determine the level of the most important taxes, that is, personal and corporate income taxes as well as value added taxes in the decision-making procedures at the federal level. These three taxes belong to the system of tax sharing. Any legal changes in this system require a majority in the lower chamber of the federal parliament, the Bundestag, as well as a majority of the states governments' representatives in the upper chamber of government, the Bundesrat. The federal government cannot therefore induce tax reforms without the consent of the German states. It autonomously decides only on the mineral oil tax, the tobacco tax, the insurance tax and on surcharges on income taxes as the four most important tax sources. Similarly, the states obtain the revenue from inheritance taxes, car taxes and so on, but can only decide on changes of the respective tax laws via the Bundesrat. This is reflected in Figure 9.4

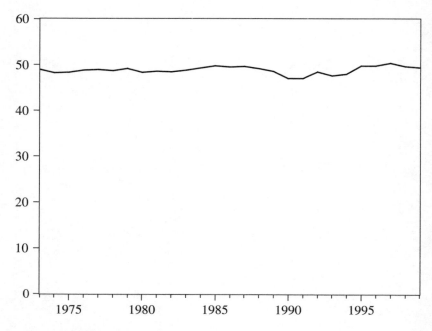

Source: Stegarescu (2005).

*Figure 9.4   Share of state and local government revenue from total revenue
of which states and local jurisdictions autonomously decide on
tax rates or tax bases or obtain revenue from joint taxation
systems in Germany (%)*

which reveals a high level of state and local tax revenue obtained via own
taxes and from tax sharing without much time variation.

The modest development of German federalism is matched by the experience of most other countries in the sample. There are only a few exceptions
to this verdict. One of them is Spain, as figures 9.5 to 9.7 show. While the
fiscal autonomy of the Spanish regions and local jurisdictions was still pretty
low during Franco's dictatorship, it increased tremendously after his death.
As Figure 9.5 indicates, spending decentralization in Spain steadily increased
from 10 per cent during 1973 to 1979 to more than 40 per cent in 1999.

Though the movements across time appear to be more cyclical, similar
trends can be observed for own tax revenue with tax rate or base autonomy
of the regions and local jurisdictions (Figure 9.6) as well as tax sharing
arrangements at the federal level (Figure 9.7). While the share of own taxes
increased from 5 per cent in 1973 to about 23 per cent in 1999, the share of

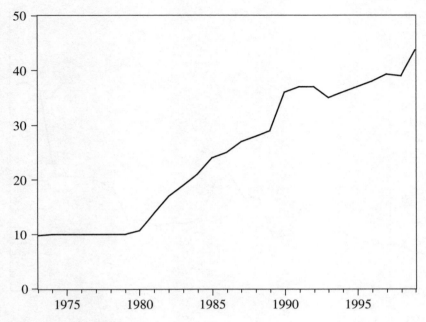

Source: Stegarescu (2005).

*Figure 9.5   Share of state and local government expenditure from total
expenditure in Spain (%)*

revenue from own taxes and tax sharing increased from 7 per cent in 1973
to 25 per cent in 1999.

The development reflects the evolution of Spain from a unitary state to
a federation. This is for instance also realized in the political data set of
Treisman (2002) who meanwhile considers Spain as a federation. Aside
from the Spanish experience, a similarly exciting time variation can only be
found in the case of Belgium and, though much less significantly, in the
cases of Italy and France. In all of these countries, decentralization processes continue although they have not yet led to such a clear-cut establishment of autonomous regions as in Spain.

9.5   THE ECONOMETRIC SPECIFICATION

In order to test the impact of fiscal decentralization on economic growth,
we adopt the national perspective by analysing economic growth of 19
OECD countries. Convergence of per capita income as well as the impact

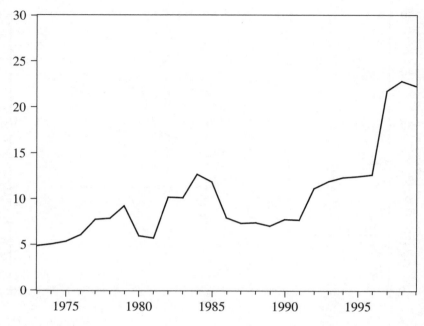

Source: Stegarescu (2005).

Figure 9.6   *Share of state and local government revenue from total revenue*
of which states and local jurisdictions autonomously decide on
tax rates or tax bases in Spain (%)

of fiscal federalism on regional economic development are left out of consideration. Aside from any ad hoc regressions of economic growth on indicators of fiscal decentralization, two different approaches can be found in the literature that are covered by the two main traditions in growth theory. First, neoclassical growth models are applied and a significant impact of indicators of fiscal federalism is interpreted as feeding into technological progress. In this case, the impact of fiscal decentralization on economic growth is only a temporary influence in the transition to the steady state. This approach follows the empirical analysis of neoclassical growth models by Mankiw et al. (1992) and is applied by Thießen (2003, 2003a) in the case of high-income countries and Feld et al. (2004) in the case of Switzerland.

Second, some authors have adapted the Barro (1990) type AK model of endogenous growth to countries with more than one layer of government. The most explicit derivation of the subsequent econometric model can be found in Davoodi and Zou (1998) and Zhang and Zou (1998, 2001).[4] In this

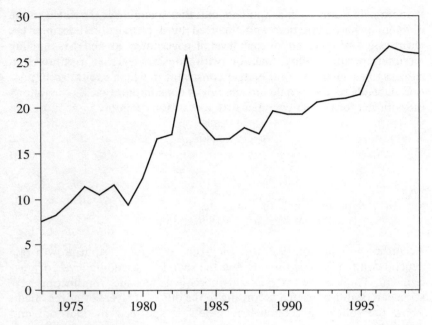

Source: Stegarescu (2005).

Figure 9.7   *Share of state and local government revenue from total revenue*
of which states and local jurisdictions autonomously decide on
tax rates or tax bases or obtain revenue from joint taxation
systems in Spain (%)

model output per capita, *y*, is explained by the private per capita capital
stock, *k*, and government spending undertaken by three different layers of
government such that the following production function obtains:

$$y = k^\alpha f^\beta s^\gamma l^\omega \qquad (9.1)$$

where

y = output per capita,
f = federal spending, $f = \theta_f g$,
s = state spending, $s = \theta_s g$,
l = local spending, $l = \theta_l g$.

There are constant returns to scale and θ_i determines the share of spending of the respective government level, while *g* denotes total government

spending. The approach simply assumes that spending is separated to the different government tiers and financed by a proportional income tax which could be specified for each level of government as well. Maximizing an intertemporal utility function with constant relative risk aversion subject to an intertemporal budget constraint in which capital accumulation depends on disposable income minus consumption yields the following solution for the per capita growth rate of the economy:

$$\frac{dy/dt}{y} = \frac{(1-\tau)\tau^{\frac{1-\alpha}{\alpha}}\alpha\theta_f^{\frac{\beta}{\alpha}}\theta_s^{\frac{\gamma}{\alpha}}\theta_l^{\frac{\omega}{\alpha}} - \rho}{\sigma} \qquad (9.2)$$

where

ρ = positive time discount rate,
σ = coefficient of relative risk aversion.

According to equation (9.2), the long-run per capita output growth rate depends on the income tax rate and the shares of spending levels of government. The income tax rate and subsequent revenue from income taxation can be differentiated according to the different layers of government. Thus, the following econometric model is specified by Davoodi and Zou (1998):

$$g_{it} = \beta_0 + \beta_1\,\theta_{it} + \beta_2\,\tau_{it} + \beta_3 D_i + \beta_4\,N_t + \beta_5\,X_{it} + \varepsilon_{it} \qquad (9.3)$$

where g_{it} stands for the growth rate of real GDP per capita. θ_{it} denotes the share of spending of sub-central jurisdictions, τ_{it} is total tax revenue in percent of GDP and X_{it} is a vector of control variables. D_i are the country specific fixed effects and N_t the time-specific fixed effects. β_0 to β_5 are the parameters of interest while ε_{it} denotes the error term.

This model has been extensively criticized in the literature as rather ad hoc (Martinez-Vazquez and McNab 2001; Thießen 2003, 2003a; Eller 2004). In fact, none of the transmission channels discussed above are satisfactorily captured by this econometric approach. In addition, it is not at all clear how the endogenous growth is derived in this model and what mechanism drives a divergence of growth performance in the long run. In particular, an explicit link between fiscal competition in models from the new economic geography (NEG) and economic growth is not considered. The latter argument provides however for the first excuse as well. Most NEG models have difficulties in establishing unique equilibria so that a clear-cut prediction for growth performances cannot be expected.

Adapting the Davoodi and Zou (1998) approach to the question of tax autonomy does not require many adjustments of equation (9.3). Instead of the ratio of total government revenue to GDP, the shares of sub-central revenue from total revenue in the case of own taxes and in the case of additional participation in tax sharing are considered. As control variables, private investment in per cent of GDP, public education spending and population growth are included. In addition, openness (in per cent of GDP), government consumption and inflation are used in order to conduct robustness tests. The analysis uses yearly data from 1973 to 1998. The subscript $i = 1, \ldots, 19$ indicates OECD countries and $t = 1973, \ldots, 1998$ indexes years. The empirical analysis is performed using a pooled cross-section time series model with time-specific fixed effects as a baseline specification and then proceeds to two-way fixed effects models. Finally, some tests on robustness of estimates to the inclusion of additional variables are performed.

9.6 RESULTS

Table 9.1 presents the baseline regressions for the pooled cross-section time series model. The overall performance of the model is satisfactory. About 40 per cent of real GDP growth is explained, while the standard explanatory variables have the expected signs and are, with the exception of public education spending as the human capital proxy, statistically significant.

Including the indicator of expenditure decentralization as it is traditionally used in this literature in the second model, a significant negative effect of fiscal decentralization on economic growth results. The same qualitative impact of fiscal decentralization on economic growth obtains when each of the revenue decentralization indicators is used alone. Tax autonomy of the state and local jurisdictions, measured by an autonomous determination of tax rates or tax bases as well as additionally measured by a co-determination of tax sharing arrangements at the federal level, appears to affect economic growth significantly negatively. Moreover, the estimated coefficients of both revenue indicators are of similar size. It is however no surprise that each of the spending or revenue decentralization measures has the same qualitative effect if the correlation between these measures is considered. The correlation coefficient between spending decentralization and autonomy in tax rates or bases is 0.71 while it is 0.69 in the case of additional co-determination on tax sharing. The correlation between both revenue decentralization measures is 0.82.

I therefore include the different decentralization measures together, starting with both revenue decentralization indicators and second adding expenditure decentralization. The estimation results in models (V) and (VI) indicate that neither spending decentralization nor sub-central tax autonomy over tax rates or bases have a significant impact on economic growth.

Table 9.1   Baseline regressions of growth of real GDP per capita on spending and revenue decentralization, 1973–98, pooled cross-section time series models

	(I)	(II)	(III)	(IV)	(V)	(VI)
Investment	0.052*	0.067**	0.074**	0.088**	0.088**	0.088**
	(2.09)	(2.68)	(2.93)	(3.52)	(3.52)	(3.51)
Public education spending	−0.054	0.064	0.083	0.061	0.060	0.046
	(0.88)	(0.92)	(1.22)	(0.97)	(0.89)	(0.65)
Population growth	−0.528**	−0.508**	−0.523**	−0.512**	−0.512**	−0.516**
	(8.96)	(8.66)	(9.03)	(8.96)	(8.95)	(8.95)
Expenditure decentralization	–	−2.142**	–	–	–	0.522
		(3.32)				(0.59)
Revenue decentralization (tax rates or bases)	–	–	−0.026**	–	0.0004	−0.001
			(4.29)		(0.04)	(0.11)
Revenue decentralization (tax rates or bases or joint taxation)	–	–	–	−0.032**	−0.032**	−0.034**
				(5.68)	(3.65)	(3.61)
Cross-section FE	no	no	no	no	no	no
Time FE	yes	yes	yes	yes	yes	yes
No. of countries	19	19	19	19	19	19
No. of observations	494	494	494	494	494	494
$\bar{R}^2$	0.378	0.391	0.400	0.417	0.416	0.415
SER	2.063	2.041	2.026	1.997	1.999	2.000

Notes: The numbers in parentheses are the t-statistics of the estimated parameters; '(*)', '*', or '**' denote significance at the 10, 5, or 1 per cent level, respectively; $\bar{R}^2$ is the adjusted coefficient of determination; SER is the standard error of regression. The computations have been performed by EViews, Version 4.1.

However, a stronger participation of sub-federal jurisdictions in joint taxation systems at the federal level induces a significantly worse growth performance. Estimating the same models with cross-section fixed effects as shown in Table 9.2 leaves none of the decentralization variables significantly different from zero. While the negative impact of sub-federal participation in joint taxation systems prevails it falls short of significance with a t-statistic of 1.23. Obviously, the reduced time variation of the decentralization variables is captured by the cross-section fixed effects.

Table 9.2 *Baseline regressions of growth of real GDP per capita on spending and revenue decentralization, 1973–98, fixed effects models*

	(VII)	(VIII)	(IX)	(X)	(XI)	(XII)
Investment	0.200**	0.200**	0.200**	0.199**	0.201**	0.200**
	(5.15)	(5.12)	(5.12)	(5.10)	(5.15)	(5.11)
Public education	0.164	0.163	0.163	0.147	0.143	0.140
spending	(1.41)	(1.39)	(1.38)	(1.24)	(1.20)	(1.17)
Population	−0.568**	−0.568**	−0.569**	−0.571**	−0.571**	−0.570**
growth	(10.06)	(9.98)	(10.04)	(10.08)	(10.07)	(10.00)
Expenditure	–	0.237	–	–	–	0.437
decentralization		(0.11)				(0.19)
Revenue	–	–	−0.004	–	0.049	0.048
decentralization			(0.11)		(0.91)	(0.90)
(tax rates or						
bases)						
Revenue	–	–	–	−0.016	−0.040	−0.040
decentralization				(0.82)	(1.22)	(1.23)
(tax rates or						
bases or joint						
taxation)						
Cross-section FE	yes	yes	yes	yes	yes	yes
Time FE	yes	yes	yes	yes	yes	yes
No. of countries	19	19	19	19	19	19
No. of	494	494	494	494	494	494
observations						
$\bar{R}^2$	0.470	0.469	0.469	0.469	0.469	0.468
SER	1.904	1.906	1.906	1.905	1.905	1.907

Notes: See Table 9.1.

This is corroborated by the further analysis. In the first two columns in Table 9.3, a federation dummy developed by Treisman (2002) is included which is 1 if the country is a federation and zero otherwise. The definition of a federation is obtained from the political science and legal literature requiring that a constitutional safeguard of the existence and the status of regional entities as states must obtain. Again, this variable is strongly time invariant with the only time variation existing in the case of Spain. The federation dummy significantly affects economic growth and has a positive effect in the pooled estimation in model XII while it has no significant effect in the model with cross-section fixed effects (model XIII). The significantly

Table 9.3   Robustness tests, 19 OECD countries, 1973–98

	(XII)	(XIII)	(XIV)	(XV)
Investment	0.095**	0.200**	0.108**	0.173**
	(3.78)	(5.06)	(4.33)	(4.52)
Public education	0.103	0.139	0.137(*)	0.147
spending	(1.36)	(1.12)	(1.74)	(1.25)
Population growth	−0.533**	−0.570**	−0.539**	−0.571**
	(9.21)	(9.99)	(9.51)	(10.52)
Expenditure decentralization	−0.269	0.415	0.360	−0.138
	(0.28)	(0.17)	(0.37)	(0.05)
Revenue decentralization	0.007	0.048	0.001	0.097(*)
(tax rates or bases)	(0.70)	(0.89)	(0.05)	(1.74)
Revenue decentralization	−0.050**	−0.041	−0.036**	0.022
(tax rates or bases or joint	(4.25)	(0.98)	(2.99)	(0.54)
taxation)				
Federalist state dummy	0.676*	0.021	0.673*	−0.416
	(2.24)	(0.02)	(2.25)	(0.44)
Openness (in % of GDP)			0.010**	0.100**
	–	–	(4.14)	(6.90)
Government consumption			0.065**	0.046*
	–	–	(3.84)	(2.03)
Inflation			−0.007	−0.027
	–	–	(0.20)	(0.56)
Cross-section FE	no	yes	no	yes
Time FE	yes	yes	yes	yes
No. of countries	19	19	19	19
No. of observations	494	494	494	494
$\bar{R}^2$	0.420	0.467	0.447	0.517
SER	1.992	1.910	1.945	1.817

Notes: See Table 9.1.

negative effect of a stronger participation in tax sharing is robust to the inclusion of the federation dummy in the pooled model, but loses significance in the fixed effects model. The final two equations show a general robustness of the models to the inclusion of additional variables like openness, government consumption and inflation. Again the estimation results for fiscal decentralization are sensitive to the inclusion of cross-section fixed effects.

Summing up, it becomes evident from the pooled regressions that tax autonomy of sub-federal jurisdictions in OECD countries does not have a robust impact on economic growth. However, the stronger the participation of sub-central jurisdictions in systems of shared taxation, the lower the economic growth. This indicates at least indirectly that fiscal decentralization on the revenue side, in particular tax autonomy, meaning the absence of joint taxation has some positive influence on economic performance of OECD countries. The problem is that tax autonomy is still not adequately measured by the data used so that the measurement problems persist. The fixed effects regressions underline this problem. The fixed effects capture the main variation of the decentralization indicators and also of the fiscal federalism dummy such that the impact of fiscal decentralization is statistically uncertain.[5] Given the extensive discussion in many OECD countries about the harmful effects of tax autonomy and subsequently induced tax competition on economic efficiency, income redistribution and regional development, these results are nevertheless encouraging. They provide some evidence that a higher tax autonomy of sub-federal jurisdictions is not economically harmful.

9.7   CONCLUSIONS

The impact of fiscal federalism or fiscal decentralization on economic growth is widely discussed in the economics and political science literature as well as in politics. Theoretical analyses do not offer clear-cut arguments as to the impact of fiscal federalism on economic growth. However, empirical results are also mixed. In this paper, we have exploited new data provided by Stegarescu (2005) on fiscal decentralization that allow us to measure different degrees of fiscal autonomy. According to our estimates, neither spending decentralization nor sub-central tax autonomy in the sense that states or local jurisdictions have the power to determine tax rates or tax bases have a significant impact on economic growth of 19 OECD countries from 1973 to 1998. However, a stronger participation of sub-federal jurisdictions in the decision-making process of tax sharing arrangements significantly reduces economic growth. In addition, the constitutional safeguarding of a regional tier of government, in the sense of a vertical division of powers, affects economic growth significantly positively.

These effects are not robust to fixed effects estimations. Including cross-section fixed effects captures most of the variation of the decentralization variables because they are relatively time invariant. These results are also robust to the inclusion of additional economic variables, such as openness, inflation and government consumption. Obviously, estimating fixed effects models with time invariant exogenous variables is not useful. This leaves some confidence as to the validity of the estimated negative effects of participation in joint taxation systems on economic growth. The more systematic analysis of the robustness of these effects is however left to further research.

NOTES

1. For a more extensive survey of the studies investigating the impact of fiscal federalism on economic growth, see Feld et al. (2007). See also Feld et al. (2004).
2. According to Strumpf (2002) this free-rider behaviour strongly depends on homogeneity and on the number of jurisdictions. Heterogeneous jurisdictions act to a lesser extent as free-riders, because it pays off for them to realize first-mover advantages with tailor-made policy innovations. Kotsogiannis and Schwager (2001) point out that in a federal country, policy innovations offer selfish politicians the opportunity of obtaining personal advantages and of letting them appear as the result of the uncertainty of policy innovations.
3. There is an earlier PhD thesis by Sang Loh Kim, quoted by Oates (1993), according to which fiscal decentralization has a significant and robust positive correlation with economic growth in 40 countries in the period 1974 to 1989.
4. Eller (2004, p. 33) summarizes the model by Davoodi and Zou (1998) in a wonderfully concise manner. We follow his presentation of the model in this section.
5. It should also be noted that it might be difficult to pick up long-run effects due to the brief time period used for the analysis (see Wohlgemuth 2006).

REFERENCES

Akai, N. and M. Sakata (2002), 'Fiscal Decentralization Contributes to Economic Growth: Evidence from State-level Cross-section Data for the United States', *Journal of Urban Economics*, **52**, 93–108.

Akai, N. and M. Sakata (2004), 'Fiscal Decentralization, Commitment and Regional Inequality: Evidence from State-level Cross-section Data for the United States', Working Paper, Kobe University.

Anderson, F. and R. Forslid (2003), 'Tax Competition and Economic Geography', *Journal of Public Economic Theory*, **5**, 279–303.

Baldwin, R.E. and P. Krugman (2004), 'Agglomeration, Integration and Tax Harmonization', *European Economic Review*, **48**, 1–23.

Bardhan, P. (2002), 'Decentralization of Governance and Development', *Journal of Economic Perspectives*, **16** (4), 185–205.

Barro, R. (1990), 'Government Spending in a Simple Model of Endogenous Growth', *Journal of Political Economy*, **98**, 103–25.

Behnisch, A., T. Büttner and D. Stegarescu (2002), 'Public Sector Centralization and Productivity Growth: Reviewing the German Experience', ZEW Discussion Paper No. 02-03, Mannheim.

Berthold, N., S. Drews and E. Thode (2001), 'Die föderale Ordnung in Deutschland – Motor oder Bremse des wirtschaftlichen Wachstums?', Discussion Paper No. 42, University of Wurzburg.

Besley, T. and A.C. Case (1995), 'Incumbent Behavior: Vote-seeking, Tax-setting, and Yardstick Competition', *American Economic Review*, **85**, 25–45.

Borck, R. and M. Pflüger (2006), 'Agglomeration and Tax Competition', *European Economic Review*, **50**, 647–68.

Brakman, S., H. Garretsen and C. Van Marrewijk (2002), 'Locational Competition and Agglomeration: The Role of Government Spending', CESifo Working Paper No. 775, Munich, September.

Brennan, G. and J.M. Buchanan (1980), *The Power to Tax: Analytical Foundations of a Fiscal Constitution*, Cambridge: Cambridge University Press.

Brueckner, J.K. (2000), 'Fiscal Decentralization in Developing Countries: The Effects of Local Corruption and Tax Evasion', *Annals of Economics and Finance*, **1**, 1–18.

Brueckner, J.K. (2005), 'Fiscal Federalism and Economic Growth', CESifo Working Paper No. 1601, Munich, November.

Davoodi, H. and H. Zou (1998), 'Fiscal Decentralization and Economic Growth: A Cross-Country Study', *Journal of Urban Economics*, **43**, 244–57.

Desai, R.M., L.M. Freinkman and I. Goldberg (2003), 'Fiscal Federalism and Regional Growth: Evidence from the Russian Federation in the 1990s', World Bank Policy Research Working Paper No. 3138.

Ebel, R.D. and S. Yilmaz (2002), 'On the Measurement and Impact of Fiscal Decentralization', unpublished manuscript, World Bank, Washington, DC.

Eller, M. (2004), 'The Determinants of Fiscal Decentralization and its Impact on Economic Growth: Empirical Evidence from a Panel of OECD Countries', unpublished master thesis, University of Vienna.

Enikolopov, R. and E. Zhuravskaya (2003), 'Decentralization and Political Institutions', CEPR Discussion Paper No. 3857, London.

Feld, L.P. (2004), 'Fiskalischer Föderalismus in der Schweiz – Vorbild für die Reform der deutschen Finanzverfassung?', series *Forum – Föderalismus 2004*, ed. Konrad-Adenauer-Stiftung, Bertelsmann-Stiftung, Friedrich-Naumann-Stiftung, Hanns-Seidel-Stiftung, Stiftung Marktwirtschaft, Berlin/Gütersloh, July.

Feld, L.P. and T.J. Goodspeed (2005), 'Discretionary Grants and Soft Budget Constraints in Switzerland', mimeo, Philipps-Universität Marburg and Hunter College, New York.

Feld, L.P., J.-M. Josselin and Y. Rocaboy (2003), 'Yardstick Competition: A Theoretical Model and an Empirical Analysis for French Regions', in A. Marciano and J.-M. Josselin (eds), *From Economic to Legal Competition: New Perspectives on Law and Institutions in Europe*, Cheltenham, UK and Northampton, MA, USA: Edward Elgar, pp. 105–19.

Feld, L.P., G. Kirchgässner and C.A. Schaltegger (2004), 'Fiscal Federalism and Economic Performance: Evidence from Swiss Cantons', unpublished manuscript, Philipps-University Marburg.

Feld, L.P., H. Zimmermann and T. Döring (2007), 'Federalism, Decentralization, and Economic Growth', in P. Baake and R. Borck (eds), *Public Economics and Public Choice: Contributions in Honor of Charles B. Blankart*, Berlin: Springer, pp. 103–133.

Gordon, R.H. (1983), 'An Optimal Taxation Approach to Fiscal Federalism', *Quarterly Journal of Economics*, **98**, 567–86.

Hayek, F.A. von (1939), 'The Economic Conditions of Interstate Federalism', in F.A. von Hayek, *Individualism and the Economic Order*, Ch. XII, Chicago 1948; quoted from the German translation: F.A. von Hayek, *Individualismus und wirtschaftliche Ordnung*, Kap. XII, Zürich 1952, 324–44.

Iimi, A. (2005), 'Decentralization and Economic Growth Revisited: An Empirical Note', *Journal of Urban Economics*, **57**, 449–61.

Inman, R.P. and D.L. Rubinfeld (1997), 'Rethinking Federalism', *Journal of Economic Perspectives*, **11** (4), 43–64.

Jin, H., Y. Qian and B.R. Weingast (1999), 'Regional Decentralization and Fiscal Incentives: Federalism, Chinese Style', unpublished manuscript, Stanford University.

Kind, H.J., K.H.M. Knarvik and G. Schjelderup (2000), 'Competing for Capital in a Lumpy World', *Journal of Public Economics*, **78**, 253–74.

Kotsogiannis, C. and R. Schwager (2001), 'Policy Uncertainty and Policy Innovation', mimeo, Zentrum für Europäische Wirtschaftsforschung (ZEW), Mannheim.

Lin, J.Y. and Z. Liu (2000), 'Fiscal Decentralization and Economic Growth in China', *Economic Development and Cultural Change*, **49**, 1–23.

Ludema, R.D. and I. Wooton (2000), 'Economic Geography and the Fiscal Effects of Economic Integration', *Journal of International Economics*, **52**, 331–57.

Mankiw, N.G., D. Romer and D.N. Weil (1992), 'A Contribution to the Empirics of Economic Growth', *Quarterly Journal of Economics*, **107**, 407–37.

Martinez-Vazquez, J. and R.M. McNab (2001), 'Fiscal Decentralization and Economic Growth', International Studies Program, Andrew Young School of Policy Studies, Working Paper No. 01-01, Georgia State University.

Martinez-Vazquez, J. and R.M. McNab (2002), 'Cross-country Evidence on the Relationship between Fiscal Decentralization, Inflation, and Growth', in National Tax Association (ed.), *Proceedings of the 94th Annual Conference on Taxation 2001*, Washington, DC, pp. 42–7.

Oates, W.E. (1993), 'Fiscal Federalism and Economic Development', *National Tax Journal*, **46**, 237–43.

Oates, W.E. (1999), 'An Essay on Fiscal Federalism', *Journal of Economic Literature*, **37**, 1120–49.

OECD (1999), 'Taxing Powers of State and Local Government', *OECD Tax Policy Studies*, **1**, OECD, Paris.

Reulier, E. (2004), 'Choix fiscaux et interactions stratégique', PhD thesis, Université de Rennes 1.

Rodden, J. and S. Rose-Ackerman (1997), 'Does Federalism Preserve Markets?', *Virginia Law Review*, **83**, 1521–72.

Rose-Ackerman, S. (1980), 'Risk-taking and Reelection: Does Federalism Promote Innovation?' *Journal of Legal Studies*, **9**, 593–616.

Salmon, P. (1987), 'Decentralization as an Incentive Scheme', *Oxford Review of Economic Policy*, **3** (2), 24–43.

Sato, M. and S. Yamashige (2005), 'Decentralization and Economic Development: An Evolutionary Approach', *Journal of Public Economic Theory*, **7**, 497–520.

Scharpf, F.W. (1988), 'The Joint-Decision Trap: Lessons from German Federalism and European Integration,' *Public Administration*, **66**, 239–78.

Schnellenbach, J. (2004), *Dezentrale Finanzpolitik und Modellunsicherheit: Eine theoretische Untersuchung zur Rolle des fiskalischen Wettbewerbs als Wissen generierender Prozess*, Tübingen: Mohr Siebeck.

Sinn, H.-W. (2003), *The New Systems Competition*, Oxford: Blackwell.

Stansel, D. (2005), 'Local Decentralization and Local Economic Growth: A Cross-sectional Examination of US Metropolitan Areas', *Journal of Urban Economics*, **57**, 55–72.

Stegarescu, D. (2004), 'Public Sector Decentralization: Measurement Concepts and Recent International Trends', Working Paper, Centre for European Economic Research, Mannheim.

Strumpf, K.S. (2002), 'Does Government Decentralization Increase Policy Innovation?' *Journal of Public Economic Theory*, **4**, 207–41.

Thießen, U. (2003), 'Fiscal Decentralization and Economic Growth in High Income OECD Countries', *Fiscal Studies*, **24**, 237–74.

Thießen, U. (2003a), 'Fiscal Federalism in Western European and Selected other Countries: Centralization or Decentralization? What is Better for Economic Growth', unpublished manuscript, DIW Berlin.

Tiebout, Ch.M. (1956), 'A Pure Theory of Local Expenditures', *Journal of Political Economy*, **64**, 416–24.

Treisman, D. (2002), 'Defining and Measuring Decentralization: A Global Perspective', unpublished manuscript, Dept. of Political Science, UCLA, Los Angeles.

Weingast, B.R. (1995), 'The Economic Role of Political Institutions: Market-preserving Federalism and Economic Development', *Journal of Law, Economics and Organisation*, **11**, 1–31.

Wildasin, D.E. (1989), 'Interjurisdictional Capital Mobility: Fiscal Externality and a Corrective Subsidy', *Journal of Urban Economics*, 25, 193–212.

Wilson, J.D. (1999), 'Theories of Tax Competition', *National Tax Journal*, **52**, 269–304.

Wilson, J.D. and D.E. Wildasin (2004), 'Capital Tax Competition: Bane or Boon', *Journal of Public Economics*, 88, 1065–91.

Wohlgemuth, M. (2006), 'Learning through Institutional Competition', forthcoming in A. Bergh and R. Höijer (eds), The Institutional Race, Cheltenham.

Woller, G.M. and K. Phillips (1998), 'Fiscal Decentralization and LDC Economic Growth: An Empirical Investigation', *Journal of Development Studies*, **34**, 139–48.

Xie, D., H. Zou and H. Davoodi (1999), 'Fiscal Decentralization and Economic Growth in the United States', *Journal of Urban Economics*, **45**, 228–39.

Yilmaz, S. (2000), 'The Impact of Fiscal Decentralization on Macroeconomic Performance', in National Tax Association (ed.), *Proceedings of the 92nd Annual Conference on Taxation 1999*, Washington, DC, pp. 251–60.

Zhang, T. and H. Zou (1998), 'Fiscal Decentralization, Public Spending, and Economic Growth', *Journal of Public Economics*, **67**, 221–40.

Zhang, T. and H. Zou (2001), 'The Growth Impact of Intersectoral and Intergovernmental Allocation of Public Expenditure: With Applications to China and India', *China Economic Review*, **12**, 58–81.

10. Asia's giants in the world economy: China and India

Erich Weede

10.1 INTRODUCTION

For millennia most of mankind has survived close to starvation level. For centuries most of mankind has lived in Asia. Together China and India account for nearly 40 per cent of mankind and about half of the population of less developed countries. Moreover, China and India embody distinct civilizations and almost unite them within a single state.[1] During the nineteenth and twentieth centuries, a peninsula and subcontinent attached to Asia, that is, Europe and its North American and Australasian daughter societies overcame mass poverty (Collins 1986; Jones 1981; Landes 1998, 2006; Maddison 2001; North 1990; Weber 1923/1981; Weede 1996, 2000). Soon thereafter Japan joined the West in making economic development its top priority. After World War II, the original four tigers at the edge of East Asia – Singapore, Hong Kong, Taiwan and South Korea – followed. But most of mainland Asia, and therefore most of mankind, remained mired in stagnation and poverty at least until the late 1970s. Certainly until then, and possibly until the end of the second millennium, the gap between developed and less developed countries widened and the global distribution of income became less and less equal (Collier and Dollar 2002; *The Economist* 2004; Firebaugh 1999; Ravallion 2004; Wolf 2004, chapter 9). Once China and India, however, joined the capitalist market economies, once capitalism became truly global, it became possible to argue that mainland Asia is catching up,[2] that global growth is good for the poor (Dollar and Kraay, 2002) and that global income distributions between households and persons are finally becoming more equal again. According to Bhalla (2002, p. 187), the global middle class is no longer Western and white. Most members of it were Asians by the turn of the millennium.[3]

The rise of Asia, and of its giants in particular, might also be illustrated in a different way. Neither the so-called 'great seven' nor the 'great eight' of the global economy constitute what the names suggest. Including Canada or Russia, but excluding China and India, may be historically or politically justified; it certainly does not reflect the current and even less the likely future weight of these economies. According to data published by the World Bank (2005, pp. 292–3), the current rank order of gross national incomes in purchase power parity terms is: first, the United States; second, China; third, Japan; fourth, India; fifth, Germany; sixth, France; seventh, Britain; eighth, Italy. Three among the top five are Asian economies. Moreover, the Chinese economy might become equal to the American economy in size – but, of course, not in living standards – in a mere decade (Maddison 1998, pp. 17, 96), and India will soon surpass Japan to become the third largest economy (Das, 2006, p. 2). The rise of China and, somewhat more slowly, of India will not only make global poverty rates fall, but also affect the global balance of power.[4]

According to Maddison's (1998, pp. 40–41) admittedly crude estimates, three hundred years ago European, Chinese and Indian shares of world product were about equal. While Chinese and Indian per capita growth rates were flat in the eighteenth century, Europe forged ahead with an annual growth rate of 0.22 per cent. Although China and India demonstrated little per capita income growth until the middle of the twentieth century, China did better than India in the 1700–1820 period, and India did better than China in the 1820–1952 period in GDP growth. By the middle of the twentieth century, India seems to have been a little bit ahead of China in per capita GDP. Because of China's larger population, however, the Chinese economy was larger than the Indian one.[5] Similar, but marginally higher growth rates in per capita income in China than in India until 1978 seem to have more or less equalized GDP per capita in both Asian societies by the end of the 1970s. Nowadays, however, the Chinese gross national income per capita (in purchase power parity terms) is 1.78 times as high in China as in India. Despite an Indian per capita growth rate of better than 5 per cent, the gap is widening because of Chinese growth rates being better than 8 per cent. Partly reflecting the different population sizes, the economic size ratio between China and India is 2.1 in purchase power terms and 2.5 in dollar terms.[6]

The purpose of this chapter is to explain the divergent economic fate of Asia's giants. In Section 10.2 I will summarize why both China and India were overtaken by the West. In doing so, I shall introduce some determinants that underlay China's ability to outperform India when both economies started to grow faster than the global economy and thereby began catch-up growth. The core section of the chapter (Section 10.3) provides an analysis of Chinese and Indian growth in the last decades of the twentieth century. The theoretical challenge of the chapter is to find at least some determinants of growth which apply both to the time when China and

India fell behind the West and to the period when both of them started to catch up, but China outperformed India. Institutional competition is the key in these theoretical accounts. The fourth and final section (10.4) looks at the prospects of both economies as well as at the security implications of the rise of these two giant nations.

10.2   THE GREAT DIVERGENCE: EUROPE AND ASIA

Before the rise of the West most of mankind, that is, almost everyone excluding small ruling elites, lived close to subsistence level. For ordinary people life was miserable. Starvation was a permanent risk. Neither China nor India made significant progress in overcoming mass poverty until the end of the twentieth century. But the West did. Why did these great Asian civilizations stand still when the West grew rich? Explanatory debates are by no means settled, but the following account looks most persuasive to me.[7] Moreover, it has the additional advantage of being closely related to the explanation in the next section of why China could overtake India in the second part of the twentieth century.

Although Bernholz and Vaubel (2004) trace the basic ideas back to Hume and Kant, twentieth-century theorizing on the causes of the rise or stagnation of civilizations essentially starts with Weber's (1923/1981) economic history of which Collins' (1986) provides the most influential interpretation. In this view, capitalism, overcoming mass poverty, and the rise of the West depend on two immediate prerequisites: calculable law and a non-dualistic ethic. Calculable law is important because it informs actors about the likely social consequences of their actions. If one acts outside of the law or against the law, then one is threatened by official sanctions. If one acts in accordance with the law, one's actions – for example, a business contract – may be supported by state officials. Most importantly, the rule of law provides limits to state action, to confiscation and the predatory behaviour of officials. A nondualistic ethic demands that the same standards of morality, in particular of honesty, govern interactions with strangers and family, friends or neighbours. Such an ethic increases the size of the market by reducing the costs of transacting with strangers. The legal-political branch of Weberian thinking has been more influential than the economic ethic branch in what later developed into 'institutional economics'.[8] Especially concerning India, however, I think that religion and ethics should not be eliminated from a full explanation of development failures until the recent past.

If calculable law and limited government – these are two sides of one coin – are preconditions of capitalism and economic growth, as suggested by Weber (1923/1981) and Collins (1986), then we should ask under what conditions these institutional characteristics of societies are likely to arise. In abstract and general terms, the answer provided by Collins (1986, p. 36) is that 'The creation of a calculable, open-market economy depends upon a continuous balance of power among differently organized groups. The formal egalitarianism of the law depends upon balances among competing citizens and competing jurisdictions.' Ultimately, limited government and the rule of law are underwritten by balances of power within and between states resulting in institutional competition. Examples of such power balances within the history of the West are interstate rivalry (Jones 1981; Weber 1923/1981), or the competition between church and state (Berman 1983), or the tensions between cities and territorial rulers in the Middle Ages (Weber 1922/1964, 1923/1981).

The main reason why we need the rule of law and limited government is that otherwise there would be no safe property rights. Unless people enjoy fairly safe property rights in the fruits of their labour, there are insufficient incentives to work. This insight is at the root of classical economics and can be found in Adam Smith (1776/1976) who recognized that most people prefer to eat all the time rather than to work, unless they may acquire property. Without property rights, shirking becomes the rule and hard work becomes the exception. Competition in shirking is no prescription for growth. So, the most fundamental cause for the divergence between China and India on the one hand and the West on the other hand is safer property rights – for working subjects rather than for the ruling leisure class – and thereby better incentives in the West than in Asia (see Jones 1981; Landes 2006; Weede 2000; and Yang 1987, for evidence).

Since property rights and incentives are themselves rooted in balances of power, the historical stagnation of China after the Southern Sung period at the beginning of the second millennium poses a lesser theoretical challenge than the case of India. China was a unified empire for most of the time, first under the Ming and then under the Manchu dynasties which lasted for some centuries each. So, there was little sustained interstate rivalry during the second millennium in China. There were no autonomous cities in China which could defend themselves against the Chinese emperor. Confucianism was the ruling ideology of the state and its officials. Buddhism was persecuted when it came close to challenging state authority. In Weberian terms, the traditional Chinese empire was patrimonial. Patrimonial states do not need to respect the rights of their subjects. In particular, Chinese merchants suffered from arbitrary, high and discriminatory taxation as well as from frequent confiscation. By harassing merchants the imperial bureaucracy impeded the development of markets and commercialization and indirectly the division of labour and productivity growth.

By contrast to China, Indian empires tended to be short-lived and less successful in uniting the entire civilization. Even the Mughal Empire never extended to the southern tip of India. Typically, there were numerous states in Indian history which made war against each other. If balances of power do contribute to safe property rights and limited government and ultimately to economic growth, then India does not seem to fit the theory, as argued by Lal (2004). In my view, however, the misfit between the Indian case and development theories focusing on limited government, safe property rights, and incentives is apparent rather than real. By contrast to fairly persistent political units in Europe, the Indian state system was much more fluid. Principalities and kingdoms disappeared fairly frequently. Under such circumstances rulers cannot expect that their sons and grandsons will still be rulers of the same territory. Without such an expectation, there is less reason for rulers to respect the property rights of their subjects for the long-term benefit of the economy as well as of the ruling dynasty.

Although rivalry between rulers of unstable political units in India did not produce the beneficial consequences of rivalry between more persistent political units observable in Europe, India conspicuously lacked other background conditions of limited government as well. Indian artisans and merchants did not acquire political power within self-ruling cities as European artisans or merchants did. As outlined by Weber (1921/1978) this is related to Hinduism and the caste system. For orthodox Hindus warmaking and defence were assigned to warrior castes. Since artisans or merchant castes must *not* defend themselves, they could not acquire political power. During the first millennium of the common era many inhabitants of Indian cities, in particular merchants, were not Hindus, but Jainas or Buddhists. These religions disarmed their adherents, too. They were prohibited from killing animals by their faith and this extended to humans, too. So, Indian ruling classes in contrast to European ones were safe from what may be called middle-class challenges to their prerogatives. Whereas a strong Catholic Church during the Middle Ages also contributed to containing the secular power of rulers (Berman 1983), no comparable counterweight to political power can be found in Indian history. Hinduism has always lacked a strong organization such as that of the Catholic Church in the West.

An analysis of Indian history has to consider that huge parts of India were ruled by Muslims for most of the second millennium. In Weber's (1922/1964) terms, Muslim rule in India qualifies as 'sultanism'. Sultanism is the most extreme subtype of patrimonialism. Whereas Western history was characterized by feudalism, mainland Asia suffered from patrimonialism. In feudalism the ruler is assisted by vassals, that is, by men of independent means who own their weapons, who own their land and who might even command troops loyal to themselves. Feudalism implies the idea of reciprocity. At least some of the vassals, and not only the ruler, enjoy rights. Given their status and resources the ruler had an incentive to respect his vassal's rights. Beginning with Magna Carta in the thirteenth century, the idea of some subjects enjoying some rights spread. Of course, it took many centuries before property and civil rights extended to commoners, but feudalism contributed to the ideas of limited government and the rule of law. In Muslim India, by contrast, rulers were assisted by foreigners and slaves who enjoyed no support in society. They absolutely depended on the ruler and his grace. The more dependent on his grace the staff of the ruler are, the more reliable an instrument of arbitrary rule it becomes. That is why sultanism provides the weakest protection of property rights.

In essence, I blame the stagnation of China and India on the weakness of property rights in both societies compared to Europe. Weak property rights for peasants and artisans reduce the incentives for hard work. Weak property rights for merchants reduce the formation and size of the market, thereby the division of labour, and thereby productivity and growth, as already analysed by Smith (1776/1976). It has to be admitted that statements about the differential degrees of safety of European and Asian property rights are debatable and questionable for a number of reasons. First, there has always been variation in place and through time, as historians like to point out. Although such variation does not rule out some kind of averaging, historians hesitate to do so. Second, histories relying on primary sources refer either to China or to India or to Europe – or even to small parts of these huge areas. They have not been written with cross-civilization comparisons in mind.[9] Whereas Jones (1981), Landes (2006) or Yang (1987), for example, claim that European property rights were safer than Asian ones with beneficial consequences for European commerce and the negative consequences for commercialization in Asia, Elvin (1973) or Pomeranz (2000) disagree with this reading of history. The more I read about the economic history of Asia and Europe, the less I expect an agreement about the comparative safety of property rights or commercialization in different civilizations. Although assertions about property rights have to be crucial parts of explanations of why countries or civilizations grow rich or remain mired in stagnation, in practice these assertions can neither be verified nor falsified because of persistent disagreements among historians and country specialists.

If one wants to test assertions about the rise and fall of civilizations one has to proceed differently. In my view, there is much less debate and disagreement about the order of magnitude of per capita growth rates in the last three hundred years in China, India and Europe, or about the degree of political fragmentation in these civilizations than about the relative

degrees of safety of property rights or commercialization. Although assertions about the link between political fragmentation and property rights or
commercialization and growth might not be testable, assertions about the
link between political fragmentation and economic growth rates are
falsifiable. Nobody seems to dispute that per capita income growth in
Europe was much better than in Asia between the late eighteenth and the
late twentieth centuries. Nobody doubts that Europe was politically fragmented into many kingdoms and principalities whereas Ching or Manchu
China (until 1911) was not. Nor have I yet found arguments claiming that
the Chinese or Indian bourgeoisie ever achieved similar degrees of self-rule
as their European counterparts did in at least some cities. Nor have I ever
heard doubts expressed about the obstacles to collective action faced by
Indian lower and middle classes because of caste barriers. Even if statements about property rights or commercialization remain un-testable, theorizing built around these concepts may be falsifiable by reference to the
determinants and consequences of property rights and commercialization.

Moreover, I suspect that the disagreements in the literature about the
comparative safety of property rights might arise because these differences
have not been ones of order of magnitude. Possibly, producers and traders
have been easy prey for rulers everywhere. Nevertheless, some differences
seem to have existed. Small differences in the safety of property rights
might have dramatic consequences in the long run, just as the small
difference between European per capita growth rates (0.22 per cent according to Maddison, 1998, pp. 40–41) and essentially zero growth rates in Asia
during the eighteenth and nineteenth centuries had dramatically affected
economic and political power as well as living standards by the early twentieth century. Concerning rulers' respect for the property rights of their subjects and the contrast between Europe and Asia, I fully endorse Jones's
(1988, p. 177) view: 'Competition for subjects and power among the states
and nobles seems in the end to be the answer. It abridged the worst behavior – not much, and only on average, but more than in other great societies
of the world.'

This explanatory sketch of the divergence between Europe and Asia is
not only built on incentives to work based on the differential safety of property rights which should ultimately be traced back to balances of power
within and between states resulting in institutional competition. 'Getting
the prices right' or the existence of scarcity prices also matters. In the early
twentieth century, Mises (1920) instigated a debate about prices when he
argued that socialism is bound to end in failure because of a lack of scarcity
prices for production inputs. Under socialism all factories or means of production belong to the people in ideology. In practice, they are at the disposal of the political leadership. Since there is no competition between

different owners of the means of production for land, workers, machines or other production inputs, there is no information about the demand for and scarcity of these inputs. Opportunity costs remain hidden. Without competition and scarcity prices, however, there can be no rational allocation of resources. This basic idea can also be adapted to the explanatory problem of the great divergence of Europe and Asia. Then the question becomes: Under which conditions can free or scarcity prices ever arise?

Traditional or pre-capitalist societies in Europe as well as in Asia knew the notion of 'just' or 'fair' prices. Of course, such prices have always been an ideal frequently more honoured in the breach. Owners of scarce resources must have been tempted to raise prices. Buyers must have resented unexpectedly high prices. The perception of 'just' or 'fair' prices everywhere depended on traditions. In essence, 'just' or 'fair' prices always differed from scarcity prices in their lack of flexibility. That is why economic efficiency or a rational allocation of resources depends on overcoming 'fair', 'just' or traditional prices. Such prices are most easily overcome in cross-border trade where nobody has the necessary authority to enforce the traditional terms of trade on both sides of the border. Once people get used to scarcity prices and flexibility in cross-border trade, this type of pricing is likely to spill over into domestic trade, too. Once again, it is hard or even impossible to find reliable evidence about the differential degree of scarcity pricing in Europe, India, and China. Once again we are on much firmer ground in asserting that the political background conditions of scarcity prices, that is, territorial fragmentation of power, were given to a much greater degree in Europe than in Asia. That is why one should have expected much better growth rates between the late nineteenth and the late twentieth centuries in Europe than in Asia, which is exactly what happened.

The first two elements – incentives and scarcity prices – of my explanatory sketch of the great divergence between Europe and Asia derive from Smith (1776/1976) and Mises (1920), the third one can be traced back to Hayek (1945, 1960). His concern is the exploitability of knowledge. In Hayek's view, human knowledge is a broad concept. It refers not only to academic or book knowledge which can be acquired at universities. It also consists of practical knowledge to be acquired by experience, whether in farming or in business. It may refer to what grows best on a particular field or to which producers of intermediate goods are most likely to deliver quality products in time, as promised. Some knowledge is necessarily local. Or, it is tacit, that is, nobody ever tried to make it explicit. Even illiterate peasants may be bearers of knowledge, especially of tacit and local knowledge. Hayek's main postulate about the character of knowledge is that it can never be centralized by some authority. In order to exploit the knowledge scattered across thousands or millions of heads people need the freedom to take decisions for themselves and the incentive to arrive at decisions beneficial not only to themselves but also to others. The first Hayekian point is new. It asserts the productiveness of economic freedom. Knowledge is wasted without economic freedom and decentralized decision-making. Then the economy works below its potential. Hayek's second point is essentially Smith's point again. We need incentives to make people work. Under freedom of contract and exchange, everyone has an incentive to do what s/he knows best and to exchange it for something which others can produce more cheaply. Whoever wastes talents or disregards the needs of potential exchange partners or customers suffers the consequences.

The Hayekian contribution to the explanation of the great divergence between Europe and Asia is as follows. Europe could outgrow China and India because of a greater degree of economic freedom, because of its more decentralized economic decision-making. Economic freedom, of course, is closely related to decentralized property rights and independent decision-making arising out of the fact that property owners are free to invest their property as they see fit – within the constraints of the law. In essence, the Hayekian insights cast some more light on the necessity of private property ownership. Private property and limited government are inconceivable without each other. Ultimately the great divergence between Europe and Asia is explained here by better incentives in Europe than in Asia, by more scarcity prices in Europe than in Asia, by making better use of scattered knowledge in Europe than in Asia. All of this is tied to private property and limited government, which are least likely to arise under conditions of vast empires in contrast to systems of rival states, under conditions of patrimonialism or sultanism rather than feudalism, in the absence of self-governing cities, or where religious and secular authorities are monolithic and symbiotic rather than pluralistic and competitive.

10.3   CHINA AND INDIA IN THE COLD WAR ERA

From the 1950s to the late 1970s per capita incomes in China and India were fairly similar. Per capita incomes in both countries grew more slowly than global averages (Maddison 1998, pp. 40–41). The great divergence between China and India on the one hand and the West on the other continued. Both China and India pursued 'leap-forward strategies' which focused on heavy industries in spite of capital scarcity and labour abundance. Comparative advantage was neglected (Lin et al. 2003: chapter 2). It could not be exploited until the focus on heavy industry and import-substitution was mitigated or given up. China and India were afflicted with socialism and an emphasis on planning.[10] Of course, a development strategy that defied comparative advantage would have been impossible in a market economy.[11] The more centralized economic decision-making becomes, the bigger the errors that can be made.[12] Whereas China suffered from a repressive and radical variety of socialism, India tried a democratic variety. Both countries, even democratic India, more or less disengaged from the global economy. In the late 1940s when India became independent, its share in global exports was 2.4 per cent. In the early 1990s, it was only 0.4 per cent (Bhagwati 1993, p. 58).

The poor performance of the world's most populous countries was not inevitable. In principle, they should have enjoyed the 'advantages of backwardness'and benefited from 'conditional convergence' (Barro and Sala-i-Martin 1995; Helpman 2004; Levine and Renelt 1992; Levine and Zervos 1993; Olson 1996). Although not all backward economies do converge, although not all of them exploit the potential 'advantages of backwardness', in principle the followers of the global development process enjoy some advantages over the pioneers. They may borrow technologies: imitation is faster and cheaper than innovation. They easily find opportunities for productive investment and are unlikely to run into the problem of decreasing returns. They can reallocate labour from less productive employment in agriculture to more productive employment in industry and, later, in services. Possibly, they do not yet suffer from the social and psychological consequences of material affluence and prosperity which may undermine achievement motivation and materialist values (Inglehart 1997).

Whether or not a backward economy develops and catches up depends on other factors. Without investment or human capital formation economic growth is unlikely. Where central planning prevails, as it did in China until Deng Xiaopings's reforms in the late 1970s, we usually lack decent data about investment, but the qualitative evidence points to problems of efficiency rather than to a lack of investment effort as such. Since India remained a much more open society than China and never abolished private property in the means of production, its data are much better. Again, there has been no lack of investment. Instead the productivity of investment left much to be desired (Bhagwati 1993, pp. 40ff.). Part of the reasons for the low productivity of Indian investments may have been the fact that much of it was public rather than private (Joshi and Little 1998, p. 31, n. 21). Investment in China and India in the1950s to 1970s was big enough, but not productive enough, for realizing the advantages of backwardness.

Human capital formation is another candidate to explain this. Here, China and India differ. As early as 1950, the Chinese had benefited from a little bit more schooling than the Indians (Maddison 1998, p. 63). By the late 1970s, about 90 per cent of all Chinese in the 15 to 19 years age group knew how to read and to write. A decade later, only about three-quarters of Indian males and about half of Indian females of the same age group were literate (Dreze and Sen 1995, p. 64). Even today China scores much better in adult literacy than India, that is, 91 against 61 per cent (World Bank 2004, p. 256). But one may do better than merely looking at literacy or school enrolment ratios. Hanushek and Kimko (2000, p. 1206) have developed a measure of labour force quality from international mathematics and science test scores which strongly contributes to growth in cross-country regressions. On this measure, India scores more than two standard deviations below average, and China about one standard deviation above average. Although taking national average test scores from intelligence tests as an alternative measure of human capital stocks would reduce the size of the Sino-Indian gap somewhat (Lynn and Vanhanen 2005, p. 30), China's superiority over India would not be questioned by switching the measure. So, human capital formation and its difference between Asia's giants may help us to understand why China outperformed India.[13] But the impact of different degrees of human capital formation on growth was delayed, as would be expected. It takes some time before schoolchildren become full members of the workforce. Since the difference in human capital endowments between China and India grew over the second part of the twentieth century, this contributed to the (until recently) widening difference in growth rates.

Compared to the global economy both China and India did poorly in the 1950s, 1960s and 1970s. Advantages of backwardness were not realized in spite of sufficient investment and, at least in China, sufficient human capital formation. This poor economic performance was to be expected, if the explanation of the great divergence between Europe and Asia provided above and inspired by Weber (1923/1981) and Jones (1981, 1988), by Smith (1776/1976), Mises (1920) and Hayek (1945, 1960) is true. Take the easier explanatory case of China first. Under Communism and central planning, incentives must have been poor. An egalitarian ideology ruled out big differences in material rewards between those who worked hard, carefully, and effectively and those who did not, or between those who produced what was needed by others and those who produced something else. Insofar as differences in income and material living standards persisted, they were more likely to result from differences in political power than from differences in effort, skill or market success. Since the means of production were also nationalized, there were no scarcity prices, least of all in input markets for production. Thus, it became possible to combine valuable inputs with the production of shoddy goods which nobody outside of a command economy with its persistent scarcity of almost everything would have bought.

Finally, few people enjoyed the opportunity of exploiting their knowledge for the benefit of themselves, of their families, and their exchange partners. Obeying commands from above instead of private initiative and the personal taking of responsibility had become the ideal. If economic freedom is productive and incompatible with big errors like a comparative-advantage-defying development strategy, as argued above, then its abolishment under central planning should guarantee slow growth rates and persistent poverty. This is exactly what happened in China.

Mao Zedong's 'great leap forward', 1959–62, is a perfect illustration of the suffering resulting from socialism. By the middle of the 1950s most Chinese agriculture had become collectivized. But most collectives still consisted of a single village. Some Chinese villages consisted of a single extended family, others of a few such extended families. Chinese peasants were used to sharing the fruits of their labour within the family. So, the damage done by collectivization to incentives remained limited during the early phase. Then, in the late 1950s, the small collectives were combined into huge people's communes often encompassing a couple of villages. Agricultural property rights were further diluted. Incentives to work hard were eliminated. Standards of living became dependent on the prosperity of the commune and no longer on individual effort. The prosperity of the commune, however, resulted from the work of others. Moreover, the local and tacit knowledge of peasants – for example, what grows best when and where – was no longer applied.[14] Cadre arrogance substituted for peasant decision-making. Moreover, time-consuming political indoctrination was high on the political agenda. So were local autarky and efforts at achieving the industrialization of the countryside. Opportunity costs were not even perceived. The 'great leap forward' became a great disaster. More than 30 million people starved to death (Fu 1993, pp. 235, 304; Lin et al. 2003, p. 58; Sandschneider 1998). No famine like this happened in equally poor, but democratically governed India. Like Sen (1999, p. 181), I find it 'hard to imagine that anything like this could have happened in a country that goes to the polls regularly and that has an independent press. During that terrible calamity the government faced no pressure from newspapers which were controlled, and none from opposition parties, which were absent'.

Although the 'great leap forward' in China is the best and most tragic demonstration of the contrasting effects of more and less economic freedom in the countryside, or of property rights more or less well aligned with the need to reward hard work and investment, Indian agriculture provides some illustrations, too. In some parts of India, including Bengal and Bihar, the British colonial rulers imposed or reinforced landlord property rights. Elsewhere, including Tamil Nadu and Maharashtra, the property rights of cultivators were respected and protected. It can be demonstrated that this historical difference in property rights and its incentive effect on investments still affects productivity patterns in post-independence India.

By and large, the assignment of property rights to cultivators leads to higher yields of agricultural products than an assignment to landlords (Banerjee and Iyer 2005).

India became and remained a democracy after its independence. It never nationalized all the means of production. Nevertheless, India was inspired by the Soviet model for decades (Lal 1998, p. 129). Influenced by the British Fabians, Congress administrations were always more likely to perceive market failure than state failure. Bureaucratic controls of the economy were expanded. One should not forget that the long-ruling Congress Party contained many members who aspired to public office (Mitra 1996, p. 683). Although Congress rule in India was never as bloody and repressive as Communist rule in China, some economic effects were quite similar: slow growth and persistent poverty. Bureaucratic controls and interventions weakened incentives, severely restricted entrepreneurial decisions, especially on hiring and firing, and distorted prices. Import substitution and protectionism also contributed to weak competition and the establishment of a rent-seeking society (Buchanan et al. 1980) where favoured enterprises, cartels, and even monopolies enjoyed an easy and profitable life at the expense of consumers. According to Das (2002, p. ix), the bureaucratic state killed India's industrial revolution at birth.

The political economy of India was characterized by 'licence-permit raj' (FICCI 1999, p. 165). The worst example of this has been described by the Federation of Indian Chambers of Commerce and Industry (FICCI 1999, p. 151) in the following terms:

> The most crippling measure against private enterprise came in 1966 with the introduction of the Monopolies and Restrictive Trade Practices (MRTP) Act. All firms above a certain asset base were restricted from free entry into almost all sectors of Indian industry. Even expanding one's own plant required permission of the government 'case-by-case'. Thus, there was no room left for profit-driven investment decisions. Allocational efficiency was not on the front-burner, nor were cost reducing strategies or, for that matter, export competitiveness.

Constraining the private sector was supplemented by expanding the public sector. From 1960 to 1991, its share in gross domestic product increased from 8 to 26 per cent (Yergin and Stanislaw 1998, p. 216). Even in the late 1980s, the Indian public sector took about 70 per cent of all workers employed by big enterprises (Bhagwati 1993, p. 64). It accounted for about 6 per cent of the economically active population and twice as many people as private employers of more than ten workers (*The Economist* 1997, p. 13). So, except for the impoverished informal sector and agriculture, public enterprises were dominant in India. As elsewhere, public enterprises in India tended to be less efficient than private enterprises

(Majumdar 1998). When public sector companies still employed 55 per cent of the industrial workforce, the public sector's share of production was only 27 per cent (Das 2002, p. 161).

Congress administrations always paid lip service to the concerns of the poor. Firing workers became close to impossible before an enterprise went bankrupt (Bhagwati 1993, pp. 65, 86; Joshi and Little 1998, pp. 211ff.). Strong job protection in the formal sector, however, came at a price. It has been estimated (World Bank 1995, p. 90) that employment in the formal sector was reduced thereby by at least 18 per cent. Workers in big enterprises earned a multiple of agricultural wages, in steel production eight times as much (World Bank 1995, pp. 76, 83). Although Indian socialism benefited a minority of workers, it did so at the expense of the poorest strata of society who were denied access to formal employment. Like totalitarian socialism in China, democratic socialism in India provided little hope for the poor or their children.

10.4   CLIMBING OUT OF THE SOCIALIST TRAP

China fell deeper into the trap of socialism, but it also started to get out of it sooner than India. During the Cultural Revolution, in the late 1960s and early 1970s, Mao Zedong unleashed fanatical youths on the bureaucracy. Leading cadres, including Deng Xiaoping and his family, suffered. Bureaucratic rule was replaced by chaos. Higher education was interrupted for nearly a decade. Millions were humiliated, tortured, and murdered, first by the 'red guards' and then by the 'people's liberation army' when it re-established 'order' (Dittmer 1994, p. 72; Rummel 1994, p. 100). The Cultural Revolution produced only one positive effect. It seriously undermined the grip of the party on the countryside and eroded collective agriculture (Domes and Näth 1992, p. 62). For this reason, the number of victims remained much smaller than during the 'great leap forward'.

After Mao's death and Deng Xiaoping's rise to power, the Chinese government switched from ideology to efficiency, from radical communism to creeping capitalism. In China, economic reform was a learning process rather than another exercise in planning. The Chinese themselves compare it to 'crossing the river by groping the stones' (Lin et al. 2003, p. 177). Reforms began where one ought to begin in an economy dominated by agriculture, in the countryside. Although the state retained ownership of the land, the communists under the competent leadership of Deng Xiaoping returned rights to work the land to small groups of families, to families, and even to individuals. Peasants had to pay rent and to sell part of the harvest to the government at fixed prices. Nevertheless, incentives to work were re-established. Peasant judgement replaced cadre decision-making. As implied by the label of the new policy, 'household responsibility system', those who made the decisions again had to suffer the consequences. Since surplus production could be sold in free markets, scarcity prices got a toehold in the Chinese countryside. Chinese peasants responded forcefully to the reforms. Agricultural output grew about 6 per cent annually and 42 per cent between 1978 and 1984 (Lin et al. 2003, p. 145). Within less than a decade, per capita incomes in the countryside doubled. Simultaneously, the urban-rural income disparity decreased from a factor of 2.36 in 1978 to 1.72 in 1985 (Wu 1996, p. 66). Remarkably, the first step toward capitalism resulted in better growth rates and more equality. Thereafter, however, the disparity between urban and rural incomes has grown vigorously again (*The Economist* 2006a, p. 6; Pei 2006).

Soon, agricultural reforms were complemented with urban and industrial reforms. The comparative-advantage-defying strategy was replaced by a comparative-advantage-following strategy (Lin et al. 2003, p. 101). The preferences for heavy industry and import substitution were overcome. So-called township and village enterprises were established. In the first two reform decades they enabled 120 million peasants to move from agricultural to industrial employment (Lin et al. 2003, p. 199). Township and village enterprises have to compete with each other. The reach of 'their' local government is not long and strong enough to protect them. Even if the ownership is still public or collective, most township and village enterprises have to compete as if they were private enterprises. Then, truly private enterprises were tolerated. Prices were permitted to reflect supply and demand. By the early 1990s, most prices were determined by scarcities rather than political fiat (Lin et al. 2003, p. 172; Schüller 1998, p. 279). Entrepreneurs, even cadre entrepreneurs, became residual claimants to profits. Local governments became residual claimants to taxes (Qian 2000, pp. 154–5). By contrast to township and village enterprises and the increasing number of truly private enterprises, state-owned enterprises frequently incurred losses without suffering bankruptcy. While making state-owned enterprises profitable has been difficult and remained elusive for a long time, China soon succeeded in reducing their weight and importance. In the late 1970s, when the reform process began, they accounted for more than three-quarters of industrial output. Two decades later their share was down to about a quarter (Lin et al. 2003, p. 187). Better still, most of them have become profitable. According to the World Bank (and *The Economist* 2006c, p. 72), state-owned enterprises made profits estimated at 6.5 per cent of China's GDP in 2004.

Recently, not only the importance of state-owned enterprises but also of township and village enterprises has declined. Although the delimitation of types of enterprises in China – whether they are private, township and

village enterprises, or state-owned enterprises – is not always straightforward, it has been estimated that private enterprise began to contribute at
least half of industrial output in 2000 and more than two-thirds in 2002.
By contrast, the share of state-owned enterprises has been cut from 32 to
17 per cent and of township and village enterprises from 17 to 9 per cent in
just three years, between 1999 and 2002 (England 2005, pp. 47–50). Since
the private sector is most productive, and state-owned enterprises are least
productive, this growth of private enterprise is a positive development.

In the account of economic growth presented here, incentives are crucial.
But incentives presuppose safe property rights and ruling communists
always tend to interfere with other people's property rights. Thus, it is hard
to understand how the Chinese economy has been able to do so well since
the late 1970s, given the absence of limited government, given the absence
of the rule of law and without a full commitment to private property rights
rather than ambivalence about the degree to which it might be tolerated. In
my view, the most convincing answer to this question has been provided by
the theory of 'market-preserving federalism' (Montinola et al. 1995;
Weingast 1995) which analyses the benefits of domestic institutional competition. What is crucial in this theory is that political decision-makers
affect only part of the market and that they have to compete with each
other. The highly centralized character of the Communist Party of China
does not undermine, but might rather reinforce market-preserving federalism. Economic success at a lower level of government is a better basis for a
later career at a higher level than economic failure. By delegating much economic decision-making authority to provincial and local governments, the
Chinese provide incentives for better governance and may even have
invented a partial and preliminary substitute for the rule of law.

Competition between provinces and local governments enforces some
respect for private property rights by the authorities. If regional governments arbitrarily interfere with business or impose more arbitrary taxation
than other provinces do, if they are more corrupt than others, then they lose
capital, business, and even qualified labour. So, 'federalism, Chinese style'
imposes effective constraints on politicians and thereby generates opportunities for growth. Mutual competition forces local and regional governments to act as if they wanted to respect private property rights. This
reminds one of the political fragmentation that propelled Western Europe
toward modernity and helped it to overcome mass poverty.

In addition to de-collectivization in the countryside, township and
village enterprises and the re-establishment of private enterprises, the toleration of free markets and the reintroduction of price flexibility, the
Chinese government opened up its economy. Instead of pursuing autarky
as China did under Mao,[15] Deng proceeded to exploit the opportunities of

export-led growth and globalization, as the four tigers of the Pacific Rim had done so successfully. By the end of the twentieth century, China had exported between 20 and 30 per cent of its gross domestic product (Lin et al. 2003, p. 195; Noland et al. 1998, p. 58). Currently, exports constitute nearly 40 per cent and foreign trade about 75 per cent of GDP. By contrast, the trade to GDP ratio in India is only about 30 per cent (*The Economist* 2005f, p. 66). Moreover, China became a magnet for foreign direct investment.[16] At the end of the twentieth century, it attracted more than ten times as much foreign investment as either India or Russia (World Bank 2000, pp. 314–15). By the mid-1990s, foreign direct investment contributed about 15 per cent to gross fixed capital formation, about 20 per cent to industrial output, and about 41 per cent to exports (Gallagher 2002, p. 347). China is vigorously participating in globalization. From 1990 to 2003, its share in global exports increased from 1.9 to 5.8 per cent, its share in global imports from 1.6 to 5.3 per cent. In 2004, China overtook Japan and became the third largest trader in the global economy, behind the US and Germany, but ahead of Japan. As *The Economist* (2005b, p. 6) observed: 'For the third year running, the increase in China's trade was larger than India's total foreign trade.' As an exporter, India does not equal in importance even the Republic of China on Taiwan (*The Economist* 2005e, p. 101). Although China is already India's second most important trade partner, India accounts for only 1.2 per cent of China's trade (*The Economist* 2005c, p. 54). By simultaneously attracting foreign direct investment and opening up its economy for foreign trade, China tapped a source of synergy. After all, foreign direct investment is least beneficial where foreign affiliates produce for protected domestic markets (Moran et al. 2005).[17]

Whereas China is one of the four most important trade partners of the US, India had to be satisfied with twenty-fifth place at the turn of the millennium (Cohen 2001, p. 288; Sivasubramonian 2002, p. 116). Of course, trade in manufactured goods is China's comparative advantage. India might have a comparative advantage in services, in particular in software exports.[18] Moreover, the 1.5 million-strong and affluent Indian-American community of doctors, engineers, businessmen and software experts (Cohen 2001, pp. 287–8) may link India at least as closely to the United States as Sino-American trade does for China. Conceivably, Indian expatriates might contribute to India's future globalization as much as Chinese expatriates have already done for China by direct foreign investment in the past. Certainly, there is little reason to doubt that more trade openness and globalization should help India. As Panagariya (2005, p. 14) has pointed out, before liberalizing its economy India's per capita growth rate in the1960s and 1970s was only 1.1 per cent. After modest liberalization in the

1980s and deeper liberalization in the 1990s, the record for these two decades improved to 3.8 per cent.

For China, creeping capitalism and globalization paid off. While China did not even double its per capita income in purchase power parity terms between 1960 an 1980, that is, before the reforms could pay off, per capita incomes more than quadrupled in the 1980 to 2000 period (Bhalla 2002, p. 218). According to the World Bank (1992, p. 76; 2004, pp. 256–7) Chinese per capita incomes corresponded to 7.6 per cent of American incomes in purchase power in 1985, but to 9.1 per cent in 1990, and to 13.3 per cent in 2003. Although the share of the poorest quintile of the Chinese population fell from 7.9 per cent in 1960 or 1980 to 5.9 per cent in 2000 (Bhalla 2002, p. 218), the smaller share of the pie going to the poor was more than compensated by the rapidly increasing size of the pie. Even focusing only on the fate of the poor, creeping capitalism in China was much better than totalitarian socialism.

Whereas China reformed its economy ahead of the bankruptcy of the Soviet model, India took its time. In 1990, India's economy was more socialist than China's according to some evaluations (Das 2002, p. 161). One reason for this tardiness might be that independent India's economy grew much better even under Nehru than in the preceding colonial period (Cohen 2001, p. 95). From a backward-looking point of view the Indian record still appeared satisfactory – although a glance at the East Asian tigers could have told India how much better they could do. By 1991, however, the Indian economy faced a crisis. Neither public finances nor the current account were sustainable. Public sector deficits rose.[19] Foreign currency was in short supply and became ever more so. After the dissolution of the Soviet Union, the main source of foreign aid had disappeared. The reforms consisted of the following measures. Most of the industrial licensing system was abolished. Industries previously reserved for the public sector were opened to private enterprise. Only defence industries, nuclear energy and railways remained firmly within the public sphere (Ahluwalia 2002, p. 72). Reluctantly, foreign investment was welcomed. The Indian currency was devalued. The dream of autarky was given up. Tariffs were cut dramatically. Whereas the average rate was 125 per cent in 1990–91, it became 71 per cent three years later. The peak rate fell from 355 per cent to 85 per cent in the same period (Joshi and Little 1998, p. 70). Although the Indian economy did not switch as vigorously from inward to outward orientation and export promotion as China did, there was significant movement in the right direction. Since growth rates improved in the early 1990s,[20] especially in manufacturing, since the current account deficit fell and foreign exchange reserves strongly recovered while the primary deficit of the central government also fell, the liberalizing reforms paid off (Joshi and Little 1998, pp. 17, 35).[21] But neither in openness to trade, nor in export growth, nor in attracting foreign direct investment could India come close to China.

In contrast to China, India had never abolished private property in land and private farming. Nevertheless, agriculture suffered from serious distortions. According to Joshi and Little (1998, p. 89):

> the prices of all major agricultural products have been largely determined by the central government's total control of foreign trade in them. The prices of cereals – rice, wheat, and coarse grains – and cotton have been held below world prices in most years by controlling exports. Except for fertilizers, farmers had to pay more than world prices for inputs, e.g. machinery and pesticides . . . on balance agriculture has been heavily disprotected.

The Indian government tried to undo part of the damage it had inflicted on the sector employing more Indians than any other by subsidizing electricity and water. Unfortunately, these subsidies were not only inefficient, but they tended to help richer farmers more than poorer ones and to promote a capital-intensive instead of a labour-intensive agriculture. 'Urban bias' or the political preference for urban industry over agriculture (Lipton 1977) neither contributed to equity nor to growth. Although opening up the Indian economy and devaluing the currency alleviated the problems somewhat, progress has been painfully slow. Nevertheless, Indian agricultural exports grew vigorously during the 1990s (Ahluwalia 2002, p. 77). It has to be admitted, however, that the agricultural protectionism of Europe and Japan also contributed to the problems of agriculture in poor countries, India included.

Compared to China, India seems to possess four advantages. First, because of the British heritage, India seems much closer to the rule of law than China.[22] Unfortunately, the lawfulness of India leaves much to be desired. Cohen (2001, p. 115) recently observed: 'In some states, it is difficult to separate the politicians from the criminals; in others, the police are under the sway of high and middle castes and are used to hunt down and kill lower-caste or tribal leaders in what are euphemistically called "police encounters".' Even in big cities property conflicts may still be 'settled' by gangs of bullies rather than by courts of law (Kakar 1996). Thus, problems of law enforcement may reduce the impact of this Indian advantage. Since Indian states are on the way to becoming more assertive, enterprising and powerful, it is conceivable that they will become engaged in a 'race to the top' where they compete with each other in providing a good business environment. 'Federalism, Indian style' may provide some hope for the future.[23] So far, however, India benefits less from its putative advantage in the rule of law than it suffers from the legacy of 'license-permit raj' (FICCI 1999, p. 165). According to *The Economist* (2005b, p. 14), 'Indian bureaucracy continues to slow things down . . . it takes 89 days to receive all the permits needed to start a business in India, compared with 41 in China. Insolvency procedures take ten years, compared with 2.4 in China.' Slow administration may undermine the putative advantages of the rule of law.

Second, a real Indian advantage is the fact that most educated Indians, and all natural scientists, engineers and economists, speak English fluently – very much in contrast to the modest foreign language skills of the Chinese. So, India should be in a position to acquire technology from the West much faster than China. Third, in the 1990s young Indians enjoyed much better access to higher education than the Chinese. Until recently Indians had six times as good a chance of entering a university as the Chinese (Dreze and Sen 1998, pp. 91, 181). More recently, however, Chinese universities are pulling ahead of their Indian counterparts. China also sends more than twice as many students abroad as India (*The Economist* 2005g, pp. 15–16).

Fourth, a conceivable Indian advantage might be its edge in economic freedom. According to the ratings published by Gwartney and Lawson (2005, p. 18), the Indian economy always was a little bit freer than China's. The most important aspect of this seems to be that India has generally provided more space for entrepreneurship than China – with the possible exception of the 1980s. According to Das (2006, p. 3), 'what is most remarkable is that rather than rising with the help of the state, India is in many ways rising despite the state'. In particular, Indian entrepreneurs make decisions about investment whereas the Chinese government and still largely state-controlled banks decide who may get a loan. 'Only 10 percent of credit goes to the private sector in China even though the private sector employs 40 percent of the Chinese workforce. In India, entrepreneurs get more than 80 percent of all loan' (Das 2006, p. 7). The Chinese arrangement is more at risk of squandering scarce resources than the Indian arrangement.

In spite of these potential advantages, so far the Indian performance remains less impressive than the Chinese. Although Bhalla's purchase power parity data (Bhalla 2002, p. 218) put India's per capita incomes ahead of China in 1960 and 1980, in 2000 Chinese incomes were ahead of India's by a factor of 1.6. Whereas China more than quadrupled its per capita income in the last two decades of the twentieth century, India's per capita income just failed to double. A marginally rising income share of the poorest quintile in India, from 8.5 to 8.7 per cent, still cannot compensate the poor for insufficient Indian growth rates. According to World Bank estimates and *The Economist* (2005b, p. 6), 35 per cent of Indians, but only

17 per cent of Chinese still have to survive on a dollar a day or less. Persistent poverty in India may well undermine the capability of future Indian workers to be productive and to climb out of poverty. In this context some numbers reported by *The Economist* (2005b, p. 6) are a special cause for concern: 'Some 47 % of India's under-five-years-olds are underweight, compared with 10% in China.' Since inadequate nutrition reduces the intelligence of its victim (Lynn and Vanhanen 2005, p. 46), since intelligence definitely contributes to economic growth rates (Weede and Kämpf 2002; Jones and Schneider 2006; Lynn and Vanhanen 2005), the malnutrition of so many Indian children might be part of a vicious circle where poverty leads to malnutrition and reduced cognitive abilities which then lead to slow growth and the persistence of poverty.

A persistent disadvantage of India – even in 2006 – is its overregulated labour market. Establishments with more than one hundred workers must not lay off employees without the permission of the state government where the factory is located. Of course, this deters hiring labour as effectively as firing workers. But the trade unions and the Communist parties on whose support the Congress government depends want to protect their rank and file. According to *The Economist* (2006b, p. 12), 'this means that the unemployed and even most workers in the "unorganized" sector are being held ransom by the tiny minority – some 30 m(illion), or about 7 per cent in "organised" employment.'

10.5 CONCLUSION

Both Asian giants face severe problems and vulnerabilities, albeit not exactly the same ones. It has been quipped (*The Economist* 2005b, p. 13) that 'China's trouble is capital that costs zero, India's is zero capital.' If the opportunity cost of capital and investment seems to be zero, there is likely to be much waste. Chinese savings and investment ratios are very high. But capital is frequently not used productively. State banks in China prefer to provide loans to state-owned enterprises. Although many of them have recently become profitable (*The Economist* 2006c), they are least likely to invest the money productively. Therefore, China suffers from a protracted, albeit still hidden banking crisis and lots of non-performing loans – possibly, more than a quarter of all loans by the late 1990s (*The Economist* 2005b; Lardy 1998; Lin et al. 2003, p. 221).[24] Actually, some estimates of non-performing loans run as high as 45 per cent of all loans and a similar share of Chinese GDP (England 2005, p. 54).[25] By contrast, India should raise its investment rate. Moreover, India needs to raise public investment significantly in order to improve its infrastructure. Since the Indian public sector is already deeply in deficit, this will be difficult. Forty-four per cent of recurrent expenses in India service the public debt (*The Economist* 2005b, p. 14). So the legacy of past profligacy undermines India's capability to improve its infrastructure. Worse still, India's government depends to a significant degree, that is, about one-sixth of its tax revenue (*The Economist* 2005b, p. 15), on customs duties, on barriers to trade and globalization. Poor infrastructure, poor productivity, and bigger barriers to trade make it unlikely that India can repeat China's success in attracting foreign capital in order to compensate for the weakness of domestic investment.[26] Although difficult, China's problems with investing capital productively look more amenable to a solution than India's problems.

Until recently population growth was considered a problem and reducing it was believed to be part of the solution to the problem of overcoming poverty. China has been successful in reducing its population growth rate. In the 1980s, China's population grew by 1.5 per cent, in the 1990s by 1.1 per cent. By contrast, India's population grew by 2.1 and 1.8 per cent (World Bank 2000, p. 278). Although the Chinese labour force grew more rapidly than the Indian labour force in the 1980s, by the 1990s India's labour force grew more strongly than China's. This is likely to continue for the next decades. Since 2000, the Chinese fertility rate of then 1.9 births per woman has been below the replacement level and falling. By contrast, India's fertility rate of 3 births per woman guarantees that India's population will increase by hundreds of millions (World Bank 2003, pp. 64, 109). By 2035, India is likely to overtake China as the most populous nation on the globe (*The Economist* 2005b, p. 5).

Like the West, China is destined to age – without, however, having become a rich country. By 2020, China's population will stagnate. By 2015, 120 million Chinese or about 9 per cent of the population might be older than 65 (Eberstadt 1998; England 2005, p. 17). Or, since the mandatory retirement age for male employees is still 60 and for females it is 55, this lower age threshold might be more relevant. In 1990, about 9 per cent of the Chinese population was over 60, in 2030 it is likely to be about 22 per cent, that is, in the order of magnitude of 300 million people (Williamson and Shen 2004, p. 3). Another decade later the percentage might be 26 and the number of old people about 400 million (England 2005, p. 23). Then China's share of old people might be higher than the Chinese share of the global population. Currently, the Chinese state has promised pension benefits to only about 10 per cent of these hundreds of millions of future retirees. Whether paid for privately by their children or publicly by the state, support for the elderly will soon become a significant burden on the Chinese economy.[27] Although China cannot continue to grow by increasing inputs, whether capital or labour, as it did so massively and successfully in the past, the size of its labour force will continue to grow for another twenty years and then start to decline gently. Moreover, internal migration from the countryside to the cities will contribute to the avoidance of a European-type labour shortage and contribute to growth (England 2005, p. 118). Nevertheless, given the already high level, major increases in capital investment are inconceivable. The workers needed for increasing the input of labour simply will no longer be available.

Worse still, on top of the ageing problem China faces a major imbalance between men and women. Given that there might be 16 to 20 per cent more men than women, about every sixth Chinese man will not be able to find a wife (Eberstadt 1998, p. 63; Poston 2004).[28] Small and rich countries might close this gap by inviting foreign women to make up the short fall. But the world's most populous country, and still a comparatively poor one, cannot solve its home-grown problems in this way. Conceivably, China's gender imbalance will even contribute to future political instability (Hudson and Boer 2002; Poston 2004). India's sex ratio is also skewed in favour of boys, but to a lesser extent (*The Economist*, 2005b, p. 5). Moreover, India as a whole[29] does not suffer from both Chinese problems at once, below replacement fertility and a skewed sex ratio. If India could succeed in improving its human capital endowment by better care for its poor youngsters and education for all of them, including rural girls, this could go a long way in providing India with a chance to catch up with China again in terms of per capita incomes.

China's one-child policy may have been the last policy success of authoritarian central planning. India's policy-making by debate and its lack of administrative decisiveness ruled out a sustained and effective population policy. Possibly, China's past 'success' will generate greater problems for the future than India's 'failure' in controlling its population size. In rural Asia, children were and are supposed to support their ageing parents. In China they will frequently become overburdened. Imagine the offspring of two one-child families marrying each other. Can they support two parental families or four persons? Although there are some tentative and under-funded programmes in urban China, a solution to the problems of rural China is not yet conceivable (England 2005).

It has been demonstrated in a cross-national econometric study (Bloom and Williamson 1998) that economic growth rates are affected by differential growth rates of dependent and working-age populations. In future, China's growth rate will be reduced by a stronger growth rate of its dependent population, whereas India's growth rate will be improved by a stronger growth rate of its working-age population. China's future growth prospects may be reduced by some future scarcity of working age people and a premature graying of the population – premature compared to the

Western sequence of first becoming rich and greying thereafter. Despite the flow of labour from the countryside to the cities, Chinese labour abundance might disappear in about a generation. By contrast, India has enough people now and for at least another half century. But inadequate nutrition for nearly half its youngsters and the likely effects of this on the development of cognitive abilities raises the question whether Indian labour force quality will be good enough for underwriting much improved growth rates.

NOTES

1. Elsewhere, for example in the West, nation-states (like Britain, France, or the USA) constitute mere components of civilizations. Although even China and India do not encompass all of their civilizations, they nearly do so. Exceptions for China are obviously Taiwan and, debatably, Singapore, Vietnam, and Korea. Exceptions for India are Nepal and, arguably, at least parts of Sri Lanka.
2. According to Maddison (2002, p. 1), in 1950 the Asian share of world population was 58 per cent, but the Asian share of world GDP was only 18.5 per cent. By 1998, the Asian share of world GDP had doubled.
3. Of course, such statements depend on definitions. In Bhalla's view, a daily income between 10 and 40 US dollars makes one a member of the global middle class.
4. Although the rise and decline of nations has historically been associated with threats to peace, I am optimistic about our chances of accommodating the rise of China and India (Weede 2005).
5. In the mid-twentieth century, China's gross domestic product was still about twice as big as Japan's. Thirty years later, it was less than Japan's GDP (Lin et al. 2003, p. 2).
6. These numbers are based on World Bank (2005, pp. 292–3) data.
7. The purpose of my chapter is to propose a theory and an explanation, not to discuss divergent or 'revisionist' theoretical approaches which play down the European contribution to modern or capitalist civilization, such as Pomeranz (2000) or Hobson (2004). For some criticism of these alternative approaches, see Duchesne (2006) or Landes (2006). In my view, pointing to 'the Eastern Origins of Western Civilisation' (as Hobson does) can only deepen the explanatory puzzle of how Europe could ever overtake the great Asian civilizations.
8. In the humanities, of course, the most influential analysis of Weber (1920/1972) is his 'Protestant Ethic'. For reasons discussed in detail elsewhere (Weede 2000), I find Weber's (1922/1964, 1923/1981) 'institutional' theorizing more plausible than most of his cultural theories. His analysis of India (1921/1978), however, looks more appealing to me than his analyses of Protestantism or Confucianism.
9. Take, for example, Kolb (2003). In comparing district magistrates and their underlings to 'greedy predators', and in pointing to the 'chaotic' weights and measures in traditional China (Kolb 2003, pp. 213 and 243) he implicitly supports a position which explains China's delayed economic development by weak property rights and other impediments to market development. But he never commits himself to this or any other theoretical position. Instead he underlines the error-proneness and uncertainty of all our data about China, including even population and mortality data.
10. In my view, the option of planning and import substitution by many poor countries, including China and India, has two important roots. One is the spirit of the time and the tendency of development economists to exaggerate market failure and to overlook state failure. The second is the desire to achieve national security by heavy industrialization, autarky, and, at least in the Chinese case, building a strong army.

11. As Lin et al. (2003, p. 78) observe: 'Driven by profit, manufacturers would have invested resources in labour-intensive industries and would have made every effort to employ technology that used less capital and more labour.'

12. Exactly this insight is missing in accounts of 'state-directed development' (Kohli 2004). If he had included China in addition to South Korea, Brazil, India, and Nigeria, Kohli probably would have found out that not only weak states, like Nigeria, but also strong states, like Mao's China, may obstruct economic development.

13. Even in the early twenty-first century the Chinese advantage persists. According to the World Bank and *The Economist* (2005b, p. 10), Chinese workers are 50 per cent more productive than Indians, but cost only 25 per cent more.

14. The people's communes were abolished two decades later in the 1970s, before Chinese peasants had forgotten their knowledge, and Chinese agriculture could recover rapidly. A more general treatment of lost knowledge in Chinese history is provided by Landes (2006).

15. Between the early 1950s and the late 1970s, the ratio between trade and output in China fell from more than 8 to less than 6 per cent (Lin et al. 2003, p. 83).

16. It has even been claimed that China prefers foreign capital and discriminates against domestic private firms (Pei 2006, p. 32).

17. It has been argued that the Indian economy relies on domestic capital and entrepreneurs to a greater degree than China, that it therefore is more resilient than China (Thakur 2006, p. 7). Whereas I agree with the descriptive statement, I am not convinced of the concluding evaluation.

18. Information technology (IT) and IT-enabled services employed less than a million people in 2004 and accounted for about 4 per cent of Indian GDP. In 2005, the IT and business process outsourcing industry employed 1.3 million people and accounted for about 5 per cent of the Indian GDP. By 2007, these numbers might grow to 4 million people and 7 per cent of GDP. The value of IT-related exports might triple in 3 years (*The Economist* 2005d, p. 69; *The Economist* 2006b, pp. 4, 8).

19. By contrast to India, China's public debt is under control. Although it rose strongly in the late 1990s, it was less than a quarter of GDP in 2005. But liabilities for future pension payments to the mere third of urban employees who are entitled to get them might add another 70 per cent of GDP (*The Economist* 2006a, pp. 9, 13).

20. Actually, Indian growth rates had already improved in the 1980s. But one may doubt the sustainability of growth in the 1980s because it was fuelled by a build-up of external debt (Ahluwalia 2002).

21. Das (2002, p. 221) summarizes what the reforms of the early 1990s did *not* achieve: 'The government had not begun to privatize the public sector, which was bleeding the economy. It had not introduced labor reforms – it is still impossible to lay off a single worker even if there is no production. It is still impossible to close a private company even when it is bankrupt. It had not opened agriculture or banking. It had not dared tackle the vast subsidies which were slowly eating away the financial health of the country and were primarily responsible for the unacceptably high fiscal deficit.'

22. As Kohli points out, the British built a much more effective administrative service in India than they did in some of their African colonies, such as Nigeria. Unfortunately, however, 'affirmative action' for the benefit of backward tribe, low-caste and untouchable (or dalit) Indians must have undermined the quality and effectiveness of the bureaucracy. In 1990, 49 per cent of central government positions were set aside for these groups (van Praagh 2003, p. 201).

23. Whereas China's market-preserving federalism is essentially a gift of the central government to lower levels of government, Indian federalism enjoys some support from the constitution, from the Supreme Court, from the regionally fragmented party system, and from the necessity to include regional parties in governing coalitions at the center (Rudolph and Rudolph 2000; Sinha 2005).

24. Although China has plenty of private savings, it is not only the banks that fail to channel them toward productive investment. The Chinese stock market also does a poor job in allocating capital (*The Economist* 2005a, pp. 67–8).

25. The government is aware of the problem. It has provided the banks with capital injections. It has permitted the four biggest banks to shift dud loans into separate state-backed asset management companies. It has permitted them to attract foreign investors, but not yet foreign takeovers. In spite of significant improvements in the recent past, it remains an open question whether bad loans in the entire banking sector are finally under control (*The Economist* 2005h; 2006a, p. 12).

26. For a long time sociologists believed that foreign investment is less productive than domestic investment. Actually, however, foreign investment tends to be significantly more productive than domestic investment (de Soysa and Oneal 1999). By contrast to domestic investment, foreign investment frequently goes together with new technology and opportunities to gain access to new markets.

27. Of course, this number is nothing better than a crude guess. It was 'confirmed' at the IIS Conference in Beijing in July 2004 by John B. Williamson who has done research on old-age security in China together with Chinese social scientists. What matters for the purposes of this chapter is not whether the true number is 8 or 19, but the fact that most rural Chinese cannot even look forward to public promises for their old age. Since about one-third of them do not have sons, who are traditionally responsible for supporting them, their prospects are bleak. If they have to work during old age, they suffer the consequences of little formal schooling and no working experience beyond the low-income agricultural sector (Eberstadt 2006).

28. Pre-natal sex identification by sonar technology and female abortion is a likely cause of this imbalance (Poston 2004). One should note, however, that imbalanced sex ratios were also reported in imperial China, most probably because of female infanticide (Helbling 2003, pp. 100–101).

29. But there is a lot of variation within India. Fertility is already below replacement level in its biggest cities and in much of the south, that is, exactly in those areas where schooling is best. Fertility is highest in the undereducated north (Eberstadt 2006).

REFERENCES

Ahluwalia, Montek S. (2002), 'Economic Reforms in India since 1991: Has Gradualism Worked?' *Journal of Economic Perspectives*, **16**(3), 67–88.

Banerjee, Abhijit and Lakshmi Iyer (2005), 'History, Institutions, and Economic Performance: The Legacy of Colonial Land Tenure Systems in India', *American Economic Review*, **95**(4), 1190–213.

Barro, Robert J. and Xavier Sala-i-Martin (1995), *Economic Growth*, New York: McGraw-Hill.

Berman, Harold J. (1983), *Law and Revolution: The Formation of the Western Legal Tradition*, Cambridge, MA: Harvard University Press.

Bernholz, Peter and Roland Vaubel (2004), *Political Competition, Innovation and Growth in the History of Asian Civilizations*, Cheltenham, UK and Northampton, MA, USA: Edward Elgar.

Bhagwati, Jagdish N. (1993), *India in Transition*, Oxford: Clarendon.

Bhalla, Surjit S. (2002), *Imagine There's No Country: Poverty, Inequality and Growth in the Era of Globalization*, Washington, DC: Institute for International Economics.

Bloom, David E. and Jeffrey G. Williamson (1998), 'Demographic Transitions and Economic Miracles in Emerging Asia', *World Bank Economic Review*, **12**(3), 419–55.

Buchanan, James M., Robert D. Tollison and Gordon Tullock (eds) (1980), *Towards a Theory of the Rent-seeking Society*, College Station: Texas A & M University Press.

Cohen, Stephen Philip (2001), *India. Emerging Power*, Washington, DC: Brookings Institution Press.

Collier, Paul and David Dollar (2002), *Globalization, Growth and Poverty*, New York: Oxford University Press for the World Bank.

Collins, Randall (1986), *Weberian Sociological Theory*, New York: Cambridge University Press.

Das, Gurcharan (2002), *India Unbound: The Social and Economic Revolution from Independence to the Global Information Age*, New York: Anchor (Random House).

Das, Gurcharan (2006), 'The India Model', *Foreign Affairs*, **85**(4), 2–16.

De Soysa, Indra and John R. Oneal (1999), 'Boon or Bane? Reassessing the Productivity of Foreign Direct Investment', *American Sociological Review*, **64**(5), 766–82.

Dittmer, Lowell (1994), *China under Reform*, Boulder, CO: Westview.

Dollar, David and Aart Kraay (2002), 'Spreading the Wealth', *Foreign Affairs*, **81**(1), 120–33.

Domes, Jürgen and Marie-Luise Näth (1992), *Geschichte der Volksrepublik China*, Mannheim: BI- Taschenbuch.

Dreze, Jean and Amartya Sen (1995), *Economic Development and Social Opportunity*, Delhi: Oxford University Press.

Duchesne, Ricardo (2006), 'Asia First?' *Journal of the Historical Society*, **VI**(1), 69–91.

Eberstadt, Nicholas (1998), 'Asia Tomorrow, Gray and Male', *National Interest*, **53**, 56–65.

Eberstadt, Nicholas (2006), 'Growing Old the Hard Way: China, Russia India', *Policy Review*, **136**, 15–39.

The Economist (1997), 'Survey: India's Economy', **342**(8005), 22 February.

The Economist (2004), 'More or Less Equal?' **370**(8366), 13 March, 73–5.

The Economist (2005a), 'China's Stockmarket. A Marginalised Market', **374**(8415), 26 February, 67–8.

The Economist (2005b), 'Survey: The Tiger in Front', **374**(8416), 5 March.

The Economist (2005c), 'China and India. Too Early to Tell', **375**(8422), 16 April.

The Economist (2005d), 'The Bangalore Paradox', **375**(8423), 23 April, 67–9.

The Economist (2005e), 'Top Exporters', **375**(8423), 23 April, 101.

The Economist (2005f), 'From T-shirts to T-bonds', **376**(8437), 30 July, 65–7.

The Economist (2005g), 'The Brains Business. A Survey of Higher Education', **376**(8443), 10 September.

The Economist (2005h), 'A Great Big Banking Gamble', **377**(8450), 29 October, 77–9.

The Economist (2006a), 'Balancing Act. A Survey of China', **378**(8470), 25 March.

The Economist (2006b), 'Now for the Hard Part: A Survey of Business in India', **379**(8480), 3 June.

The Economist (2006c), 'Dividends in China: Can't Pay, Won't Pay', **380**(8488), 29 July, 69–72.

Elvin, Mark (1973), *The Pattern of the Chinese Past*, London: Eyre Methuen.

England, Robert Stowe (2005), *Aging China. The Demographic Challenge to China's Economic Prospects*, Westport, CT: Praeger (for the Center for Strategic and International Studies, Washington, DC).

FICCI (1999), *Indian Business through the Ages*, Delhi: Oxford University Press.

Firebaugh, Glenn (1999), 'Empirics of World Income Inequality', *American Journal of Sociology*, **194**(6), 1597–630.

Fu, Zhengyuan (1993), *Autocratic Tradition and Chinese Politics*, New York: Cambridge University Press.

Gallagher, Mary E. (2002), 'Reform and Openness: Why China's Economic Reforms Have Delayed Democracy', *World Politics*, **54**(3), 338–72.

Gwartney, James and Robert Lawson (2005), *Economic Freedom of the World, Annual Report 2005*, Vancouver, BC: Fraser Institute, and Potsdam: Liberales Institut.

Hanushek, Eric and Dennis D. Kimko (2000), 'Schooling, Labor Force Quality, and the Growth of Nations', *American Economic Review*, **90**(5), 1184–208.

Hayek, Friedrich August von (1945), 'The Use of Knowledge in Society', *American Economic Review*, **35**(4), 519–30.

Hayek, Friedrich August von (1960), *The Constitution of Liberty*, Chicago: The University of Chicago Press.

Helbling, Jürg (2003), 'Agriculture, Population and State in China in Comparison to Europe, 1500–1900', in Rolf Peter Sieferle and Helga Breuninger (eds), *Agriculture, Population and Economic Development in China and Europe*, Stuttgart: Breuninger Stiftung (Foundation), pp. 90–199.

Helpman, Elhanan (2004), *The Mystery of Economic Growth*, Cambridge, MA: Harvard University Press (Belknap).

Hobson, John M. (2004), *The Eastern Origins of Western Civilisation*, Cambridge: Cambridge University Press.

Hudson, Valerie M. and Andrea Den Boer (2002), 'A Surplus of Men, A Deficit of Peace: Security and Sex Ratios in Asia's Largest States', *International Security*, **26**(4), 5–38.

Inglehart, Ronald (1997), *Modernization and Postmodernization. Cultural, Economic, and Political Change in 43 Societies*, Princeton, NJ: Princeton University Press.

Jones, Eric L. (1981), *The European Miracle*, New York: Cambridge University Press.

Jones, Eric L. (1988), *Growth Recurring*, Oxford: Clarendon.

Jones, Garett and W. Joel Schneider (2006), 'Intelligence, Human Capital, and Economic Growth: A Bayesian Averaging of Classical Estimates Approach', *Journal of Economic Growth*, **11**, 71–93.

Joshi, Vijay and I.M.D. Little (1998), *India's Economic Reforms 1991–2001*, Delhi: Oxford University Press.

Kakar, Sudhir (1996), *The Colors of Violence. Cultural Identities, Religion, and Conflict*, Chicago: The University of Chicago Press.

Kohli, Atul (2004), *State-directed Development: Political Power and Industrialization in the Global Periphery*, New York: Cambridge University Press.

Kolb, Raimund (2003), 'About Figures and Aggregates', in Rolf Peter Sieferle and Helga Breuninger (eds), *Agriculture, Population and Economic Development in China and Europe*, Stuttgart: Breuninger Stiftung (Foundation), pp. 200–275.

Lal, Deepak (1998), *Unintended Consequences: The Impact of Factor Endowments, Culture and Politics on Long-Run Economic Performance*, Cambridge, MA: MIT Press.

Lal, Deepak (2004), 'India', in Peter Bernholz and Roland Vaubel (eds), *Political Competition, Innovation and Growth in the History of Asian Civilizations*, Cheltenham, UK and Northampton, MA, USA: Edward Elgar, pp. 128–41.

Landes, David S. (1998), *The Wealth and Poverty of Nations*, New York: Norton.

Landes, David S. (2006), 'Why Europe and the West? Why Not China?' *Journal of Economic Perspectives*, **20**(2), 2–22.

Lardy, Nicholas R. (1998), *China's Unfinished Economic Revolution*, Washington, DC: Brookings Institution Press.

Levine, Ross and David Renelt (1992), 'A Sensitivity Analysis of Cross-country Growth Regressions', *American Economic Review*, **82**, 942–63.

Levine, Ross and Sara J. Zervos (1993), 'What Have We Learned about Policy and Growth from Cross-country Growth Regressions?' *American Economic Review*, **83**, 426–30.

Lin, Justin Yifu, Fang Cai and Zhou Li (2003), *The China Miracle: Development Strategy and Economic Reform*, Hong Kong: The Chinese University Press.

Lipton, Michael (1977), *Why Poor People Stay Poor*, London: Temple Smith.

Lynn, Richard and Tatu Vanhanen (2005), 'The Role of Human Capital and Intelligence in the Economic Development of the Asian Economies', in John B. Kidd and Franz-Jürgen Richter (eds), *Infrastructure and Productivity in Asia*, Basingstoke: Palgrave, pp. 28–50.

Maddison, Angus (1998), *Chinese Economic Performance in the Long Run*, Paris: OECD Development Centre.

Maddison, Angus (2001), *The World Economy: A Millennial Perspective*, Paris: OECD.

Maddison, Angus (2002), 'Introduction: Measuring Asian Performance', in Angus Maddison, D.S. Prasada Rao and William F. Shepherd (eds), *The Asian Economies in the Twentieth Century*, Cheltenham, UK and Northampton, MA, USA: Edward Elgar, pp. 1–4.

Majumdar, Sumit K. (1998), 'Assessing Comparative Efficiency of the State-owned, Mixed and Private Sectors in Indian Industry' *Public Choice*, **96**(1–2), 1–24.

Mises, Ludwig von (1920), 'Die Wirtschaftsrechnung im sozialistischen Gemeinwesen', *Archiv für Sozialwissenschaft und Sozialpolitik*, **47**(1), 86–121.

Mitra, Subrata K. (1996), 'Politics in India', in Gabriel A. Almond and G. Bingham Powell (eds), *Comparative Politics Today. A World View*, New York: HarperCollins, pp. 669–729.

Montinola, Gabriella, Yingyi Qian and Barry Weingast (1995), 'Federalism Chinese Style. The Political Basis of Economic Success in China', *World Politics*, **48**(1), 50–81.

Moran, Theodore H., Edward M. Graham and Magnus Blomström (2005), *Does Foreign Direct Investment Promote Development?*, Washington, DC: Institute for International Economics.

Noland, Marcus, Li-Gang Liu, Sherman Robinson and Zhi Wang (1998), *Global Economic Effects of the Asian Currency Devaluations*, Washington, DC: Institute for International Economics.

North, Douglass C. (1990), *Institutions, Institutional Change and Economic Performance*, New York: Cambridge University Press.

Olson, Mancur (1996), 'Big Bills Left on the Sidewalk: Why Some Nations Are Rich, and Others Poor', *Journal of Economic Perspectives*, **10**(2), 3–24.

Panagariya, Arvind (2005), 'Miracles and Debacles: Do Free-Trade Skeptics Have a Case?' Federal Reserve Bank of Dallas, http://www.Columia.Edu/ap 2231/.

Pei, Minxin (2006), *China's Trapped Transition: The Limits of Developmental Autocracy*, Cambridge, MA: Harvard University Press.

Pomeranz, Kenneth (2000), *The Great Divergence: China, Europe, and the Making of the World Economy*, Princeton, NJ: Princeton University Press.

Poston, Dudley L. (2004), 'The Demographic Destiny of China, South Korea and Taiwan: Changes and Implications for the Family', paper presented at the 36th World Congress of the International Institute of Sociology, Beijing, 7–11 July.

Qian, Yingyi (2000), 'The Process of China's Market Transition (1978–1998)', *Journal of Theoretical and Institutional Economics*, **156**(1), 151–71.

Ravallion, Martin (2004), 'Pessimistic on Poverty?', *The Economist*, **371**(8370), 10 April, 70.

Rudolph, Lloyd I. and Susanne H. Rudolph (2000), 'Chandrababu Meets the World: Liberalization and Economic Performance in India's Federal System', paper presented at the 18th International Political Science Association Congress, Quebec, Canada, 5 August.

Rummel, Rudolph J. (1994), *Death by Government*, New Brunswick, NJ: Transaction.

Sandschneider, Eberhard (1998), 'Die kommunistische Partei Chinas an der Macht: Politische Entwicklungen bis zum Ende der Ära Deng Xiaoping', in Carsten Hermann-Pillath and Michael Lackner (eds), *Länderbericht China*, Bonn: Bundeszentrale für Politische Bildung, pp. 169–85.

Schüller, Margot (1998), 'Reform und Öffnung: Der chinesische Weg zur Marktwirtschaft', in Carsten Hermann-Pillath and Michael Lackner (eds), *Länderbericht China*, Bonn: Bundeszentrale für politische Bildung, pp. 278–301.

Sen, Amartya (1999), *Development as Freedom*, Oxford: Oxford University Press.

Sinha, Aseema (2005), 'Political Foundations of Market-Enhancing Federalism. Theoretical Lessons from India and China', *Comparative Politics*, **37**(3), 337–56.

Sivasubramonian, Siva (2002), 'Twentieth Century Economic Performance in India', in Angus Maddison, D.S. Prasada Rao, and William F. Shepherd, *The Asian Economies in the Twentieth Century*, Cheltenham, UK and Northampton, MA, USA: Edward Elgar, pp. 102–42.

Smith, Adam (1776/1976), *An Inquiry into the Nature and Causes of the Wealth of Nations*, Oxford: Oxford University Press.

Thakur, Ramesh (2006), 'Der Elefant ist aufgewacht: In wenigen Jahren hat Indien es geschafft, zur globalen Wirtschaftsmacht aufzusteigen', *Internationale Politik*, **61**(10), 6–13.

Van Praagh, David (2003), *The Greater Game: India's Race with Destiny and China*, Montreal: McGill-Queen's University Press.

Weber, Max (1920/1972), *Gesammelte Aufsätze zur Religionssoziologie, 1. Band*, Tübingen: Mohr.

Weber, Max (1921/1978), *Gesammelte Aufsätze zur Religionssoziologie, 2. Band*, Tübingen: Mohr.

Weber, Max (1922/1964), *Wirtschaft und Gesellschaft*, Köln: Kiepenheuer und Witsch.

Weber, Max (1923/1981), *Wirtschaftsgeschichte*, Berlin: Duncker and Humblot.

Weede, Erich (1996), *Economic Development, Social Order, and World Politics*, Boulder, CO: Lynne Rienner.

Weede, Erich (2000), *Asien und der Westen*, Baden-Baden: Nomos.

Weede, Erich (2005), *Balance of Power, Globalization and the Capitalist Peace*, Berlin: Liberal Verlag.

Weede, Erich and Sebastian Kämpf (2002), 'The Impact of Intelligence and Institutional Improvements on Economic Performance', *Kyklos*, **55**(3), 361–80.

Weingast, Barry R. (1995), 'The Economic Role of Political Institutions: Market-preserving Federalism and Economic Development', *Journal of Law, Economics, and Organization*, **11**(1), 1–31.

Williamson, John B. and Ce Shen (2004), 'Do Notional Defined Contribution Accounts Make Sense as Part of the Old-age Security Mix for China?' paper presented at the 36th World Congress of the International Institute of Sociology, Beijing, 7–11 July.

Wolf, Martin (2004), *Why Globalization Works*, New Haven, CT: Yale University Press.

World Bank (1992), *World Development Report 1992*, New York: Oxford University Press.

World Bank (1995), *World Development Report 1995*, New York: Oxford University Press.

World Bank (2000), *World Development Report 2000/2001*, New York: Oxford University Press.

World Bank (2003), *Little Data Handbook*, Washington, DC: World Bank.

World Bank (2004), *World Development Report 2005: A Better Investment Climate for Everyone*, New York: Oxford University Press.

World Bank (2005), *World Development Report 2006: Equity and Development*, New York: Oxford University Press.

Wu, Zhengzhang (1996), 'Transitional Economy and Regional Development: The Case of China', in Asfaw Kumssa and Haider A. Khan (eds), *Transitional Economies and Regional Development Strategies: Lessons from Five Low-income Developing Countries*, Nagoya: United Nations Center for Regional Development, pp. 63–76.

Yang, Tai-Shuenn (1987), 'Property Rights and Constitutional Order in Imperial China', PhD dissertation, Indiana University (Department of Political Science), Bloomington.

Yergin, Daniel and Joseph Stanilaw (1998), *The Commanding Heights. The Battle between Government and the Marketplace that is Remaking the Modern World*, New York: Simon and Schuster.

Index

Acquis communautaire 83–4
actor 2–13, 18–25, 70–75, 141, 232
advantages of backwardness 239
aid to families with dependent children (AFDC) 184
allocative efficiency 53, 166, 203
anarchy 5, 21, 29, 36, 164
Asia 32, 49, 57, 110, 170, 230–53
Australia 169, 171–7, 213
Austria 170–77, 213
Austrian economics 13, 45, 68–69, 73, 156, 165

balance of power 231–3
Bangladesh 170
Belgium 171–7, 213, 217
Bolivia 170
Botswana 170
bureaucracy 46, 93–4, 186, 233, 242–3

Cameroon 170
Canada 171–3, 175–7, 213, 230
capital export neutrality 133–4, 141
capital import neutrality 141
capitalism 48, 95, 230–33, 243–4
cartels 21, 59, 281–3, 96–7, 103, 126, 130–31, 242
    see also tax cartels
centralization 36–8, 81–3, 100–102, 208, 237–9
    see also decentralization
China 14, 30–32, 48, 161–2, 203, 211, 230–53
Church 31, 51, 234
citizens' interests 118, 121–2
command economy 240
comparative advantage 162, 238–9, 244–6
competition 29–30, 71–3, 92–7, 113–14, 117, 156–8, 202, 232–7
    as a discovery procedure 71

see also institutional competition; market competition; political competition; tax competition
constitution 35–7, 73, 80, 95, 102, 115–17, 225
consumer interests 121–3
consumer preference 17, 130
cooperative federalism 202–209
coordinating rule 1, 16–19
corrective force 117
Côte d'Ivoire 170
Cyprus 171, 174
Czech 174, 213

decentralization 34, 40–6, 53, 80–83, 90, 103–104, 202–208, 212–5
    see also centralization
democracy 46–18, 67, 75–9, 93–7, 113–18, 125, 135, 163–6, 187, 207, 242
Denmark 170–77, 185, 190–93, 213
division of knowledge 69–70, 76

ECOFIN 129, 136, 183
economic development 94–7, 204–212, 230
economic freedom 238–49
    see also freedom; liberty
efficiency 43, 55–8, 68–9, 80–2, 100, 105, 134, 157, 196–8, 202–209, 237, 243
England 53, 206
    see also United Kingdom
entrepreneurship 72–3, 158–9, 242–5
equilibrium 2–7, 5, 69–72, 78, 97, 211
Estonia 158, 174
European Union 83–4, 90, 101, 129, 182, 158
experimentation 40, 68, 81–2, 104, 196, 203
externality 58, 103, 143